THE WRITINGS OF
EVELYN WAUGH

THE WRITINGS OF
EVELYN WAUGH

Ian Littlewood

BASIL BLACKWELL · OXFORD

© Ian Littlewood 1983

First published 1983
Basil Blackwell Publisher Limited
108 Cowley Road, Oxford OX4 1JF, England

British Library Cataloguing in Publication Data

Littlewood, Ian
    The writings of Evelyn Waugh.
    1. Waugh, Evelyn—Criticism and interpretation
    1. Title
    823'.912   PR6045.A972/

    ISBN 0—631—13211—2

Typesetting by System 4 Associates Limited
Gerrards Cross, Buckinghamshire
Printed in Great Britain by Billings, Worcester

For my Mother and Father

Contents

Acknowledgements

Tony Nuttall and Stephen Medcalf went through the first draft of this book and made numerous helpful suggestions — as did Norman Vance when he read the opening chapters. Anne-Barrie Hunter has given me valuable assistance at a later stage. Other friends who at some time helped with information or advice were Graham Benton, Andrew Gibson, Peter Stallybrass, Patrick and Edwina Conner, Graham and Jan Clarke, and Jeffrey and Valerie Meyers. I am very grateful to them, and also to Jill Willder, who copy-edited the book while I was abroad; she did much to help me.

Extracts from the writings of Evelyn Waugh are included by kind permission of the Estate of Evelyn Waugh and A.D. Peters and Company, London.

Chronological Table

—————

1903	Born at 11 Hillfield Road, Hampstead (28 October).
1907	Family moves to North End Road, Hampstead.
1910—17	Day-boy at Heath Mount preparatory school.
1917—21	Lancing College, Sussex.
1922—24	Hertford College, Oxford.
1923	'Antony, Who Sought Things That Were Lost', a short story, published in *The Oxford Broom* (June).
1925	Schoolmaster at Arnold House in Wales. Attempts suicide.
1926	Schoolmaster in Aston Clinton, Buckinghamshire. 'The Balance: A Yarn of the Good Old Days of Broad Trousers and High Necked Jumpers', published in *Georgian Stories.*
1927	Schoolmaster in Notting Hill, London. Employed on the *Daily Express.*
1928	*Rossetti, His Life and Works* (Waugh's first book). Marriage to Evelyn Gardner (27 June). *Decline and Fall, An Illustrated Novelette* (September).
1929	Mediterranean cruise — basis of *Labels*. Illness of Evelyn Gardner on the trip. Evelyn Gardner leaves Waugh for John Heygate (July). (Waugh was at work on *Vile Bodies* at the time.)
1930	*Vile Bodies*. Literary and social success. *Labels* (Waugh's first travel book).

Received into the Roman Catholic Church (September).

To Abyssinia to attend the coronation of Haile Selassie. Travels in East and Central Africa. Leaves England October 1930, returns March 1931. Trip becomes the basis of *Remote People* and *Black Mischief.*

1931   *Remote People* (November).

Christmas with the Lygons at Madresfield.

1932   Journalism. Short visits to France, Italy and Spain. Meets Lady Diana Cooper (summer).

Black Mischief (September).

Leaves England in low spirits for Georgetown, British Guiana (December). Arduous journey in British Guiana and Brazil, recorded in *Ninety-Two Days.* Basis of the South American section of *A Handful of Dust.*

1933   Returns to England in May.

'The Man Who Liked Dickens'.

Mediterranean cruise (late summer) in the course of which he meets Laura Herbert.

1934   Winters in Morocco.

Ninety-Two Days, The Account of a Tropical Journey through British Guiana and Part of Brazil.

Completes the stories later published with 'Mr Loveday's Little Outing'.

Trip to Spitzbergen (July—August).

A Handful of Dust (September).

1935   Reports Italian—Abyssinian war for the *Daily Mail.* Basis of *Waugh in Abyssinia* and *Scoop.*

Edmund Campion: Jesuit and Martyr.

1936   *Mr Loveday's Little Outing and Other Sad Stories* (June).

Annulment of his marriage to Evelyn Gardner confirmed (July).

Returns to Abyssinia to assess latest developments (July—August).

Waugh in Abyssinia (October).

1937   Marriage to Laura Herbert (17 April).

Moves to Piers Court, Stinchcombe, Gloucestershire (September).

1938   *Scoop, A Novel about Journalists* (May).
        Visits Hungary.
        Visits Mexico, having been commissioned to write a book exposing the socialist government of General Cardenas.

1939   *Robbery Under Law, The Mexican Object-Lesson.*
        Works on the fragment later to be published as *Work Suspended.*
        Joins the Royal Marines (December).

1940   Participates in the unsuccessful Dakar expedition.
        Transfers to Commandos.

1941   To Egypt. Takes part in the battle for Crete.
        Growing disillusionment with the war.
        Returns to England and the Royal Marines (September).

1942   Spent in the UK on routine duties.
        Put Out More Flags (March).
        Work Suspended (December), two chapters of an unfinished novel.

1943   Dispiriting period of inactivity.
        Death of his father, Arthur Waugh (June).
        Resigns from Commandos after dispute with Lord Lovat (July).
        Joins the Special Air Service Regiment (October).
        Parachute training (December).

1944   On leave in Devon, writing *Brideshead Revisited* (January–June).
        Accompanies Randolph Churchill to Yugoslavia as part of 37th British Military Mission to the partisans (July). Stationed at Topusko.
        Liaison officer in Dubrovnik (December).

1945   Writes report on religious toleration in Yugoslavia.
        Brideshead Revisited: The Sacred and Profane Memories of Captain Charles Ryder (May).

Wide popular success, especially in America.
Attends the Nuremberg trials (spring).

Attends international conference in Madrid
(June). Basis of *Scott-King's Modern Europe.*

1947 In America to discuss possible film treatment
of *Brideshead Revisited* (January—March).

Summer — works on *The Loved One*, inspired
by his frequent visits to Forest Lawn cemetery
in Los Angeles.

1948 *The Loved One: An Anglo-American Tragedy*
published in *Horizon* (February).

Developing friendship with Ronald Knox.

Lecture tour in America (November and early
December).

1949 Returns to America to complete his lecture
tour (January—April).

At work on *Helena.*

1950 Travels to Italy in the spring.

Helena (October). Waugh disappointed by its
reception.

1951 Travels in Near East for *Life* magazine (January
—March). Articles collected as *The Holy Places*
in 1952.

At work on *Men at Arms.*

1952 Travels to Sicily with Harold Acton.

Men at Arms. The first volume of the trilogy
based on his war experiences.

Christmas in Goa.

1953 Returns in February.

*Love Among the Ruins: A Romance of the
Near Future.*

Interviewed for BBC radio programme,
'Frankly Speaking'. The experience features
prominently in *The Ordeal of Gilbert
Pinfold.*

1954 Voyage to Ceylon and breakdown (January—
March). Recorded in *The Ordeal of Gilbert
Pinfold.*

At work on *Officers and Gentlemen.*

Death of his mother, Catherine Waugh.

1955   Winters in Jamaica as the guest of Ian and Ann Fleming.
              Officers and Gentlemen (June).

1956   Moves to Combe Florey, near Taunton, Somerset.

1957   *The Ordeal of Gilbert Pinfold.*
              Death of Ronald Knox. Waugh starts research for the biography.

1958   At work on the life of Ronald Knox. Travels to Rhodesia to collect material.

1959   To Africa again (January—April) with a commission from the *Sunday Times* for travel articles. His journey is the basis of *A Tourist in Africa.*
              The Life of the Right Reverend Ronald Knox (October).

1960   Trip to Europe (January—February), financed by articles for the *Daily Mail.*
              At work on *Unconditional Surrender.*
              A Tourist in Africa.

1961   *Unconditional Surrender.*
              Trip to British Guiana, financed by an article for the *Sunday Times.*

1962   Returns to England in February.

1963   *Basil Seal Rides Again, or The Rake's Regress,* published after being serialized in the *Sunday Telegraph.*
              At work on his autobiography.

1964   *A Little Learning, The First Volume of an Autobiography.* Waugh's last book.

1965   Worsening health and spirits.

1966   *Sword of Honour.* The one volume recension of the war trilogy.
              Dies at Combe Florey on Easter Sunday, 10 April.

Abbreviations

Introduction

Those who make their living from the study of literature have a strong incentive to take it seriously. Comic novels, like children in church, can be a source of embarrassment. For the critic they pose an obvious problem: their humour is a potential affront to the seriousness of his own endeavour. Unless they can be deftly converted into a semblance of something more respectable, works of comic fiction are likely to receive from him only grudging attention. There is more to this than an awareness that the rest of the world finds his activities quite frivolous enough already. In many cases it derives from an unstated conviction that life tenders more substance for gloom than for gaiety and that it is the business of a novel to reflect this disproportion. Those which fail to carry their weight of suffering have fought shy of their obligations. Unable, or unwilling, to lay claim to profundity, such books seem foreign to the language in which the study of the novel is justified.

Few are more delinquent in this respect than the novels of Evelyn Waugh. They are themselves escapes and they are concerned with strategies of escape; they are about ways of avoiding reality and they offer in themselves an avoidance of it.

Waugh's last book ends with a description of how, as a young man, he once tried to commit suicide. His post as a teacher was irksome to him, the hope of an alternative job with Scott Moncrieff[1] had come to nothing, his friend Harold Acton was unenthusiastic about the early chapters of his novel. One evening, his thoughts full of death, he went

---

[1] The translator of Proust.

down to the beach, left with his clothes a quotation from
Euripides about the sea which washes away all human ills,
and began to swim out from the shore:

> It was a beautiful night of a gibbous moon. I swam
> slowly out but, long before I reached the point of no
> return, the Shropshire Lad was disturbed by a smart
> on the shoulder. I had run into a jelly-fish. A few more
> strokes, a second more painful sting. The placid waters
> were full of the creatures.
>
> An omen? A sharp recall to good sense such as Olivia
> would have administered?
>
> I turned about, swam back through the track of the
> moon to the sands which that morning had swarmed
> under Grimes's discerning eye with naked urchins. As
> earnest of my intent I had brought no towel. With
> some difficulty I dressed and tore into small pieces my
> pretentious classical tag, leaving them to the sea, moved
> on that bleak shore by tides stronger than any known
> to Euripides, to perform its lustral office. Then I
> climbed the sharp hill that led to all the years ahead.
> [LL 220]

The outlines of the episode are simple: despair, attempted
suicide, failure, the resumption of normal life. But the threads
of response which can be detected in Waugh's account of it
are more various. There is, first of all, the reticence which
has withdrawn from view the emotional springs of the
action; there is the detachment of tone which places the
whole performance, 'the excursion', at a distance that is
more than just temporal; there is the response of the romantic — of the young man, certainly, with his thoughts full of
death and his tag from Euripides, but perhaps also, in the
subtler tones of the penultimate sentence, of the older man
who looks back on him. There are other points of view as
well, perspectives allowed to Waugh by the distance he puts
between himself and his subject. It is a comic scene, and also
one with a certain aesthetic appeal: the would-be suicide is
both the butt of Nature's failure to live up to the occasion
and the figure in an empty seascape, turning alone into the

track of a gibbous moon. ('Pure Turner,' says Crouchback, as bombs illuminate the night sky over war-time London.) Finally, there is the presence of the story-teller, ordering and manipulating these other perspectives to fashion the incident into a proper conclusion to his book, making out of it, in spite of the duller course that events took in reality, an artificial turning-point in the hero's fortunes, a boundary to mark the end of this work, and, as it turned out, of his life's work.

'At my present age,' Waugh comments, 'I cannot tell how much real despair and act of will, how much play acting, prompted the excursion.' Yet even to sustain the play acting a measure of real despair must have been necessary. We are given details, but not of this despair; the description is centrifugal from that core of feeling which set the whole episode in motion. Waugh's account has more to do with outwitting suicide than committing it. The details he does give us point away from it to the devious strategems by which, despairing or not, we survive.

Those I have indicated — reticence, humour, romanticism, detachment of tone, aestheticism, the shaping prerogative of the artist — might be seen as a sort of defensive armoury, weapons that have been deployed in varying combinations at different stages of the writer's career to secure immunity from the incursions of a world grown more and more outrageous to his sensibilities. The list is incomplete and oversimplified. It suggests nothing of the role of nostalgia in Waugh's writings, nor of the range of his irony, nothing, most importantly, of the deepening influence of religion in his work. It does, however, convey something of the direction which this study is intended to take.

Waugh's temperament is not sunny, nor are his books — even the funniest of them. From *Decline and Fall* to *Unconditional Surrender* they are shot through with an awareness of most of the things that tempt men to despair: whatever lies between social boredom and the concentration camp, disappointment in love and the decline of a civilization. But equally present in the novels is the strain of opposition to these things, the refusal to accept them as definitive features of the novelist's world. Above I have listed rather starkly some of the ways in which Waugh seeks to resist their urgency. Put briefly, my project is to examine the elements of escapism in his art and to gauge their limits. Escapism here is no retreat into fantasy. I have in mind more curious processes: the omissions and distortions, deflections, exaggerations and denials by which a novelist can try to cheat reality of its power to oppress him.

There are six chapters, the first five of which follow a similar course. In each case I have taken a particular mode of response and tried first to survey its role in Waugh's writing, then to trace the stages by which its effectiveness declined. Headings of some sort are a necessary convenience, and those I have chosen — 'humour', 'romanticism', 'nostalgia' and so forth — are offered here as broad categories within which can be subsumed the range of literary manoeuvres that interest me.

The aim of these chapters is straightforward: to explore recurrent patterns in Waugh's writing and to suggest how they relate to one another. It is the texture of the novels rather than the theoretical implications of my approach to them that I have sought to examine. Implicit in this approach, however, is an assumption about the relationship between Waugh's life and his work which could not go unexplained. The final chapter is an attempt to gather together the critical arguments that have threaded the rest of the book and to set them within the context of this issue. My own account goes only to the point where the precarious balance between the writer's real and his imaginative life tipped over into crisis. Waugh himself takes up the analysis in *The Ordeal of Gilbert Pinfold*. This book I have reserved for the Conclusion.

There are two aspects of my approach which require a word of explanation. First, its bearing on other works of criticism. In England Waugh has received less critical attention than is his due, and for this he would perhaps have been thankful. In

America he is the subject of a scholarly newsletter which takes annual stock of a more and more daunting bibliography. There were already, a few years ago, enough books on Waugh to fill several long afternoons. My excuse for proposing an addition to them is implicit in what was said at the start of this Introduction. It seemed to me that the critical emphasis on his novels had from the beginning been unbalanced by a misguided eagerness to rescue them from the charge of triviality. By contrast, I wanted to argue that his comedy should be seen as a way of challenging seriousness, not as a covert way of purveying it. This was the position from which I started. Since then, increasing interest in Waugh has accelerated moves to qualify him as a 'serious writer' — with predictable consequences. The exigencies of academic life have developed in most of us a robust belief in the ability of butterflies to survive the wheel, but an essay on *Decline and Fall* which begins by declaring that 'Symbols are always the key to Waugh's art'[2] can still cause a faltering of the spirits.

Symbols there are, of course, of varying importance, but they are facets of Waugh's art, not the key to it. In most of his early fiction there is the skeleton of a serious novel which can be uncovered by the exercise of a little ingenuity. It is not coincidental that in *Decline and Fall* the half-hearted Church of England clergyman should be done to death by a Calvinist lunatic, that the film in *Vile Bodies* should be a historically garbled life of Wesley, that the incident in *Black Mischief* which finally brings the 'progressive' Emperor of Azania to grief should be a pageant in support of birth control. Such threads run through the novels and we need to be aware of them, but to thrust them into prominence is to distort their function. It results from a confusion between two different kinds of critical practice: to emphasize patterns that have taken shape beneath the conscious surface of a work is a legitimate procedure of the critic; to emphasize patterns which are a part of that conscious surface and which the author has chosen not to emphasize is a failure of

---

[2] Jerome Meckier, 'Cycle, Symbol, and Parody in Evelyn Waugh's *Decline and Fall*'.

critical sympathy. However consistent the analysis, it will have little in common with our response to the original work. Too often the novels come back to us replete with significance but drained of all the erratic vitality that made them distinctive.

'Waugh's private meaning,' says Jeffrey Heath in his recent book, 'is so well concealed that the uninitiated reader might question its presence.'[3] This is an ominous prelude to a discussion of comic fiction. No doubt there are writers whose novels have kept their true colours hidden from all but a few initiates. I am not persuaded that Waugh is one of them. He was quick enough to complain when he felt that people were missing the point of *Brideshead Revisited* or had misconstrued the ending of the war trilogy. Yet there are no similar complaints that either the general public or his personal friends had failed to do justice to the seriousness of his earlier work. The note he added to the first edition of *Decline and Fall* suggests that any misgivings he may have had were on quite the opposite count: 'Please bear in mind throughout that IT IS MEANT TO BE FUNNY'. For a novelist whose fundamental concern is with the moral and religious import of his work, this is carrying obliquity to an extreme. The undertow of moral seriousness provides a crucial tension within these books, but it does not dominate them. We are right to be more struck by their comedy, and my argument has tried to reassert that priority.

I have said little in this study about the social background of the inter-war years; the subject has already been treated at length elsewhere. But it would be a damaging consequence if this were to leave the impression of Waugh as a figure isolated from his time. The point needs to be made at the outset that many of the characteristics I have attributed to him belong also to his generation. Indeed, his responses to English society in the wake of the First World War were so far from being unique that he could even at one stage see himself as a possible spokesman for the 'English youth movement'.[4]

The basis of at least some of these shared attitudes is

---

[3] *The Picturesque Prison*, p. 59.
[4] Cf. letter to W. N. Roughead [*Letters* 30].

suggested by a remark that Paul Fussell makes of Waugh's friend, and later enemy, Robert Byron: 'He lived by means of frantic antipathies: to the tame, the tedious, the color-less — his forays into the Middle East were largely searches for "colored architecture" as a relief from the principle of greyness obtaining in England.'[5] This could be a description, almost word for word, of that side of Waugh which I have chosen to investigate. It points to an important perspective that he holds in common not just with Byron but with a con-siderable number of his contemporaries. The world revealed by his letters in the twenties and thirties is a world of initials and nicknames, intimate slang and private jokes — an insider's world. It implies a shared landscape; and this is what the tone and humour of his books reflect. Their dedications are more than a conventional gesture; Waugh wrote for his friends.

In later years the insider's world tended to be that of the Roman Catholic Church. This was the 'Household' of which he had membership, the source of that 'family unity' from which even 'the most earnest outsider' was cut off [Letters, 271-2]. Here again was a body of shared perceptions which linked Waugh in various ways to fellow writers. Almost thirty years ago Donat O'Donnell had already noted that the sense of exile which permeates his writing — and which is central to my own discussion of him — was a theme common to many of his Catholic contemporaries. What is not common, and what is the main subject of the ensuing pages, is the precise verbal form that Waugh gave to these responses.

There is, in conclusion, one other sort of kinship which has been largely omitted from my study, but this for different reasons. Efforts to define Waugh's purely literary context have on the whole yielded unimpressive results. He is not a writer who lends himself to such treatment. 'The Auden generation' is a literary category; 'the Waugh generation', if one were to use the phrase, would be a social category. Earlier critics who have attempted to classify him in terms of his literary affinities have left us with a bewildering assort-ment of names. For Stephen Greenblatt, he is a modern satirist beside Huxley and Orwell, for Terry Eagleton, an

[5] *Abroad*, p. 81.

author of upper class novels along with Woolf and Forster, for Donat O'Donnell, one of a group of Catholic writers in the company of Greene and Mauriac. Waugh himself acknowledged debts to Hemingway, Wodehouse, Firbank, Saki, Norman Douglas and others — these just in the twentieth century. Meanwhile, references in his work constantly draw us back to the nineteenth century, to Morris and Pater, Lear and Carroll, Browning, Tennyson and Dickens.

To accumulate names is easy; their significance, outside the context of specific allusions, remains a matter of speculation. There is no one close enough to Waugh to demand consideration, too many in the middle distance who have a claim to it. We can pick up an echo of Huxley's *Antic Hay* here, an echo from Proust there, a triple echo of Ford's *Parade's End* over here. All of them have their interest; they are identifiable strands of the cultural web within which a writer's work comes into being. But how close do they take us to the heart of Waugh's achievement? With reference to his own writing, he may not have been wholly unfair when he dismissed the search for 'Influence' and 'Movements' as 'convenient inventions for the thesis writer....'[6] He himself, in *The Ordeal of Gilbert Pinfold*, directed us to the late eighteenth century. Is this, then, his true context: an age, he suggests, of elegance and variety of contrivance? Or should we place him even further back — among those writers, perhaps, for whom the world could still be mastered by the precise language, pure syntax and balanced rhythms of Augustan prose? It is one more possibility, inconclusive like the rest. Other names could be invoked, remoter centuries. From these widening circles we shall turn back to the books themselves.

[6] Frederick J. Stopp, *Evelyn Waugh: Portrait of an Artist*, p. 212.

1

Detachment of Tone

Adolescence is probably as good a place to start as any.
For a study in ways of eluding pain, it is the obvious place.

When Waugh was sixteen, he broke a penknife belonging to
Francis Crease. The man was an amateur scribe, an artist,
whose friendship was treasured. Along with J. F. Roxburgh,
he was one of the 'Two Mentors' to whom Waugh devoted a
separate chapter of his autobiography. Roxburgh's cosmo-
politan panache and the reclusive aesthetic preoccupations
of Crease provided two stylistic models that continued to
exercise a powerful influence over the course of Waugh's
life. It was an important relationship, and this incident
with the penknife marked the 'first and to some extent
decisive rift' in it.

In Crease's absence and without his permission, Waugh
had borrowed a delicate blade for cutting quills. It shattered
under his hand. The episode is recounted in detail in *A Little
Learning* — as is Crease's reaction: Waugh 'had betrayed his
trust and ruined his life as a scribe'. The account continues:

> I was radically shocked, not so much by his magnification
> of his loss as by his imputation to me of presumption
> and curiosity. By the next post another letter came
> saying that the first had been written in momentary
> vexation...But the wound did not heal....He remained
> a friend for many years...But after the incident of the
> broken blade the old bright, confident morning light
> never shone on our friendship. [*LL* 147]

The vividness with which this letter is recalled over forty
years later, and the prominence given to it, suggest that the

whole affair had left an enduring mark. It is therefore interesting to see how Waugh set about dealing with it at the
time. He records in his diary for 31 May 1920:

> The day which might have been rather a pleasant one
> was spoiled by a letter from Crease at breakfast. He is
> very bored about my breaking his knife and says that I
> had no right to be using it at all. All he intended to lend
> me was his ink and he had put the box of other things
> away purposely.... I am very hurt that he should take
> that line about it. If anywhere in this bloody place, I
> did look for kindness and sympathy at Lychpole. Oh
> well another broken pencil point.... [*Diaries* 80]

The entry shows Waugh caught between two inclinations:
the natural impulse to indulge his distress is being countered
by the desire to formulate a response that will shrug it off.
His choice of the word 'bored' is a calculated gesture of self-
defence. The event, both bitter and important to him, is met
by a word that refuses to acknowledge either its bitterness or
its importance. The effort is not sustained in this passage, but
the cryptic last phrase is obviously in the same character.
What it signifies is an awareness on the part of the schoolboy
that the contours of an experience can be modified by the
way in which it is recorded; Waugh has begun to grasp the
importance of tone. It is to this perception that the pre-war
novels owe much of their insolent composure. The writer's
aim in choosing his words is less to convey the reality of an
experience than to suggest an attitude to it.

'A modern dandy'[1] was Peter Quennell's description of him
in his early days at Oxford, and this is the dandy's traditional
strategy. The impact of experience, both moral and emotional, is turned aside by his studied refusal to accord it any
significance that is other than aesthetic. Matters of normal
concern leave him unmoved; in fact they bore him — to be
bored is his characteristic response. It is, of course, a word —
and a style — that commonly attracts the sophisticated adolescent, but its occurrence at a crucial point in Waugh's diary

---

[1] *Evelyn Waugh and his World*, ed. David Pryce-Jones, p. 37.

was indicative of more than a passing phase. We can compare
his use of it eight years later in another context which might
have provoked unwelcome emotion. This is his diary entry
for 22 June 1928:

> Evelyn and I began to go to Dulwich to see the pictures
> there but got bored waiting for the right bus so went
> instead to the vicar-general's office and bought a mar-
> riage licence. Lunched at Taglioni. Went to Warwick
> Square to see Harold and show him our licence. With him
> to Alec where we drank champagne. [*Diaries* 294-5]

Again, the word implicitly denies any emotional claims
which the situation might make. ('Darling, I *am* glad about
our getting married.' 'So am I. But don't let's get intense
about it.' [*VB* 44]) The tone of the passage is carefully
chosen — urbane, stylish...disengaged. It must have seemed
exquisitely right to be so blasé where one's parents' generation would have been so serious — *were* being so serious.
The insouciant note Waugh strikes is intended to reflect a
relationship conducted according to the demands of a particular style.

What was lacking was any sense of the limits of that style.
Waugh had failed to determine how far it could safely extend
beyond the literary bounds of the lover's diary. After a few
months of marriage, Evelyn Gardner, with an acute sense of
stylistic propriety, moved on to another partner. It was
probably the most painful experience of Waugh's life, and
its shock waves can be felt through successive novels for the
rest of his career. How well was the style of the dandy able
to accommodate it? Waugh communicated the news to
Harold Acton on 4 August 1929: 'A note to tell you what
you may have already heard. That Evelyn has been pleased
to make a cuckold of me with Heygate & that I have filed a
petition for divorce.' [*Letters* 38] The literary style is
beautifully intact; the elegant archaism of the phrase puts
Waugh at just enough distance from its bitterness. But the
social style has disintegrated. Instead of reaching for the
cocktail shaker, he is petitioning for a divorce. 'Are you
so very male in your sense of possession?' Acton writes back.

The pained incomprehension places him in an earlier world; and a second, more emotional letter to him from Waugh points up the gulf between them: 'I did not know it was possible to be so miserable & live but I am told that this is a common experience.' [Letter of September ? 1919; *Letters* 39]

That it was an event which impinged on Waugh morally as well as emotionally is suggested by a remark he made to his brother shortly after Evelyn Gardner's defection: 'The trouble about the world today is that there's not enough religion in it. There's nothing to stop young people doing whatever they feel like doing at the moment.'[2] It has the tone of an article he wrote for the *Spectator* at about the same time, in which he taxes the younger generation with rebelling against 'the widest conceptions of mere decency' [*LOr* 12]. The result, he says, is in many cases 'the perverse and aimless dissipation chronicled by the gossip writers of the Press'. His attitudes have stiffened. The break-up of his marriage was not something that could be pronounced a bore; it had shattered the diarist's pose.

Such risks are inherent in the pursuit of style, for its aim is to shape life by the principles appropriate to a work of art. The episode was for Waugh a cruel demonstration of how far apart the two are in reality — and how much more manageable is the work of art. This latter point is important; it must have confirmed Waugh's sense of the protective possibilities of his trade.

Broken relationships can be handled so easily in a novel:

'Oh, I say. Nina, there's one thing — I don't think I shall be able to marry you after all.'
'Oh, *Adam*, you are a bore. Why not?' [*VB* 34]

The italicized name is impeccable: how maddening of him. How 'boring' of him. Nina has no trouble in finding the right word. And for her there is no risk of emotional retribution — even when Adam sells her to Ginger for £78 16s 2d.

[2] Alec Waugh, *My Brother Evelyn and Other Profiles*, pp. 191-2.

'Oh, but Adam, I think this is beastly of you; I don't
want not to see you again.'

'I'm sorry....Good-bye, Nina, darling.'

'Good-bye, Adam, my sweet. But I think you're
rather a cad.' [*VB* 198]

The threatening claims of emotion and morality have been
defeated. The style which in life had foundered has triumphed
in the novel. It is a concise illustration of the literary manoeuvres with which we are concerned in this chapter.

Vile Bodies deals freely in occasions for misery — the frustrations that embitter private or public life, the incidental
chances that dictate good or evil fortune, the aimlessness
that afflicts those who live without convictions. But such
stuff is teased fine; we scarcely recognize in it the origins of
unhappiness. The emotional distress of the letter to Acton
and the moral gravity of the *Spectator* article are excluded
from the novel by its prevailing tone. And it is the nature of
this tone that we must now examine — the accents of sophistication on one side, on the other that element of childishness
which is their counterpart.

The point made in the Introduction is of some relevance
here, for the tone in question was not Waugh's alone; it
was available to him as part of the social currency of his
time. He himself implies as much in *A Little Learning*: 'We
were in some respects more sophisticated than our successors,' he writes of his generation at Oxford, 'but in others
barely adolescent.' [*LL* 163] This mixture of qualities was not
confined to the undergraduate world of Oxford. The same
outlines are apparent in Dudley Carew's description of
Evelyn Gardner at the time of her marriage to Waugh:
'there she was, with a kind of puppyish eagerness to appre-
ciate and embrace everything and everybody — I think that
I underrated at that time a certain strain of toughness and
sophistication in her.'[3] The same two aspects are singled out
by Martin Green in his analysis of 'modernity' in the 1920s.
He notes both a taste for 'corruption', reflected in plays by
Noël Coward and Frederick Lonsdale, and a correlative taste

[3] *Evelyn Waugh and his World*, ed. David Pryce-Jones, p. 42.

for childishness expressed by, amongst other things, the popularity of Daisy Ashford's *The Young Visiters* and the drawings of Pamela Bianco. It was a pattern in the social history of the decade, and my choice of *Vile Bodies* as a point of reference for this discussion is intended to reflect the fact. More clearly than any other of Waugh's early books it illustrates the extent of his debt to the language and attitudes of the social world he took as his subject.

In an attempt to avert the crisis which culminates in his suicide, Lord Balcairn makes a heartfelt appeal to Adam over lunch:

> 'It's so damned unfair. All my cousins are in lunatic asylums or else they live in the country and do indelicate things with wild animals...except my mamma, and that's worse....They were furious at the office about Van getting that Downing Street "scoop". If I miss this party I may as well leave Fleet Street for good...I may as well put my head into a gas-oven and have done with it....I'm sure if Margot knew how much it meant to me she wouldn't mind my coming.'
> Great tears stood in his eyes threatening to overflow.
> [*VB* 86]

Here is the combination of childishness and sophistication — the pettishness and tears matched by a casual acceptance of insanity and sexual aberration. Balcairn is both a Bright Young Person and a little boy 'who got into awful trouble about spelling the other day'. This very English conjunction is the basis of Waugh's tone, and the starting point for any analysis of it must be linguistic.

'Sophistication' is itself an unsatisfactory term. For lack of a better, I use the word to cover a range of responses, characteristic of the early Waugh, which have in common the refusal to be shocked, disoriented, embarrassed or involved. As the diary entries suggest, it is an outlook that tends to assert itself through minor deflections of language; at the simplest level, a word like 'bored' is substituted for 'enraged' or 'desolated'. In Balcairn's speech the sophistication is focused in the word 'indelicate'. What, according to the conventions of the time, should have been judged morally is instead judged aesthetically; the issue becomes one of delicacy rather than degeneracy. It is by blithe realignments of this sort that the Bright Young People affirm their eccentric perspective on the world, and it is for this reason that they are so closely identified with a certain form of language. Words conventionally associated with one kind of situation are shifted out of their usual context and applied to another. In this way new values are defined.

Adam, waking from an afternoon nap in Doubting Hall, notes that it would be a good place to go for the day 'after a really serious party'. It is not easy to conceive what else the word could be applied to in this world. When Adam's engagement has finally been broken off, it is a party that Miss Runcible proposes to him as an alternative to suicide, just as earlier she had led him away from his encounter with the customs officer, telling him 'all about a lovely party that was going to happen that night'. This, just after he has watched the autobiography on which his livelihood depends being dispatched to the incinerator — 'Adam, angel, don't fuss or we shall miss the train.' [VB 26] The reaction is typical. 'Such a fuss,' complains Lottie Crump in the aftermath of Flossie's death.

Ecstasy and despair are responses as appropriate, if not more so, to what is irredeemably trivial as to what is normally considered important. 'Divine', 'adorable', 'awful', 'terrible', relentlessly applied to social trivia, reduce all the other contexts in which they are used to the same level of social triviality. It is not that the enthusiasm implied by saying 'how divine' is necessarily factitious, merely that it is an enthusiasm quite without commitment. A comparable effect is achieved by the use of the word 'rather'. The term loses any force of qualification and simply registers in passing a degree of disengagement on the part of the speaker. 'They sat on our knees and embarrassed us rather,' Waugh says of some friendly Egyptian prostitutes, 'so we made our escape…' [*L* 84]. It is just one example of the way his tone in these early writings tends to draw on the linguistic mannerisms of his characters. The 'very heavenly' party he attends on board his cruise ship in *Labels* would no doubt have been described in just those words by Agatha Runcible. It is a vocabulary that has withdrawn all substance from its terms of praise and blame, flaunting its allegiance to what lies on the surface, its indifference to what lies beneath. The terms like 'shy-making' and 'drunk-making', which Waugh did much to popularize, reflect the same priorities; they indicate only the response to an experience, ascribing to the speaker a purely passive role which tacitly disclaims involvement in it.

These brittle forms of speech have emotional analogues that are equally typical of the pre-war novels. Paul Pennyfeather, after his final interview with Margot, 'was greatly pained at how little he was pained by the events of the afternoon' [*DF* 196]; and the thin paradox exemplifies a standard level of response. Emotional threats are neutralized by the bland assumption that emotions don't run deep enough to constitute a threat. Basil Seal has been having an affair with Prudence, but the discovery that he has eaten her at a cannibal banquet casts no shadow over his return to London. William Boot has been in love with Kätchen, yet he watches without bitterness as she and her porcine 'husband' are swept away into the dawn. In time Waugh's characters will become susceptible to pain, but for the moment they treat the betrayals and infidelities of personal life with as little concern as Balcairn displays over his aberrant relatives.

The random incisions of chance into this world are accommodated with no less poise. Adam's £1,000, casually acquired and as casually surrendered, create scarcely a ripple. Ringing up to tell Nina once again that after all they will be unable to get married, he explains that he has put the money on a horse:

> 'That was silly. Can't you get it back?'
> 'I gave it to a Major.'
> 'What sort of a Major?'
> 'Rather a drunk one. I don't know his name.'

'Well, I should try and catch him. I must go and eat now. Good-bye.' [*VB* 46]

This is not how Fred Vincy and Mary Garth would have played the scene. But then in *Middlemarch* Fred was being educated towards maturity and a sense of responsibility, whereas the adult notion that the business of life is to struggle and endure is precisely what the Bright Young People have set themselves against. Prime Ministers change week by week, fortunes come and go, but these are the concerns of a serious world. It is acceptable to look worn, as Basil does, from dissipation, but not from care.

That Balcairn should end by putting his head in the oven in no way alters this condition. The details of the episode belong unmistakably to the social world he is leaving behind. Preceded by a cocktail and interrupted by a frivolous impulse of professional jealousy, it is, like the £1,000 or the broken engagement, just another event, though admittedly a final one, in the perspectiveless world of a Bright Young Person. The scene is untainted by distress.

The element of childishness in Balcairn's speech is less easy to place within the context of this general outlook, but it nonetheless works to the same end. We can perhaps get a better idea of its importance by looking at the diary entry that was quoted earlier. Its veiled emphasis was on the nonchalance with which Waugh and Evelyn Gardner were going about their marriage, but here too there is a whisper of something else: 'Went to Warwick Square to see Harold and show him our licence.' It gives an inkling of what lay behind Nancy Mitford's description of them as being 'like two little boys' — or Cyril Connolly's remark that their house was 'like a smart little bandbox'. The story of Waugh himself contributing to the interior decoration of the place by sticking postage stamps to the coal scuttle is a congruent detail from the period.

It is evident that the childish accents of Balcairn's speech were more than a coincidental aspect of the characterization. Comparable images of the persistence of childhood come readily to mind: Adam waiting for Nina at Lady Metroland's ('If only you *knew* how sweet you looked skipping about in

Margot's hall all by yourself' [*VB* 80]); Basil, thwarted by
General Connolly, his expression 'insolent, sulky and curiously
childish' [*BM* 122]; Prudence and William as child lovers
('Listen, I've got a whole lot of new ideas for us to try'
[*BM* 55]); Brenda Last, who, after her visits to London,
'went completely to pieces quite suddenly and became a
waif' [*HD* 55]; Peter Pastmaster, taken on by Molly only
when he has shown himself to be in reality 'an adorable
little boy' [*PF* 158]. The list of examples could be extended,
but the point is clear: many of the characters who move at
ease in an atmosphere of social sophistication and moral
licence have, like Balcairn, a side to them which is naive
and immature.

Where then does this leave our notion of Waugh's detachment of tone? It surely gives life to just those parts
of the early novels which come closest to a denial of detachment, to the occasional stirrings of emotion we are
allowed to glimpse beneath the social hedonism. The
memory of Adam skipping in the hall is taken up again
a few pages later — 'You did look happy, you know, Adam,
and so sweet. I think I really fell in love with you for
the first time when I saw you dancing all alone in the
hall.' [*VB* 83] And again — 'In the train Nina said: "It's
awful to think that I shall probably never, as long as I live,
see you dancing like that again all by yourself." ' [*VB* 83]
The stress, three times repeated, on the fact that Adam
was alone is an invitation to sentiment. Later, at Margot
Metroland's party, 'Nina thought how once, only twenty-
four hours ago, she had been in love.' [*VB* 100] The past
tense makes its own muted appeal; it is a prediction of the
future:

> Later he said: 'I'd give anything in the world for some-
> thing different.'
>   'Different from me or different from everything?'
>   'Different from everything...only I've got nothing...
> what's the good of talking?'
>   'Oh, Adam, my dearest...'
>   'Yes?'
>   'Nothing.' [*VB* 192]

Here, if anywhere, one might feel that the glacial detachment of tone has been broken. Thus abstracted from the
rest of the novel, these passages suggest a relationship heavy
with melancholy, and although that may not be our experience in reading the book, the vein of emotion does exist.
Indeed, because the texture of the novel is so alien to it, this
emotion seems almost excessive, hovering at times, as in some
of the other novels, on the edge of sentimentality. Yet in the
end such passages do not upset the dominant tone of the
books. What links them to the author's attitude of ironic
detachment is precisely what links the elements of naivety
to those of sophistication in the characters: both are indicative of a refusal to engage life on what is conventionally
regarded as an 'adult' level.

It is consonant with this that the childishness and the
sophistication, the sentimentality and the indifference tend
to coexist most strikingly in the presentation of sexuality.
(Not by chance are Havelock Ellis and *Wind in the Willows*
Peter Beste-Chetwynde's favourite reading.) The first piece
of information we are given about the Bright Young People
is that 'They had spent a jolly morning strapping each other's
tummies with sticking plaster (how Miss Runcible had
wriggled).' [*VB* 11] The childishness of the exercise —
presumably intended as a precaution against sea-sickness —
is accentuated by 'jolly', 'tummies', 'wriggled', but there is
also a pointed element of sexuality. The acceptance of
unconventional forms of sexuality that we noted in the case
of Balcairn is a customary mark of sophistication in these
novels. Relationships in the early Waugh tend to be compounded of extremes of naive romance and urbane cynicism;
Paul's affair with Margot is perfectly reflected in the fact
that she is both an image of the first breath of spring in the
Champs-Elysées and the owner of a chain of brothels in
South America.

The middle ground on which relationships usually struggle
for survival is quite absent. When disaster occurs, the choice
is between Basil's indifference and Nina's melancholy. The
second is really no more painful than the first; it makes the
same assertion that what has gone wrong is nothing to do
with oneself. In Nina's response quoted above there is no

sense of a situation open to analysis or individual action. Occasions of sadness are adult problems, out of a child's range. Instead, there is just a general sense that the world has been unkind, that it is, in other words, a 'sad-making' place. Painful emotion is diffused into sentimental melancholy. Its sources are never studied. Whether they are sentimentalized or ignored, they remain equally remote. The responses of the child and the sophisticate achieve the same result.

It is this avoidance of the areas of commonplace adult enterprise and engagement which gives the early novels their endearing strain of frivolity. But even in a fictional world this tone is subject to pressure — most insistently from the older generation, for it is they who embody all the claims that are being denied. In the tensions between children and parents we can at times detect an element of stress that is not a conscious part of the novel's design.

There is, for example, the uncomfortable interchange in *Vile Bodies* between Peter Pastmaster and his step-father, whom he rebuffs with drunken brutality. It is a scene that comes immediately after Father Rothschild's sententious analysis of the Younger Generation ('But these young people have got hold of another end of the stick...' [*VB* 132]) and it produces in the reader a similar feeling of uneasiness. Neither passage is quite as it should be: one is too harsh, the other too heavy. And the chapter closes with a third scene which takes up the same subject and raises comparable doubts about the author's control. It is a finely turned conversation in which the Duchess of Stayle, with inexorable sweetness, arranges her protesting daughter's marriage. The tone is carefully maintained on the edge of exaggeration until the last sentence, 'It's a real joy to see the dear children so happy.' [*VB* 136] The line does not ring true: an adjective too many has tipped the balance, giving the scene a slight but perceptible burden of over-emphasis.

Vile Bodies was a novel that Waugh wrote quickly and

wrote, in part, under adverse conditions. Nowhere else in his fiction does one find so many incidental errors of clumsiness. Perhaps the end of this chapter was just one of the casualties. On the other hand, it is a suggestive fact that in these three successive scenes, all of which have a similar point of focus and which, taken together, may be said to constitute a semi-serious core to the novel, Waugh seems momentarily to lose his perfect pitch.

These hints of seriousness point to the possibility of areas that cannot properly be contained by Waugh's chosen tone. Later, in that part of the book he wrote after the break-up of his marriage, he interjects, with the emphasis of a separate paragraph, 'It hurt Adam deeply to think much about Nina.' [VB 185] Again the tone has faltered; there is nothing in the previous account of their relationship in which a comment of this nature can take root. A painful splinter of the writer's life has pierced the smoother surface of his art. As it does, perhaps, in the desolation of the final chapter. Is not the irony of its title, 'Happy Ending', a little too bitter for the rest of the book?

The strain is emotional, of course — Waugh's broken marriage and his fraught relationship with his father are there in the background — but it is also moral. We can sense behind these scenes the continual pressure of a more austere response: 'The trouble about the world today is...' Against this, too, Waugh must hold the line.

His tone is naturally antagonistic to moral judgements. 'I was interested,' he comments, in describing his visit to a Paris night club, 'to see the fine, manly girl in charge of the cloakroom very deftly stealing a silk scarf from an elderly German.' [L 23] The spectacle is one of craftsmanship, not of moral delinquency. A barely raised eyebrow is the most that can be provoked by anything encountered on his travels. In the course of an evening's brothel-going in Port Said he fetches up at the 'Maison Dorée'. 'Some of the ladies took off their frocks and did a little dance,' he remarks, 'singing a song which sounded like ta-ra-ra-boom-de-ay.' [L 84] An interesting variation on the entertainments offered in Mayfair. The humour depends on an appeal to the standards of polite society, but although it presupposes them, it does not, as

satire would, endorse them; it merely profits from the disparity
they reveal. The irony of tone is Olympian rather than insular.
It defends the author rather than any particular code of
values or behaviour. The traveller's interest is impartial, his
fastidiousness a mark of how remote he is from the touch of
what he sees.

The American edition of *Labels* was called *A Bachelor
Abroad*. Waugh was not in fact a bachelor at the time and
Evelyn Gardner was with him on the trip, but this new title
was in line with the persona he chose to adopt in writing the
book. He is a man without ties; he can regard the absurdities
of life around the Mediterranean — and later in Africa —
as dispassionately as he regarded the absurdities of life in the
worlds of *Decline and Fall* and *Vile Bodies*. Danger, disease
and depravity are accepted with equal unconcern. Real events
impinge no more sharply than fictional ones. In *Remote
People* he appends a footnote about the tribal interest in
telegraph wire. Having mentioned that the government dealt
with a few men who may have been implicated in thefts by
mutilating and then exhibiting them, he comments: 'no
doubt the example was salutary, but the telegraph service
remained very irregular' [*RP* 23]. The icy tone separates
him from the creatures he describes as effectively as a sheet
of sterilized glass. It is the same voice that we hear in his
fiction. When a foreign commercial agent is knifed in Azania,
Amurath responds by executing the culprits in front of the
Anglican Cathedral — 'and with them two or three witnesses
whose evidence was held to be unsatisfactory' [*BM* 13]. The
episode is related with a suavity that leaves no room for
indignation.

Only when Waugh's aesthetic sense is offended do we get
a movement of revulsion. On the journey from Port Said to
Malta he elects to travel second class — and soon regrets it.
There are too many people, and moreover 'the three or
four public seats were invariably occupied by mothers
doing frightful things to their babies with jars of vaseline'
[*WGG* 45]. It is the reaction — and language — of one of
the Bright Young People. Waugh does not at this stage
create an authorial perspective consistently separate from
that of his characters. To do so would be to expose them to

...u feel the
...f tone broken —
...n to the author's
...onic detachment
...t links the elements
...o those of sophistication,

...es — both indicate
...engage life on
...ly regarded as an 'adult'
level

| Ian Little |

- such pauses – w
glacial detachme
what links
attitude of
is precisely
of naivety
in he chan

ae refusal
hat is co

judgement, and it is their immunity from judgement, like
their immunity from pain, which is his line of defence.

Yet even in the pre-war novels this immunity is sometimes
precarious. The substitution of aesthetic for moral termin-
ology is not always a way of withdrawing from judgement.
Take the account in *Black Mischief* of Prudence's afternoon
rendezvous with Basil Seal. She goes into a shabby room
rank with tobacco smoke. Unshaven, Basil rises to meet her.

> He threw the butt of his Burma cheroot into the tin
> hip-bath which stood unemptied at the side of the bed;
> it sizzled and went out and floated throughout the
> afternoon, slowly unfurling in the soapy water.…
> Below, in the yard, Madame Youkoumian upbraided
> a goat. Strips of sunlight traversed the floor as an hour
> passed. In the bath water, the soggy stub of tobacco
> emanated a brown blot of juice. [*BM* 141]

Again our attention is directed towards what is aesthetically
displeasing about the scene, but we have only to compare the
effect of Balcairn's use of the word 'indelicate' to see the
difference. Rather than acting as an evasion of moral judgement, this description is pressing hard towards one. Only the
predominating mood of farce prevents it from being achieved.

In *A Handful of Dust* the pressure is predictably stronger.
It is not just that the humour is more muted; the writer's
detachment is under far greater strain from the autobio-
graphical realities out of which he created the book. His
presentation of a figure like Jenny Abdul Akbar conveys
more than social distaste. Even the description of her eating
muffins suggests a rapacity that goes beyond the physical:

> 'Muffins stand for so much,' said Jenny.
> She ate heartily; often she ran her tongue over her
> lips, collecting crumbs that had become embedded
> there and melted butter from the muffin. One drop of
> butter fell on her chin and glittered there unobserved
> except by Tony. [*HD* 85]

With John Andrew, Tony's son, this unappealing character
has an immediate success:

What a heavenly child...I love children. That has been
my great tragedy. It was when he found I couldn't
have children that the Moulay first showed the Other
Side of his Nature. It wasn't my fault...you see my
womb is out of place... [*HD* 87]

So powerfully charged with disgust, these images of vulgarity come close to delivering a moral judgement. As much
as anything else, Brenda's infidelity is presented as a colossal,
and partly conscious, failure of taste. The set into which she
moves, presided over by Mrs Beaver, is characterized by a
barbarity that reveals itself most obviously in the plans for
transforming Hetton, Tony's country house. The fate of
King's Thursday some years earlier was viewed with a much
cooler irony, and it is hard not to see in Waugh's presentation
of the aesthetic and emotional crudity of these people the
embodiment of a criticism that is basically moral. The
author's tone remains detached, but the involvement that
underlies it is evident.

A Handful of Dust occupies a pivotal position in the
development of Waugh's writing; it is poised between the
carelessness of disengagement and the consolations of faith.
The resulting sense that it is closer to the author's nerve ends
than any of his other fiction makes us perceive the restraint
of his tone as a singular triumph. Nevertheless, it marks an
important revision in the outlook that prevailed through the
earlier novels. Implicit in the book is a recognition that
those attitudes of sophisticated detachment which had been
part of the glamour of the social milieu to which he once
aspired were, from the inside, potentially vicious.

The old positions were never entirely abandoned. In the sad
introduction to his last book of travel reminiscences, Waugh
speculates about the history of the Cook's representative in
Paris: 'As happier men watch birds, I watch men. They are
less attractive but more various.' [*TA* 18] The principle is
still in essence defensive. As Waugh explained in his diary,

'to watch one's fellow-countrymen, as one used to watch foreigners, curious of their habits, patient of their absurdities, indifferent to their animosities — that is the secret of happiness in this century of the common man' [9 May 1962; *Diaries* 787]. But though an attitude of detachment might continue to attract him, it was not one that could be sustained indefinitely. *A Handful of Dust* had already exposed its limitations and in the later thirties two factors combined to weaken it. There was first the increasing pull of personal and domestic commitments and then, at the end of the decade, the demands made by the war. Both of these found a reflection in the work that followed Waugh's second marriage, and it is to a consideration of some of his later books that we must now turn.

'To write of someone loved, of oneself loving, above all of oneself being loved — how can these things be done with propriety? How can they be done at all?' [*WS* 151] The questions are asked in *Work Suspended*, the novel that was interrupted by the outbreak of the Second World War, and they suggest the distance travelled since *Decline and Fall*. Bereavement and the process of falling in love are the respective concerns of the book's first and second parts, and in each we find the same recognition of the potential treachery of words. Of his grief John Plant says:

> For the civilized man there are none of those swift transitions of joy and pain which possess the savage; words form slowly like pus about his hurts; there are no clean wounds for him; first a numbness, then a long festering, then a scar ever ready to re-open. Not until they have assumed the livery of the defence can his emotions pass through the lines; sometimes they come massed in a wooden horse, sometimes as single spies, but there is always a Fifth Column among the garrison ready to receive them. [*WS* 130]

It is quite evidently a world of emotional pressures more intrusive than any dreamed of by earlier characters. Moreover, the defensive role of words is not to be relied on; their powers can betray. In both these passages, the one concerning

love, the other grief, we have the sense of a writer contem-
plating the range and limitations of his medium. It is as
though, in *Work Suspended*, Waugh is taking stock of the
materials of his trade as a preliminary to some new departure.

Certainly, the fragment has an emotional density greater
than that of any of his previous works. The sort of statements which in an earlier book would have been neutral in
their detachment now carry a suggestion of something less
acceptable. Roger, we are told, did not resent his wife's
pregnancy:

> It was as though he had bought a hunter at the end of
> the season and turned him out; discerning friends, he
> knew, would appreciate the fine lines under the rough
> coat, but he would sooner have shown something
> glossy in the stable. He had summer business to do,
> moreover; the horse must wait till the late autumn.
> [*WS* 173]

The degree of Plant's involvement with Lucy, elaborated as
no previous emotional relationship has been in Waugh, edges
the husband's contrasting detachment into callousness.
Speaking of Simmonds's earlier affairs, Plant says, 'Trixie
had been Roger's last girl. Basil had passed her on to him,
resumed the use of her for a week or two, then passed her
back.' [*WS* 148] It is a pattern of relationships that, presented with less brutality, would have fitted comfortably into
the early novels. But the coarse note of 'resumed the use
of her' makes no concessions to any glamour in such sophisticated nonchalance. We have the feeling, as elsewhere in *Work
Suspended*, that attitudes which served in the past are now
unsatisfactory, even perhaps reprehensible.

It is significant that the central action of these pages
should turn on Plant's new 'sense of homelessness' and his
consequent attempts to find a house. The abandoning of
geographical detachment has obvious emotional parallels
which can be traced in Waugh's own life as well as in that of
his character.

Plant's new house is found, but the outbreak of war
enforces other claims. In *Put Out More Flags* we are shown

how one by one the 'race of ghosts' from the period of
Decline and Fall, *Vile Bodies* and *Black Mischief* respond
to them. Sonia Trumpington gives a tentative explanation of
Alastair's enlistment:

> 'You see he'd never done anything for the country and
> though we were always broke we had lots of money
> really and lots of fun. I believe he thought that perhaps
> if we hadn't had so much fun perhaps there wouldn't
> have been any war. Though how he could blame himself
> for Hitler I never quite saw....At least I do now in a
> way,' she added. 'He went into the ranks as a kind of
> penance or whatever it's called that religious people are
> always supposed to do.' [*PF* 106]

Sonia's hesitancy, almost embarrassment, is partly the
author's. Waugh is not quite certain how seriously he can
present the case, but its emphasis is clear: membership of a
society imposes obligations of which the Bright Young
Things have taken too little care.

The war is a chance to make reparation, but what must
first be sacrificed is the aesthetic detachment of the artist.
In *Put Out More Flags* the dismissal of this viewpoint is
played out in the opposition between Basil Seal and Ambrose
Silk. For all Silk's absurdity, there is plenty of evidence in
the book to suggest his kinship with Waugh. 'Born after his
time' [*PF* 42] is how he describes himself — a figure unbap-
tized into the modern world: 'I belong, hopelessly, to the
age of the ivory tower.' [*PF* 35] His ideal of Chinese scholar-
ship and a life of withdrawal is satirized by Mr Bentley's
parallel with Godfrey Winn, but the extent of its attraction
is fully evident in the description of Cedric Lyne making his
way across to the Loamshires in the middle of a battle:

> As he walked alone he was exhilarated with the sense of
> being one man, one pair of legs, one pair of eyes, one
> brain, sent on a single intelligible task; one man alone
> could go freely anywhere on the earth's surface; multi-
> ply him, put him in a drove and by each addition of his
> fellows you subtract something that is of value, make

him so much less a man; this was the crazy mathematics of war...there's danger in numbers; divided we stand, united we fall, thought Cedric, striding happily towards the enemy, shaking from his boots all the frustration of corporate life. He did not know it, but he was thinking exactly what Ambrose had thought when he announced that culture must cease to be conventual and become cenobitic. [*PF* 207-8]

The terms of this new engagement are harsh; the pressures of war obliterate the individual and exalt the group. The formula could hardly be more repugnant.

Angela Lyne is another isolated figure. Her face tells nothing: 'It might have been carved in jade, it was so smooth and cool and conventionally removed from the human.' [*PF* 25] She exemplifies the individual as work of art in both its barrenness and its beauty. Later, she says to Basil:

'In the old days if there was one thing wrong it spoiled everything; from now on for all our lives, if there's one thing right the day is made.'
'That sounds like poor Ambrose in his Chinese mood.' [*PF* 218]

She, like her husband and Ambrose Silk, is identified with an impulse of withdrawal that is inappropriate to the hour. Their self-isolating preoccupation with things aesthetic — Angela with herself, Cedric with his grottoes, Ambrose with his art (and it is made clear that he *is* an artist [*PF* 188]) — makes them victims of the war. The contrasting enthusiasm for battle of Alastair, Basil and Peter Pastmaster may be boyish, but in the end enthusiasm is what the novel endorses.

When Cedric finds the tattered remains of the Loamshires, he asks the subaltern in command what happened. '"It was all rather a nonsense," said the subaltern, in the classic phraseology of his trade which comprehends all human tragedy.' [*PF* 209] The subaltern's words might neatly have defined the view of human tragedy taken by the early Waugh. Now, however, the phrase has a different emphasis; its tone is no longer that of disengagement but of the charged and committed understatement of an English tradition of heroism.

In *Sword of Honour* there is from the start a sharper recognition of the human cost of this commitment. ('Oh, Guy, you're too young to remember,' [*MA* 32] his sister tells him, when she sees his keenness to get to France.) But in other respects the trilogy extends and deepens the earlier critique of disengagement. Guy's seclusion in his Italian castle is presented unambiguously as a symptom of emotional deprivation. The journey back 'to his own country to serve his King' is a rediscovery of the springs of life.

> Eight years of shame and loneliness were ended. For eight years Guy, already set apart from his fellows by his own deep wound, that unstaunched, internal drain-ing away of life and love, had been deprived of the loyalties which should have sustained him. [*MA* 12]

The emotional void is filled − to overflowing − by the attachment he develops towards his regiment.

> Guy loved Major Tickeridge and Captain Bosanquet. He loved Apthorpe. He loved the oil-painting over the fireplace of the unbroken square of Halberdiers in the desert. He loved the whole corps deeply and tenderly. [*MA* 53]

It is an emotion, like his later 'deep affection' for X Com-mando, that derives from a newly found sense of community among men who say 'Here's how' before swallowing their pink gin, play rugger in the mess, and think lightly of sexual conquest. There is a certain relish for Ritchie-Hook's total lack of aesthetic sense as he lavishes praise on a hideous calendar of gnomes and toadstools; it is an element in Guy's affection.

When his love for the army is betrayed on Crete, his response is to seek refuge in the old isolation. He detaches himself physically from the world around him by refusing to speak:

there was an orchestra pit, footlights, a draped proscen-
ium, between him and all these people. He lay like an
explorer in his lamp-lit tent while in the darkness outside the anthropophagi peered and jostled. [*OG* 226]

The two images summarize classic attitudes of defensive
withdrawal: life as a spectacle, other humans as an alien —
and barbarous — species.

It is at this point that Julia Stitch comes on the scene. She
has survived dazzlingly intact from the days before the war.
Her stylish charm as she drives recklessly through Alexandria
in search of a pair of crimson slippers is an apparently un-
muted echo of the scene in *Scoop* in which she drove through
London in search of a carpet shop. She retains from an earlier
decade the priorities which for others have been revised by
the demands of war and the responsibilities of patriotic allegiance. She is detached from the wartime concerns to which
Guy had committed himself, and in his revulsion from the
army it is to her that he responds.

But his alliance with her can only be temporary. Her
attractiveness has become, with the changing situation, a
dubious quality: 'Three or four times a day she was at his
side with the hypodermic needle of her charm.' [*OG* 239]
The phrase has a sinister undertone; it seems to involve an
admission, perhaps in the wake of *Brideshead Revisited*,
that charm can be a drug, the attraction of style no more
than a pain-killer. It is Julia who delays Guy's return to
England and who drops into a wastepaper basket the soldier's
identity disc that he had brought back from Crete. When she
fondly kisses him goodbye, we are forced to confront the
fact that the seductive attitudes of a pre-war lifestyle cannot
without taint survive the pressures of a war.

It is in the nature of things that Julia's act of betrayal (and
I take it that her kiss, along with the reference to Hérédia's
image of Cleopatra,[4] is intended to make this word apposite)

---

[4]   Et sur elle courbé, l'ardent Imperator
   Vit dans ses larges yeux étoilés de points d'or
   Toute une mer immense où fuyaient des galères.
('Antoine et Cléôpatre', José-Maria de Hérédia). Julia's eyes, as she sees Guy off,
are described as 'one immense sea, full of flying galleys'.

should be committed in defence of Ivor Claire. Both of them
are linked in Guy's mind to memories of the past, he to an
afternoon in the Borghese Gardens, she to a luncheon party
on the Tyrrhenian coast. Both retain the priorities appropriate to these memories and to the styles of life that go with
them. In Ivor Claire Waugh embodies an admission even
bitterer than his disillusionment with the army, for Claire,
like Julia Stitch, only more poignantly so, is a late and
cherished bloom of Waugh's first love. Exquisite, incorrigible, impeccable, Ivor Claire is 'the fine flower of them all'
[OG 114]; he is graced with just the qualities of style that
have fired Waugh's imagination since the first vision of
Margot Beste-Chetwynde stepping from her Hispano-Suiza.
An unrepentant remnant of aristocracy in the century of
the common man, he more than anyone is the focus of
Waugh's residual admiration for the detached invulnerability
of the dandy. But the detachment that gives Claire his style
is also what cuts him off from those commitments which
could have checked his drift into dishonour. There is no
logical objection to his argument in favour of desertion; the
only counter to it would be an appeal to loyalties from which
he has withdrawn himself. When the treacherous decision
has been taken, Guy looks at him and sees, ironically, just the
image that had originally attracted him: 'Guy could see him
clearly in the moonlight, the austere face, haggard now but
calm and recollected, as he had first seen it in the Borghese
Gardens.' [OG 221]

There is no way back from the Cretan débâcle. Conceived
in terms of style, detachment has shown itself fatally liable to
corruption. As an emotional condition, its pathos is re-
emphasized in Guy's disoriented wanderings across the island.
Caught at one point between Hookforce and the Halberdiers,
he recognizes his isolation:

And all the deep sense of desolation which he had
sought to cure, which from time to time momentarily
seemed to be cured, overwhelmed him as of old. His
heart sank. It seemed to him as though literally an organ
of his body was displaced, subsiding, falling heavily like
a feather in a vacuum jar; Philoctetes set apart from his

fellows by an old festering wound; Philoctetes without
his bow. Sir Roger without his sword. [*OG* 210]

It is not just that isolation, so far from being the defence he
had tried to make of it in Italy, is perceived as a fundamental
evil; the passage also marks Guy's recognition that the attach-
ments by which he had sought to break his isolation were
illusory ones. Claire's defection and Guy's disenchantment,
both of which are the substance of the concluding pages of
Officers and Gentlemen, go some way to explain a certain
flatness in the final volume of the trilogy. Gaiety, charm,
grace, style are notably lacking in its characters, partly
because it is a meaner world than it seemed at the beginning
of the story, but partly also because these qualities no longer
command the writer's allegiance as once they used to.

The development of Kilbannock through the trilogy
provides a grim commentary. Initially, there are echoes of
Basil Seal, or at least of the Seal, Pastmaster, Trumpington
ethos. He seems to be cast in the same mould: nonchalant,
mildly caddish — a good sort rather than otherwise. His
response in the Prologue to *Men at Arms* is typical: 'I want
to be known as one of the soft-faced men who did well out
of the war.' [*MA* 26] In *Put Out More Flags* Basil had said:
'I want to be one of those people one heard about in 1919;
the hard-faced men who did well out of the war.' [*PF* 46]
But there the ways part. Kilbannock turns out to mean what
he said. *Officers and Gentlemen* leaves him a somewhat tarnished figure; his contribution to the war effort has been the
manipulation of Trimmer and the virtual prostitution of
Virginia. In *Unconditional Surrender* we find him repeating
stories in Bellamy's, like a typical club bore, and then avoiding his round of drinks. (The last person to do that was
Beaver.) Viewed in the light of his dealings with Guy and
Virginia, Kilbannock cuts a shabby figure.

He reflects in subdued tones a version of what is portrayed
in Ivor Claire. The impudence with which Claire abridges the
night operation by hiring a bus is at the time marked up to
his credit; it gives a humorous turn to his well-bred disdain
for more plodding ways of going to work; it has style. Later,
it comes to seem more ambiguous; it was also an easy way

out. Kilbannock's unscrupulous use of Guy to second his
Air-Marshall's application to join Bellamy's functions in the
same way. In both characters the seeds of corruption are
located in facets of their personality that before the war
would have been admired or unremarked. Like Jock Grant-
Menzies in *A Handful of Dust*, they were the sort for whom
people made room at the bar. People still do, but Waugh is
less enchanted.

In the course of the trilogy Guy moves as far as either
of them, though in a different direction. His final marriage
is a commitment in striking contrast to his self-dedication
at the tomb of Roger of Waybroke. The bond he forms in
adopting Trimmer's son is a deliberate acceptance of ties
with what is least congenial to him in human society. And
the religious motive for this step brings us to the final stage
of the argument.

That religion must impose other claims than those of
style was apparent before the war. In the last of the pre-
war travel books explicit moral judgements were already
beginning to force themselves into the writer's world. A
tone of detachment had been adequate for the vignette of
the Parisian cloakroom girl, but his irreverent guide to the
hidden convent of Puebla outrages him in a way that ten
years earlier would have been inconceivable:

> It was, to me at any rate, inexpressibly shocking to see
> him jingling the little penitential chains which they had
> found the nuns wearing; to hear him sneer at the under-
> ground cells where the nuns retired for meditation and
> at the three foot door through which they crept to
> Mass. [*RL* 249]

There is, of course, room for cynicism. *Robbery Under Law*
was written on commission with an acknowledged political
motive, but even if Waugh's indignation has been given a
propagandist fillip, it is still significant, when we think back
to the supreme indifference of *Vile Bodies*, that he should
have involved himself on one side of a political issue in the
first place.

To take political sides, to champion the cause of religion,

to make war for certain values — these things cannot be
done honestly without the sacrifice of a measure of detachment. They demand that judgements be made. The
locked vans rolling east and west towards the concentration
camps in *Men at Arms*, the dishonourable collapse on Crete,
the fate of the Jugoslav Jews in *Unconditional Surrender*, are
part of an order of experience that requires subtler tones
and graver concessions than lie within the range of the artist
for whom men are really no more than birds to the bird-
watcher.

In so far as these developments are the product of a
deepening religious influence in Waugh's work, the revision
they imply of many of his earlier attitudes has already been
foreshadowed in *Brideshead Revisited*. The subject is for a
later chapter. Here it is enough to note that while his religious
convictions did on one level demand from him judgements
and commitments which previously he had eschewed, they
also provided the foundation for a different, and more profound, kind of detachment. Religion in Waugh's novels is
seen primarily not as a source of social and political obligations but as a refuge from social and political disillusionment.
For Helena, for Guy Crouchback, in the end for Charles
Ryder, it constitutes an object of attachment and a realm of
stability that are in direct contrast to the squalor of loveless
marriage, foolish ambition and ignoble expediency that
characterizes the world of human affairs. What is being
offered by religion is a kind of detachment more absolute,
if more demanding, than anything that can be attained
simply through mastery of tone.

Perhaps it is this security that permits Waugh to exercise
an unusual degree of imaginative sympathy towards some of
his characters in these last novels. Earlier in his career there
was a marked disparity between the rigour of his pronouncements on the Younger Generation in his *Spectator* article and
the imaginative presentation of them in *Vile Bodies*. Fiction,
it was argued, enabled him to defuse the most painful aspects
of reality and deny its harsher laws. The result was a world
of brittle detachment, invulnerable on its own terms, but
limited in the range of experience it could comprehend. The
seriousness of the *Spectator* article cannot be superimposed

on *Vile Bodies* without doing violence to the prevailing mood of the novel.

The disparity is still present when we come to the war trilogy, but it no longer implies a contradiction. Take, for example, Waugh's remark in his interview with Julian Jebb that 'Guy is offered this chance [of salvation] by making himself responsible for the upbringing of Trimmer's child, to see that he is not brought up by his dissolute mother.'[5] The tone of such a comment is strikingly at odds with the sympathy a reader is allowed to feel for Virginia. Even when she is looking for an abortion — surely, from a Roman Catholic point of view, her most disgraceful pass — Waugh can still do justice to the 'high incorrigible candour' [*US* 83] with which she goes about it. But the sympathy is no longer incompatible with judgement. The novel can contain both without distorting them because the writer's detachment is not now primarily a mechanism of self-defence but a consequence of his security.

It is the achievement of the final novels to separate sympathy from vulnerability. Despite the realism of these books, the author of the war trilogy is paradoxically less involved with his fictional world than the author of *Decline and Fall* or *Vile Bodies*; he has less at stake because his security is invested elsewhere. Only now, towards the end, can sympathy be seen as more than a risk, detachment as more than a tone.

[5] Julian Jebb, 'The Art of Fiction XXX: Evelyn Waugh'.

2

Humour

In a paper on humour written in 1927, Freud tells the story of the criminal, led out to the gallows on a Monday morning, who remarks to his executioners, 'Well, the week's beginning nicely.' The man's response provides a convenient model of one of the ways in which defensive humour can work. Its essence is a refusal to take things at their own level of seriousness. The humorist resists the conventional claims of a situation and responds to it instead according to a different scale of values, imposed by himself. The force of circumstance yields to his rebellious perception of it; what seemed fearful is transformed into an occasion for laughter. This is his victory.

It will not be the humour of, say, George Eliot — a tolerant smile to ease our passage in a flawed world; its drift will be crueller and more mischievous. Callousness is an indispensable constituent, for it is taking us in exactly the opposite direction from that envisaged by the great nineteenth-century novelists. This is not an art that will enlarge men's sympathies; sympathy — or at least the obligations imposed by sympathy — is just what defensive humour is seeking to avoid. It functions by undermining the accepted basis of personal and social responsibility. The tyranny against which it stands is that of a concept of adult maturity. Its aim is to set the humorist outside and above the conditions of a life that is all the time hedging him round with calls on gravity and prudence and good sense — invitations to turn serious. Such invitations are not usually as pressing as the threat of execution, but they are encountered at every stage of daily life. To refuse them demands an effort of imagination and revolt.

We might take as a point of departure three images from the opening of *Decline and Fall*. First, there are the guests assembled for the Bollinger dinner — amongst them, 'ambitious young barristers and Conservative candidates torn from the London season and the indelicate advances of débutantes' [*DF* 9]. Then, as the occasion gathers momentum, we are shown the college authorities, in the persons of the Junior Dean and the Domestic Bursar, cowering in the darkness of the Senior Common Room. Finally, as the prospect of enormous fines and the consequent flow of founder's port gains on their imagination, we have the Junior Dean's somewhat heterodox prayer, 'Oh, please God, make them attack the Chapel.' In each case the humorous charge comes from a reversal of the expected order of things: débutantes as the initiators rather than the victims of indelicate advances, authority hiding from transgressors rather than prosecuting them, prayers being offered for the destruction of the Chapel rather than for its preservation. These inversions can be taken as a paradigm of much of the humour that follows.

Waugh has, moreover, in these first two pages of *Decline and Fall* outlined the three areas that are to be his most fertile sources of absurdity: sex, authority and religion. Illustrations of this are too plentiful to require much quotation. Lesbianism, pederasty, buggery and bestiality all have their adherents in the first couple of novels, and sexual irregularities are chronicled by Waugh with obvious relish. ('It was like having Puck as a member of the household,' Lady Dorothy Lygon recalls.[1]) At home and abroad pimps were among his most reliable comic stand-bys. From the leader of the Llanabba silver band to more exotic procurers like Youkoumian and Palaeologue they ply their trade with a bland insensitivity to moral scruples which delights him by its outrageousness.

Since everything is in the artist's gift, he is free to lend his characters whatever disreputable touches of colour he

---

[1] *Evelyn Waugh and his World*, ed. David Pryce-Jones, p. 50.

chooses. The special piquancy of linking sexual humour with figures of religious or secular eminence gives Mrs Ape her favourite Angel, the Nestorian Patriarch his favourite deacon and Sir Walter Outrage his oriental fantasies. The dignified and sometimes improbable associations of their office make clergymen, with or without any sexual peculiarities, particularly vulnerable to ridicule; from Prendergast onwards they have much to endure in Waugh's novels. Even in a work so relatively sober in temper as the biography of Edmund Campion, Waugh cannot resist the temptation to explain that when a harlot was introduced into the cell of the Bishop of Lincoln and the Abbot of Westminster, imprisoned in Wisbech Castle, it was 'not with the kindly, if misguided, notion of relieving their depression, but in order to damage the reputations of these aged men with the charge of incontinence' [EC 113]. He is clearly tickled by the situation. His words — 'kindly', 'misguided', 'notion', 'depression' — are just far enough off-centre to suggest irony without obtruding it. The solemn cadence of the last clause barely conceals a grin, but manages to stop short of broadening it into mockery. Often one can sense behind Waugh's writing the presence of a schoolboy who knows to a hair's breadth how to keep his impudence out of the reach of retribution — 'a prancing faun, thinly disguised by conventional apparel' was how Harold Acton described him in Memoirs of an Aesthete.

Figures of secular authority fare little better than the prelates. Maltravers and Lucas-Dockery, Outrage, Monomark, Copper, Mannering — all of them are inviting targets. In one form or another, irreverence is the staple of Waugh's early humour. But in what sense can this humour be called defensive? On the simplest level, it makes fun of what the world takes seriously. More precisely, it affirms a scale of values contrary to those by which we are accustomed to live. The humorous inversions in the opening scene of Decline and Fall are symptomatic of a much more general challenge to orthodox perspectives. How Waugh formulates this challenge is the subject of the present chapter. In this section and the next I shall be focusing on Black Mischief.

Consider Sir Samson Courteney, his Britannic Majesty's

Minister to Azania. We first come upon him sporting in his
bath with an inflated rubber sea-serpent, rapt in a daydream
of the Pleistocene age. Outside a war is being fought. William
Bland interrupts his daydream with the news that Walker has
ridden over to see him.

> Sir Samson returned abruptly to the twentieth cen-
> tury, to a stale and crowded world; to a bath grown
> tepid and an india-rubber toy.
> 'Walker? Never heard of him.'
> 'Yes, sir, you know him. The American secretary.'
> 'Oh, yes, to be sure. Extraordinary time to call. What
> on earth does the fellow want? If he tries to borrow the
> tennis marker again, tell him it's broken.'
> 'He's just got information about the war. Apparently
> there's been a decisive battle at last.'
> 'Oh, well, I'm glad to hear that. Which side won, do
> you know?'
> 'He did tell me, but I've forgotten.'
> 'Doesn't matter. I'll hear about it from him. Tell him
> I'll be down directly. Give him a putter and let him play
> clock golf. And you'd better let them know he'll be
> staying to luncheon.'
> Half an hour later Sir Samson came downstairs and
> greeted Mr Walker.
> 'My dear fellow, how good of you to come. I couldn't
> get out before; the morning is always rather busy here. I
> hope they've been looking after you properly. I think
> it's about time for a cocktail, William.' [BM 63]

The claims of office rate low on the Envoy's scale of
priorities, and he makes the engaging assumption that the
same is likely to be true for everyone else. The inconvenience
of lending the tennis marker is closer to his heart than any
concern over the current war. The phrase 'a decisive battle'
stimulates no more than polite curiosity; the tone of his
enquiry as to 'which side won' might suggest a cricket match
of rather less than usual interest. After his moment of disillusionment in the bath, the Envoy again rises above the
intrusion of 'the stale and crowded world', imposing his

own standards of judgement with effortless absurdity. Unmoved by grosser considerations, his mind turns, at the appropriate hour, to the question of cocktails.

This attitude to the fate of Azania belongs in the context of a total, though quite unconscious, refusal to respond to the world according to customary notions of what is important and what is trivial. It is a refusal that is fairly typical of Waugh's characters. Ten years after the event Lady Moping persists in regarding her husband's attempted suicide as a base betrayal on the day of her annual garden party — an act of disloyalty compounded by the fact that it was done '*in front of the Chester-Martins*'. The response is idiosyncratic, but, once one accepts a system of values in which social considerations have absolute primacy, perfectly logical. Lady Moping is impervious to human priorities, just as the Envoy is impervious to diplomatic priorities and William Boot to the harsh priorities of journalism. The latter's rambling, chatty telegrams ('PLEASE DONT WORRY QUITE SAFE AND WELL IN FACT RATHER ENJOYING THINGS WEATHER IMPROVING' etc.) are a fair example of the absurdity that results when a character fails to catch the idiom of the world in which he is moving. Boot simply carries on as though he had never left the environment of Boot Magna.

This, of course, is a traditional characteristic of the Englishman abroad. It is what makes the Legation in Azania so bizarre. While war and revolution rage outside, civilians clamour for protection and other legations disperse in panic, the British remain preoccupied with tennis and bagatelle, the growing of asparagus and the digging of the lily-pond. But the humour of the situation operates on behalf of these people as well as against them. Such total insouciance has a certain lunatic splendour to which Waugh is very much alive. Indeed, the unruffled social tone with which they meet the news of murder, loot and fire is quite close to the tone that Waugh himself sought to impose on the world both of his fiction and of his travel books. There is, after all, sound precedent for the British attitude. It is not such a large step from the gardens of the Legation to the bowling green on which Sir Francis Drake received news of the Spanish

Armada. 'There is plenty of time to finish the game…'

In England a social tone carries strong implications of class, and this brings us to the edge of one of the determining aspects of Waugh's humour. When Julia Stitch gets caught in a traffic jam, she extricates herself with her usual panache:

> She mounted the kerb and bowled rapidly along the pavement to the corner of St James's, where a policeman took her number and ordered her into the road.
> 'Third time this week,' said Mrs Stitch. 'I wish they wouldn't. It's such a nuisance for Algy.' [S 9]

What Waugh finds attractive in her is an absolute carelessness of the sort of everyday restrictions by which the lives of most of us are bound. Roads are for driving on, pavements for walking on, and there are policemen to ensure that the principle is maintained; but neither the law nor the sanctions against those who break it impinge for a moment on Mrs Stitch. It never occurs to her to consider herself bound by the regulations that govern everyone else or to bother about the consequences of ignoring them. It would be unthinkable to take policemen seriously. This is the same source of amusement as Waugh had derived from the Legation in Azania, but more clearly than in *Black Mischief* it shows how far this sort of humour is dependent on characteristically upper class attitudes to life.

The tradition is summarized in a passage in *The Leopard* by Giuseppe Tomasi di Lampedusa. (It is a novel Waugh later read with approval and commended to Nancy Mitford in a letter of May 1960 as the only good book to have appeared during the year [*Letters* 540].) At this point Padre Pirrone is trying to explain to Don Pietrino something of the mentality of the 'signori':

> They're just different. Perhaps they seem so strange to us because they have reached a stage towards which everyone who is not a saint is moving, that of the indifference to earthly goods which comes from surfeit. Perhaps it is for this reason that they are careless of

certain things which to the rest of us are of great importance....For them new fears have come into being
which are unknown to us: I have seen Don Fabrizio,
wise and serious though he is, get angry over a shirt
collar that was badly ironed, and I know for a fact that
the Prince of Lascari was for a whole night too enraged
to sleep because he had been wrongly seated at one of
the Viceroy's dinners.[2]

He goes on later to contrast this with the bearing of a nobleman who intended to commit suicide:

And then these aristocrats put a good face on their
troubles. I've seen one of them, poor man, who had
decided to kill himself the following day and who
looked smiling and spirited as a boy on the eve of his
first Communion; while you, Don Pietrino, if you were
forced to drink one of your own herbal concoctions,
would make the village ring with your laments.[3]

Behind the priest's words is the recognition that members
of the aristocracy are, traditionally, a law unto themselves,
that they have developed a hierarchy of values different
from that accepted by the mass of people, and that one
aspect of this hierarchy is the inversion, in certain areas, of
what is taken seriously and what is not; trifling matters of
form can be treated with deadly seriousness, matters of life
and death with frivolity.

Perhaps a phrase like 'indifference to earthly goods' seems
inflated in this context, but it is relevant nonetheless. In
more sober language it points to something we have observed
both here and in the previous chapter: the tone that is caught
by Raymond in *Remote People*, as he drives Waugh out to
Muthaiga — 'The windscreen of his car has been broken over-
night, and the body heavily battered. He remarks that
someone must have borrowed it.' [*RP* 177] Mrs Stitch would
no doubt have reacted in the same way. It is exactly the sort

[2] Giuseppe Tomasi di Lampedusa, *Il Gattopardo*, p. 133.
[3] Ibid., p. 135.

of carelessness of which Padre Pirrone is speaking, and although the religious turn of the priest's phrase might have baffled Raymond himself or Julia Stitch, it would have been perfectly comprehensible to Waugh.

The passage from Lampedusa must have pleased him. It traces the outlines of an attitude from which he constructed important elements of his own authorial persona. The upper classes were attractive because a tradition of wealth and privilege enabled them to live life on their own terms. And this is just the condition to which humour aspires. Set Padre Pirrone's nobleman on the point of suicide — 'smiling and spirited as a boy on the eve of his first Communion' — against Freud's comment on the intention of humour: 'It means: "Look! here is the world, which seemed so dangerous! It is nothing but a game for children — just worth making a jest about!"' This is what the man about to be hanged says with his joke; it is what the nobleman says with his behaviour. The superiority to circumstance which one gains through humour, the other has acquired through an inherited code of responses. Is it perhaps through irony that the poor man can aspire to be an aristocrat? The marks of snobbery in Waugh's writing tend to wound our modern sensibilities, but they have an evident connection at this point with the workings of his humour.

It is one of many areas where we can pick out his affinities with Dickens, whose changing attitude to upper class *désinvolture* culminates in *Our Mutual Friend* with the admiring portrait of Eugene Wrayburn. There are ways and ways of asserting superiority, and the vein of callousness in Dickens's humour is one of them; it forges a link of sympathy with even the most depraved of his heartless aristocrats. But once this sympathy becomes explicit, as in the case of Wrayburn, Dickens can barely stop short of adulation. Waugh, by contrast, will rarely allow himself to be caught in a posture of hero-worship. As the example of Lady Moping suggests, he is quite capable of seeing what is ridiculous in the aristocratic tendency to exalt social form at the expense of human sympathy. When Lady Circumference expresses vexation that her son should have died just when he has, since it may lead people to mistake her reason for refusing to

attend Paul's and Margot's wedding, we are in no doubt
about the object of Waugh's mockery.

Often, however, the direction of his class humour is
more elusive. Before leaving for Azania, Basil goes round
to see Sonia and Alastair and finds them in bed. Confined to
the house by duns, they are nonetheless acting as reluctant
hosts to a miscellaneous group of people who can't be
bothered to go anywhere else. Sonia to Alastair:

> 'Ring for dinner, sweet. I forget what there is, but
> I know it's rather good. I ordered it myself.'
> There was whitebait, grilled kidneys and toasted
> cheese. Basil sat between them on the bed and they ate
> from their knees. Sonia threw a kidney to the dogs and
> they began a fight.
> Alastair: 'It's no good. I can't eat anything.'
> Sonia's maid brought in the trays. She asked her:
> 'How are the gentlemen getting on downstairs?'
> 'They asked for champagne.'
> 'I suppose they'd better have it. It's very bad.'
> Alastair: 'It's very good.'
> 'Well it tasted awful to me. Basil, sweety, what's your
> news?'
> 'I'm going to Azania.'
> 'Can't say I know much about that. Is it far?'
> 'Yes.'
> 'Fun?'
> 'Yes.'
> 'Oh, Alastair, why not us too?'
> 'Hell, now those dogs have upset everything again.'
> 'How pompous you're being.' [BM 78-9]

It is one of the scenes of sophisticated disorder to which
bedrooms lend themselves in an upper class world — a more
sordid parallel to Mrs Stitch's levée in *Scoop*. The atmosphere can only exist as the result of a particular combination
of values, which once again depends upon stressing the pre-
eminent importance of trivia. The threat of duns must not
be allowed to interfere with the quality of one's dinner or
the extravagance of sharing it with the dogs. It may be costly

to dispense champagne, but it would be tedious to make a
fuss about it. Despite Alastair's petulance, the situation
obviously distresses him no more than it does Sonia. His
complaints about the hangers-on or the destructive and
incontinent dogs are either ignored or called pompous.
Applied to what seems an entirely reasonable grievance, the
oddity of this adjective highlights the singularity of Sonia's
viewpoint. What is Alastair accused of? Giving himself the
airs of a grown-up? In any case, he soon settles down to play
happy families with the other two.

   Like snap, happy families is a game that recurs in Waugh's
novels. To play either of them is inevitably to be an object
of the author's irony, but it is also to be marked as a character who is essentially sympathetic. Waugh is clearly charmed
by Sonia's insouciance and Alastair's petulant resignation;
there is no residue of the sharpness with which the latter was
portrayed in *Decline and Fall*. Their carelessness of just the
things that most people spend life worrying about is a source
of ironic humour, but also of envy — the sort of unreal envy
one feels for possibilities that can only exist in the simplified
worlds of fiction and memory. It is an integral part of our
response to what Enid Welsford called comedy's 'pleasing
delusion that facts are more flexible than they appear to
be'.[4] Sitting between Sonia and Alastair on the bed in this
scene, Basil is as close to his creator as he comes at any point
in the book. But there is never any question of their being
identical. That Waugh recognizes the childishness of the
tableau would alone be enough to separate them. There is in
him a Chaucerian propensity for creating imaginative projections of himself while at the same time humorously
exploiting the artist's superiority to them. He can be at once
both child and adult.

   The appeal of this combination points to a strand of
Waugh's attachment to the upper classes which has already
been touched on in our consideration of tone. It was until
recently their curious distinction to unite a lifestyle which
gave them access to all the trappings of sophistication with
certain habits of mind determined by an incorrigible

[4] *The Fool*, p. 322.

nostalgia for adolescence. Waugh's own schooldays were remembered with little enthusiasm, but he recognized that the sort of freemasonry that existed between members of the upper classes, enabling them, however remote the place or outlandish the circumstances, to regroup smoothly with their own kind, was largely a product of the years they had spent at school together. 'Beastly,' says the young vice-consul, 'Moke,' says Boot, and the relationship is re-established, while Corker, the outsider, stands by nonplussed. Although Waugh seems to like this sort of thing, or at any rate the idea of it, the theme was first broached with a good deal more cynicism in the figure of Grimes.

> 'Besides, you see, I'm a public-school man. That means everything. There's a blessed equity in the English social system,' said Grimes, 'that ensures the public-school man against starvation. One goes through four or five years of perfect hell at an age when life is bound to be hell, anyway, and after that the social system never lets one down.' [DF 28]

Perhaps Waugh was at this stage still too close to the experience for it to have gained much enchantment, but the satire in *Decline and Fall* does not really erode his basic regard for the ethos of the public school. The way people in his novels employ its characteristic phraseology can provide the reader with a fairly sensitive index of their place in the novelist's sympathies. And this is not confined to the men. The upper class woman, if she is the right sort, is likely to have absorbed something of the jargon of the public school as well. 'Foregonners,' replies Mrs Stitch, when John Boot asks if there is really no chance of his being sent to Ishmaelia as a spy. In this instance the question itself endorses by its tone the attitude behind Mrs Stitch's reply. Public school slang is attractive because it presumes a world that does not make adult demands. Love, battle, disappointment and the rest are reduced by it to the level of the schoolroom. Like the long list of metaphors drawn from the school playing fields and then applied with touching faith to the diverse crises of adult life, it implicitly denies that anything can be worse than a sticky wicket or a bad break. The scale of things diminishes; life's problems are miraculously confined within the landscape of the sixteen-year-old. 'Fact is,' Grimes confesses, 'I'm in the soup again.' More trouble with the prefects.

It is not coincidence that links the upper classes to the barbarous and the insane. They have for Waugh a common point of interest. What appeals to him is that all of them — or at least the satirical parodies of them he creates — respond to the world in the light of convictions and principles of conduct altogether foreign to the average member of England's middle classes. The resulting clash of values is what produces those sparks of surrealism which sustain Waugh's interest in life. It is to the clash of cultural values that we shall turn now.

When a hapless American schoolgirl sent Waugh a questionnaire, he returned a sorrowful letter to her headmistress, deploring this offence against modesty and speculating that its perpetrator might possibly be a Red Indian. From the standpoint of a reclusive English gentleman he is utterly unable to comprehend the modern laxity of manners which prevails on the other side of the Atlantic; that the girl must be some half-reclaimed savage is his only explanation. 'I trust,' he concludes, 'you will mete out condign punishment to this unhappy child but not take the grave step of expelling her to her Reserve.' [Diaries 663] A chance fragment of ordinary life has been seized in passage and carried off into a world of comedy. Waugh was obviously pleased with his morning's work, since he copied the letter into his diary — a successful raid on the grey spaces of another day.

In his art, such invigorating forays were easier to arrange. Azania is a place where the savage and the civilized come into collision every day. But in the dark places of Africa Waugh merely found a natural setting for the sort of confrontations that had already excited his sense of humour in more familiar surroundings. On his second visit to Doubting Hall Adam encounters a cigar smoking bishop who

jauntily informs him that, along with the other Wesleyans,
Colonel Blount is just being shot:

> 'I dare say you'd like to come round to the front and
> see the fun. I should think they'd be just singing their
> last hymn now. It's been uphill work,' he confided as
> they walked round the side of the house, 'and there's
> been some damn bad management. Why, yesterday,
> they kept Miss La Touche waiting the whole afternoon,
> and then the light was so bad when they did shoot her
> that they made a complete mess of her — we had the
> machine out and ran over all the bits carefully last
> night after dinner — you never saw such rotten little
> scraps — quite unrecognizable half of them. We didn't
> dare show them to her husband — he'd be sick to death
> about it — so we just cut out a few shots to keep and
> threw away the rest. I say, you're not feeling queer,
> are you? You look all green suddenly. Find the weed
> a bit strong?' [VB 141-2]

A linguistic misapprehension has thrust Adam into a scene
of barbarism as appalling as anything to be found in Azania.
His failure to understand one word has had the effect of
confronting him with a perspective grotesquely different
from his own. As it turns out, the bishop's cheerful acceptance of atrocity is only apparent; he is actually talking
about the shooting of a film. Nonetheless, he is a portent of
things to come. His descendants range from the cannibal
tribes of the Wanda to the morticians of Whispering Glades.
   No one tries harder to bridge the gap in cultural perspectives than Mr Youkoumian. He is on hand when Basil wants a
ticket to Debra Dowa. The train is full, but for an Englishman
Youkoumian is willing to make sacrifices:

> 'I like Englishmens. They are my favourite gentlemen.
> Look, you give me hundred and fifty rupees I put Mme
> Youkoumian with the mules. You don't understand
> what that will be like. They are the General's mules.
> Very savage stinking animals. All day they will stamp at
> her. No air in the truck. 'Orrible, unhealthy place. Very

like she die or is kicked. She is good wife, work 'ard,
very loving. If you are not Englishmans I would not put
Mme Youkoumian with the mules for less than five
hundred. I fix it for you, OK?'

'OK,' said Basil. 'You know you seem to me a good
chap.'

'Look, 'ow about you give me money now. Then I
take you to my café. Dirty little place, not like London.
But you see. I got fine brandy. Very fresh, I made him
myself Sunday.' [BM 98]

The unquestioned assumption is that his gesture will be
thought creditable in proportion to the sufferings it entails
for his wife. He therefore stresses the hideousness of the
ordeal before her with emphatic urgency ('They are the
General's mules'). Her loving and industrious nature is
adduced only to underline his case for the hundred and
fifty rupees. The propriety of shoving her in the mule truck
at all is never in question, merely the price that can reason-
ably be asked for doing so. The lack of human, as opposed to
commercial, subtlety in Youkoumian's perspective is suffi-
ciently conveyed by his prediction of Mme Youkoumian's
probable fate, 'Very like she die or is kicked.' The sense of
looking down a vista of increasing horror ('kicked, or even
die') which would have been the European perspective is
completely absent. The two possibilities exist for Youkoumian on a flat surface, and although he has grasped enough
of European attitudes to recognize that they constitute an
appeal (they are not a consideration he would have proposed
to Ali in similar circumstances), he is without the degree of
understanding necessary to organize them into the appropriate form, or even to put them in the right order. The
humour Waugh invites the reader to derive from this cultural
disjunction is seasoned by the fact that in Basil, the representative of European civilization to whom the speech is
addressed, Youkoumian has stumbled on an interlocutor
whose attitudes harmonize perfectly with his own. Ironically,
there is in this case no disjunction at all.

Youkoumian's manipulation of half-understood fragments
of another culture can be taken as the model for a whole

range of humorous effects. His offer of fresh, home-made brandy captures precisely the response of someone whose superficial contact with Europeans has taught him that, for reasons which remain a mystery, these terms, applied to food and drink, are in general a strong recommendation. It is unfortunate, but hardly predictable, that brandy should be judged by criteria different from those which obtain for milk or fruit juice. However conscientiously one tries to adapt to European attitudes, there is a basic perversity of outlook that makes them elusive.

More than anyone else, it is the Emperor of Azania himself who suffers from the absurdities of cultural confusion. Informed by Connolly that the Wanda have recently eaten his father, he decides that they need education and at once begins to speculate dreamily about the possibility of starting them on Montessori methods. His brief reign is a catalogue of such misconceptions. One after another the cultural formulae of the western world are indiscriminately transplanted and imposed upon a society to which they are wholly unsuited. Nowhere more obviously so than in the opening lines of the novel: 'We, Seth, Emperor of Azania, Chief of the Chiefs of Sakuyu, Lord of Wanda and Tyrant of the Seas, Bachelor of the Arts of Oxford University...'. It is not just the oddity of juxtaposing the emperor's BA with his other, more extravagant distinctions; what Waugh does by inserting the definite article in Seth's academic title, Bachelor of *the* Arts, is to undermine the very claim it is making: Seth has not acquired the cultural refinements of western civilization, he has not even understood the initials he is using as their symbol. The phrase suggests that he has learnt the arts of Oxford University rather as one might learn the law of the jungle. Admittedly, the two may have something in common, but that is not at all Seth's point.

This passage from the start of Black Mischief exemplifies not only Waugh's use of cultural confusion but also the linguistic finesse with which he goes about it. He is particularly sensitive to the ripples of implication that can be created by a single word or phrase knocked slightly off its accustomed course. When the engine of the emperor's official train parts company with its coaches, the stationmaster comments

balefully: 'Our only engine has gone away alone. I think I
shall be disgraced for this affair.' [BM 101] The use of 'alone'
in this context conveys, without any sort of direct statement,
the stationmaster's sense of the train engine as a mechanism
that can only with difficulty be regarded as inanimate. It is
a word which carries the suggestion of individual volition,
giving the sentence what is almost an undertone of reproach.
Here is another implicit blow to Seth's hopes of moderniza-
tion; his stationmaster is more at home in a world moved by
spirits than in one that depends on the laws of science.

With satisfying economy a word or phrase of this kind can
shoot an oblique light into an entire mental world. 'Splendid,'
says Sir Samson, when William finally discovers the Foreign
Office's cipher book in his collar drawer. 'It doesn't matter
as long as it's safe, but you know how particular the FO
are about things like that.' The use of 'particular' delicately
indicates Sir Samson's sense of their idiosyncrasy.

By similar means Waugh manages to summarize the ethos
of a whole precarious world of speculative enterprise in
talking of Mr Jagger's succession of 'quite honourable bank-
ruptcies' in Cape Town, Mombasa, Dar-es-Salaam and Aden.
'Honourable' is not an adjective that immediately suggests
itself in connection with bankruptcy, but once the slight
shift in perspective has been made, the phrase neatly resumes
the changing fortunes of a lifetime in business in Africa and
the qualities of moral flexibility and spiritual resilience
needed to survive them.

This is not a flamboyant form of humour, but it has the
same basis and works to the same end as Waugh's more outrageous flippancies. We do not have to be solemn about it
to say that humour of this kind has a serious purpose. Dictators have never doubted it: the suppression of frivolity has
long been recognized as a precondition of successful tyranny.
If we are to catch the drift of Waugh's writing, we must
understand why this should be so.

When Wenlock Jakes has no war to report for his readers,
he makes one up:

barricades in the streets, flaming churches, machine-
guns answering the rattle of his type-writer as he wrote,

a dead child, like a broken doll, spreadeagled in the
deserted roadway below his window — *you* know. [*S* 67]

At first glance, this dispatch about a non-existent war merely
casts an ironic light on the trade of foreign correspondent,
but its final effect is more ambivalent. For the space of a
paragraph the blazing church and spreadeagled child become
properties of comedy: the context forbids us to take them
seriously. We could, of course, respond by asserting simply
that this is not a fit subject for jokes, but that would be to
admit that these images could impinge on us at the level of
reality. By contrast, laughter offers us the subversive thrill
of discarding our habitual solemnity in the face of such
things and allowing them to be absorbed into the world of
comedy. We can do this, but it is a response that undermines,
however fleetingly, our conventional patterning of experience.
Similarly, in the conversation with Basil, it is Youkoumian's
immaculate callousness that is the primary object of irony,
but, granted this, our amusement cannot but be partially at
the expense of the moral standards he flouts. We do not have
to laugh. Would Theobald Pontifex have laughed?

There is in fact no need to appeal to a hypothetical response of this kind. Ernest Oldmeadow's attack on *Black
Mischief* in the *Tablet* has been subjected to a lot of understandable abuse: it is a pompous and unamiable piece of
work.[5] It is also, on its own terms, absolutely reasonable. To
laugh at Youkoumian, at Basil, at the birth control pageant,
at the fate of Prudence, is subtly to countenance the making
light of what should 'properly' be treated with gravity.
Oldmeadow's attitude may be repulsive, but it is more clear-
sighted than that of the Catholic apologists who imagine that
by ascribing it all to fun and high spirits they have disposed
of its implications.

In a grim world laughter will always be a truancy from
some claim on our seriousness. What the moralist requires is
that the writer, even the comic writer, should have a moral

[5] Oldmeadow was at the time editor of the *Tablet* (a Catholic weekly magazine),
and he took strong exception to Waugh's novel. His views are discussed in more
detail below, page 144.

stance in relation to his material. But Waugh's irony will move straight from Lucas-Dockery's views on crime to the antithetical ones of his predecessor. The author's account is impartially humorous. To the satirist it is the *object* of his humour that matters, the point of view it serves; what matters to Waugh is the humour itself: it is vital only that the texture of life should be made to yield a comic response rather than a bitter or tragic one.

Distinctions as to what is allowed to provoke this response are secondary. We can hardly read Waugh's description of the fate of the nineteenth century Europeans in Ishmaelia without thinking of Swift:

> They came as missionaries, ambassadors, tradesmen, prospectors, natural scientists. None returned. They were eaten, every one of them; some raw, others stewed and seasoned — according to local usage and the calendar (for the better sort of Ishmaelites have been Christian for many centuries and will not publicly eat human flesh, uncooked, in Lent, without special and costly dispensation from their bishop). [*S* 74]

Shades of *A Modest Proposal*? The difference is crucial. If we apply to Swift's work the hypothetical objection raised earlier — 'This is not a fit subject for joking' — the answer is quite plain: Swift is not joking. However absorbed he may be imaginatively by the project, he is in bitter earnest. But bitterness — the bitterness of personal feeling — and earnestness are precisely the qualities of response from which Waugh's early fiction is in flight. True, the novelist's irony exposes folly, ridicules absurdity — but only because they provide something to laugh at, not because it would be a better world if they did not exist. On the contrary, they are positively to be relished; Waugh's primary concern is to create a world in which there is nothing that *cannot* be laughed at. As John Felstiner has written of Max Beerbohm, 'he depended as man and artist on the survival of the context he satirized'.[6]

---

[6] *The Lies of Art: Max Beerbohm's Parody and Caricature*, p. 133.

In every case we have looked at, Waugh's irony has had an immediate object — Seth, Youkoumian, Jagger, the Envoy and so on — and if the aim had been merely to satirize incompetent diplomats, dubious businessmen, half-educated barbarians or whatever, this would have been enough. But Waugh's aim was broader. He wanted a world that could be looked at from a purely comic perspective — 'just worth making a jest about'. Not only abuses, but also the standards by which these abuses are judged must be brought within the reach of laughter. The author's irony is so deployed as to erode the dignity of anything that lays claim to seriousness. And this is just the unruly accomplishment which our examples have illustrated. It is the effect achieved in these early novels by the continual juxtaposition of disparate objects, responses and standards of judgement. There is no mystery about Waugh's preoccupation with the trinity we picked out at the start of *Decline and Fall*: sex, authority and religion are time-honoured resources of the humorist. But they are so precisely because they are the areas of life that traditionally command a respectful solemnity. They are touchstones of decorum — for Western culture in general and for the British middle classes in particular. From his Olympian vantage point Waugh lets loose on them the savages and the upper classes. The resulting collision of values makes all of them a subject for jest. All are encompassed by the superior irony of the author. Only he is unvulnerable.

The situation was not one that could last. At the end of *Black Mischief* Sonia and Alastair are still playing happy families and going out to cocktail clubs, but the mood has lost some of its freshness. Tremors from the world of grownups have been felt — 'a general election and a crisis — something about the gold standard' — and even worse, deep down in Sonia's heart there is the tiny fear that Basil is going to turn serious on them too. In Matodi Youkoumian still flourishes under the hygienic administration of the Reppingtons and the Lepperidges, but the final image is of him fastening the shutters of his café — 'New regulation. No drinking after ten-thirty. I don't want no bust-ups.' [*BM* 238]

From the start there had been a vein of seriousness in Waugh's humour. Prendy's religious doubts, Paul's reflections on the question of honour, Silenus's disquisition on Life — such aspects of *Decline and Fall* are gestures towards a seriousness which the novel does not actually sustain but which lingers in the reader's mind, half-supported by occasional moments of melancholy like the final conversation between Pennyfeather and Pastmaster. The same is true, to a greater or lesser extent, of the rest of the pre-war novels. In *Vile Bodies* there is a continuing preoccupation, not always fully integrated, with the 'problem' of the Younger Generation. *Black Mischief* and *Scoop* deal lightly with questions of colonization and the relationship between Africa and the West, but in both cases the theme is one that has a serious undercurrent. In *A Handful of Dust* the comic tone cannot altogether conceal the painfulness of the circumstances that lie behind it. There is always enough in Waugh's writing to remind us that the equilibrium of humour is not maintained without a certain effort. Comedy exists under pressure.

It is impossible to read the books chronologically without perceiving that this pressure increased with the passing of time. The fact was noted by Waugh himself. Looking back at his travel books in the Preface to *When the Going was Good*, he commented: 'Each book, I found on re-reading, had a distinct and slightly grimmer air, as, year by year, the shades of the prison-house closed.' [*WGG* 7-8] It is a mark of the same process in Waugh's humour that the word 'satire' ceases to be inappropriate. When we turn after the war to *Scott-King's Modern Europe*, *The Loved One*, *Love Among the Ruins*, we can no longer speak of the humour as being random, of its point of view as being secondary. It has in these works a new coherence and with it a sterner sense of purpose.

The world in which we are moving now is comparatively cheerless. Scott-King is a man 'fascinated by obscurity and failure' [*WS* 198], and the masters' common room at Grant-chester provides him with a suitable context:

The cold grate was used as ash-tray and waste-paper basket and was rarely emptied. The breakfast table was a litter of small pots, each labelled with a master's name, containing rations of sugar, margarine and a spurious marmalade. The breakfast dish was a slop of 'dried' eggs. [*WS* 200]

A drab scene. Pennyfeather, too, was dispirited by his first sight of the common room at Llanabba Castle; it was cramped and rather sordid. But the tone of the description sets it in a different world:

In a corner were some golf clubs, a walking stick, an umbrella and two miniature rifles....There were also a bicycle pump, two armchairs, a straight chair, half a bottle of invalid port, a boxing-glove, a bowler hat, yesterday's *Daily News* and a packet of pipe-cleaners. [*DF* 21]

The clutter of miscellaneous objects conveys a range of possibilities. It is a room instinct with potential activity and also, as the hint of incongruity suggests, potential absurdity. At Grantchester there is no potential for anything. It presents a grey landscape to which Neutralia is the bleak modern alternative. For Scott-King the only defence is afforded by the values — and language — of the past.

In different ways the worlds of *The Loved One* and *Love Among the Ruins* are just as depressing. Hollywood, Neutralia and the socialist state of the future have a common preference for the second rate and the synthetic. Their citizens are fed with lies. Waugh makes these things amusing, but not casually so. The more anarchic impulses of his humour are now being held in check.

Both *The Loved One* and *Love Among the Ruins* begin with the same joke — a description that teases us into making certain assumptions about the scene and then abruptly stands them on their head. The two Englishmen are not in some forgotten outpost beyond the pale of civilization; they are in Hollywood, at its glittering modern heart. The pleasure gardens through which Miles strolls in the 'rich, old-fashioned

Tennysonian night' are those of a prison. But Waugh is not merely inviting us to smile at the ingenuity of his initial deception. As we go through these books, it becomes apparent that the comic inversion of their openings is part of a consistent argument about the nature of the societies being satirized. Thus, for example, when the 'mortuary hostess' (in itself a curiously perverse mixture of concepts) is discussing with Dennis the appropriate site for Sir Francis's body, she mentions that Amelia Bergson has just bought a Before Need Reservation under the statue of 'the prominent Greek poet Homer'. Offered a choice between that and Shadowland, Dennis replies: 'I think he would prefer to be with Homer and Miss Bergson.' The bizarre conjunction is a modern American version of the absurdities that resulted from similar encounters between civilization and barbarism in the unreclaimed regions of Africa and South America: first Dickens among the Pie-Wie, now Homer and Miss Bergson. It is a link with the opening of the novel, but it is also part of the general attack on a society that has inverted the civilized function of art and put it to the service of death.

The point receives a good deal of emphasis. Again and again Aimée and Mr Joyboy are referred to as artists, and the connection is made explicit when Dennis asks the girl what she thinks about when she comes alone to the Lake Island in the evenings — '"Just Death and Art," said Aimée Thanatogenos simply.' Dennis takes up the cue with a quotation from Keats. The idea of being 'half in love with easeful death' is one to which Aimée responds eagerly; her imagination has conjoined Art, Love and Death in a perverted trinity. Dennis's use of scraps of poetry to woo her points to the gap between language as it has been used by the artists of traditional western culture and the language by which the artist of the New World communicates — quite literally, a language of corpses: 'When I send a Loved One in to you, Miss Thanatogenos, I feel as though I were speaking to you through him.' [LO 58] The contrasting messages of love from Dennis, debased and plagiarized though they are, carry echoes of a civilization from which Hollywood is as remote as the jungles of Africa.

In a similar way, the description of the night at the

beginning of *Love Among the Ruins* as 'Tennysonian' brings
into play associations that emphasize the grotesque inversion
of civilized values on which the society is based. '"On such a
night as this," said Miles, supine, gazing into the face of the
moon, "on such a night as this I burned an Air Force Station
and half its occupants."' [*GP* 204] The Lorenzo of the new
order finds his poetry in strange places and uncivil acts. When
Chokey said his piece in *Decline and Fall* about the poor
coloured man, the parody of Shylock ('Don't he breathe the
same as you? Don't he eat and drink?') was no more than a
random adornment; here Waugh is quarrying in the same
play, but the element of parody has a calculated direction.

There is no loss of comic poise in these books, but they do
reveal exactly the qualities which I suggested were foreign
to his earlier novels: earnestness and bitterness. 'Hollywood
is my life,' says Sir Francis, and then casts around for a suitable image:

> Did you see the photograph some time ago in one of the
> magazines of a dog's head severed from its body which
> the Russians are keeping alive for some obscene Musco-
> vite purpose by pumping blood into it from a bottle? It
> dribbles at the tongue when it smells a cat. That's what
> all of us are, you know, out here. [*LO* 15]

Waugh has never been shy of the horrific when it lends itself
to humour; Prendergast, Prudence and many others meet a
distressing end in his books. But in this passage there is nothing to laugh at. The image, an unusually revolting one, is
apparently being offered on its own merits as an analogy for
a certain way of life. And when Hollywood turns out to be
Sir Francis's death as well, the picture is equally unprepos-
sessing. It is an image, we are told, seldom out of Dennis's
mind:

> the sack of body suspended and the face above it with
> eyes red and horribly starting from their sockets, the
> cheeks mottled in indigo like the marbled end-papers
> of a ledger and the tongue swollen and protruding like
> an end of black sausage. [*LO* 39]

Again, it is a curiously unyielding image. In some measure it can no doubt be accounted for, like the book itself, by a fascination on Waugh's part with the physical details of the macabre (the parallel with Dickens's obsessive taste for visiting morgues is suggestive), but this does not affect the absence of humour. The suspended body of Sir Francis remains a stubborn fact in the novel, unnegotiable for humour or moral edification.

Harshness would perhaps be a better term than bitterness. Bitterness suggests an element of disillusionment, a sense of betrayal that is not quite consonant with the mood of Waugh's satires, for they deride a world that has confirmed rather than betrayed his expectations of it. Disillusionment is the experience of the war years, and it is in his writings about this period that it is most obviously reflected. If the coming of the Second World War was a factor in the increasing seriousness that underlay his humour, the progress of the war was the decisive source of any bitterness that became mingled with it.

The débâcle on Crete is as much of a watershed in Waugh's fiction as it was in his life. Six years after *Officers and Gentlemen*, *Unconditional Surrender* is written in its shadow. Whatever Waugh's reasons, there was a certain propriety in his suppression of Apthorpe's role when he came to write a synopsis of the first two volumes.[7] Apthorpe's dominating presence in *Men at Arms* was in one sense appropriate to Guy's early days in the army, the days of his 'happy adolescence'; but even at this stage Apthorpe is straining the defensive powers of comedy to their limit. The first volume of the trilogy records an attempt by Waugh to sustain a comic response to a grave situation. In the end it is abandoned: the materials in himself from which he sought to fashion this response could no longer quite serve his turn.

Apthorpe is a compendium of different sources of humour. He stands between Guy and the war — almost, one is tempted to say, between Guy and reality. Bruised by his humiliating reunion with Virginia, Guy returns to Southsand: the familiar surroundings would give him solace, 'the spell of Apthorpe

[7] To preface *Unconditional Surrender*.

would bind him, and gently bear him away to the far gardens
of fantasy' [*MA* 131]. The association of Apthorpe with
fantasy takes up an important passage earlier in the novel
when Guy is trying to analyse his fellow soldier:

> Yet there was about Apthorpe a sort of fundamental
> implausibility. Unlike the typical figure of the JD
> lesson, Apthorpe tended to become faceless and tapering
> the closer he approached. Guy treasured every nugget
> of Apthorpe but under assay he found them liable to
> fade like faery gold. Only so far as Apthorpe was him-
> self true, could his enchantment work its spell. Any
> firm passage between Apthorpe's seemingly dreamlike
> universe and the world of common experience was a
> thing to cherish... [*MA* 107]

Guy recognizes the potential here and turns it to his own
account. Apthorpe is being used, quite deliberately, to make
the world into a comic place. When entertainments are
organized to alleviate the corrosive boredom of life on the
immobile troop ships, Apthorpe is asked to lecture on
Africa:

> He chose, instead, an unexpected subject: 'The Juris-
> diction of Lyon King of Arms compared with that of
> Garter King of Arms.'
> 'But, Uncle, do you think it will interest the men?'
> 'Not all of them perhaps. Those that *are* interested
> will be very much interested indeed.' [*MA* 206]

Boredom is temporarily allayed, but not by Apthorpe's
lecture; it is his response to the invitation that works the
change. Impervious as ever to the humour he inspires,
Apthorpe embodies the possibility that life contains
enough potential absurdity to be redeemed from seriousness by an ironic regard. Wartime accentuates the grimness,
the seriousness, and, outside the battle zones, the tedium
of life; what makes these days tolerable is the disruption
of this perspective by absurdity: the telegraph poles
thought to be marked by fifth columnists, Apthorpe's

arsenical smoke that turns out to be sea mist, the captains from another regiment who nearly get shot on Guy's orders. Such incidents are life's uncovenanted blessing to the ironist; they offer him a purchase on ways of looking at the situation which defeat its claim to be taken seriously.

This is how Waugh has used character and incident from the start; it is how, in life, he has used his own persona. More important here, it is what Apthorpe has provided throughout *Men at Arms*. From the moment of his opening remark about porpoises, his existence is a sublimely unconscious challenge to any sane, depressing view of the war. Finland falls; the trains roll on to the concentration camps; but Apthorpe's obsession with boots remains unchanged. His minutest concerns take on the proportions of myth; national emergencies are dwarfed by the epic scale of his triumphs and tragedies.

But all the time both Guy and, behind him, the author are half-conscious that they are putting more strain on this figure than he can really bear. 'Only so far as Apthorpe was himself true, could his enchantment work its spell.' The sentence is ominous. It expresses an awareness that Apthorpe exists on the edge of a plane of fiction different from that of the rest of the novel. He is, like Grimes, one of the immortals, but one who is forced to live under a new dispensation in which no immortality can be granted. Waugh had to struggle to keep him within the bounds of this contracted world. The sense that he is always on the verge of escaping into another mode is returned to by Guy later in the novel when he thinks of him as 'gloriously over-Technicoloured like Bonnie Prince Charlie in the film' [*MA* 165]. Unfortunately, as Guy has perceived, the spell can only be effective if Apthorpe is accepted as real within the world in which he functions.

In the end, the disparity is too great: either the world which the novel has posited must change, expand, lighten to accommodate Apthorpe, or else Apthorpe himself and what he represents must be accepted as fantasy and set aside. When the campaign of the thunder-box grows into a substitute for the real war, Guy at last transfers his allegiance to Ritchie-Hook and together with him brings about Apthorpe's death. Waugh stresses the element of responsibility. The episode marks a reluctant admission, prefigured in Guy's earlier reflections, that Apthorpe was a character who paid insufficient dues to reality. It is a conclusive acceptance, after twenty-five years, of the limits of the comic vision. Apthorpe on Crete would be as impossible as Falstaff under Henry V.

The effects of his passing make themselves felt in the two succeeding volumes, and nowhere more so than in the death of the Cyclopean figure who displaced him. The romantic perspective proves as inadequate as the comic one; each of them is too closely related to a level of fantasy. Apthorpe reappears for his last illness slung in a hammock like a Victorian woodcut from a book of exploration; Ritchie-Hook goes off to his death with Sneiffel, the photographer, skipping around him like a dwarf at the heels of a Renaissance prince. The similes evoke other periods and other worlds. With Apthorpe's death the tone of these books suffers a loss of elasticity, and the fate of Ritchie-Hook perhaps seems, in consequence, the crueller of the two; its absurdity is recorded with an irony that is bitter rather than humorous, resigned rather than rebellious. There is a sort of comedy in the grotesque single-handed assault, but little is made of it. The uniformly selfish reactions of everyone else throw up only the bleakest of ironies:

> It's an odd thing. In all this war I've only twice had any part in an operation. Both have afforded classic stories of heroism. You wouldn't have thought, would you, that Trimmer and Ritchie-Hook had a great deal in common? [*US* 223]

Fittingly enough, the speaker is Kilbannock. As we have seen, he, as well as anyone, reflects the changing temper of the novels. The epitaph he pronounces on Ritchie-Hook tells how far the dimensions of this world have shrunk. In the first volume Ritchie-Hook and Trimmer were antitheses — the romantic and the anti-romantic, the courageous and

the cowardly, the anachronistic and the modern; now the
cynical expediencies of the journalist have annihilated these
distinctions; Trimmer and Ritchie-Hook both find their inglorious apotheosis as heroes of the new age.

It is not an episode, nor, finally, a war, that can be redeemed by humour. To Guy at this point there seems only
one way of making his situation more bearable; he can use
what influence he has to secure the transfer of the Jews.
This, 'in a world of hate and waste', is his chance of doing 'a
single small act to redeem the times' [US 192]. Humour has
lost much of its virtue; the lines of defence have had to be
redrawn on different ground, the nature of which is essentially religious.

This is not for the present chapter, but we must note
before we leave the subject that there was for Waugh no im-
passable barrier between the worlds of comedy and religion.
Indeed, he saw the possibility of an important link between
them. Towards the end of the first book of *Officers and
Gentlemen*, he analyses the relationship between Guy and
Ivor Claire:

> As for Guy, he had recognized from the first a certain
> remote kinship with this most dissimilar man, a com-
> mon aloofness, differently manifested — a common
> melancholy sense of humour; each in his way saw life
> *sub specie aeternitatis*; thus with numberless reser-
> vations they became friends, as had Guy and Apthorpe.
> [OG 87]

Claire is on the face of it an odd successor to Apthorpe, yet
the connection is explicitly made. It points to a change in
Guy himself. 'Melancholy' would have been a quite inaccu-
rate word to describe the sort of humour he derived from
Apthorpe. On the contrary, it was an escape from the natural
melancholy of his temperament rather than an affirmation
of it. The exchange of Apthorpe for Claire is part of the recognition that this escape is no longer possible.

But if the quality of humour is now muted, it is also associated with the faculty of seeing life *sub specie aeternitatis*.
Defensive possibilities of another sort have been brought into

play; humour is not the only perspective from which grave
things can be made to seem trifling. The phrase *sub specie
aeternitatis* defines a bond between the ironic perspective
and the religious. Both have the effect of diminishing those
concerns that attach us most insistently to the hazards of
daily life. The ironic disdain of Waugh's early humour is
different in kind from the *contemptus mundi* of religion. I
wish merely to indicate a possible line of transition between
them and to suggest that the passage quoted above ought
perhaps to be taken as a hint of this transition in process.

It would be foolish to give the impression that this shift
of emphasis can be pinpointed; the reader has glimpses of it
long before *Officers and Gentlemen*. I have argued that as
Waugh's career progresses, he tends increasingly to encounter
subjects and situations that escape the reach of irony. It may
be just as true to put it the other way round: a change in his
own perspective makes him increasingly able to confront
subjects and situations without the support of irony. When
Tangent's foot swells and turns black in *Decline and Fall*, it
is purely comic; Kurt's foot full of pus in *Brideshead* might
almost be a direct challenge to comedy — as though Waugh
were deliberately setting something down in the novel that
could only be assimilated by a perspective other than the
comic. In his earlier fiction the unrelenting callousness was
in part a symptom of the pressure under which his irony
was operating. The lunatic, the crippled and the wretched
had to be laughed at, because there was no other response
available that did not betray the writer's own vulnerability.
It is only with the shift towards a religious viewpoint that
this irony could be relieved of some of the strain.

But at this point we reach once again the boundaries of
the chapter on religion. Here, I have given the case a different
emphasis, attempting first to examine the sources of some of
Waugh's early humour and then to suggest how the comic
vision of the pre-war novels came to be modified by the
growing pressure of external circumstance. The case is a
partial one. In outline it commands assent: Ritchie-Hook's
death is *not* as funny as it would have been thirty years
earlier; the irony *is* more bitter than humorous; the mood
has changed from rebellion to resignation. But this is not

the whole truth. The single-handed attack, 'which had no precedent in Clausewitz', is still funny; the irony still has its humorous side; and a hint of rebellion still lurks in the conclusion:

> Perhaps the body was not really Ritchie-Hook's — they had his full biography — but that of a sacrificial victim. Ritchie-Hook was being preserved for some secret enterprise. Warning orders were issued throughout the whole 'Fortress of Europe' to be vigilant for one-eyed men. [US 222]

There is no foothold here for tragedy or pathos — our feelings have again been spared. Breached, but not entirely overrun, the defences of humour are still functioning.

3

Romanticism

From time to time, no doubt, impatient of life, men have left their clothes at the water's edge and swum out along the track of a gibbous moon towards a solitary release. Probably they were not turned back by idling jellyfish; some of them must have held their course and died with unshaken dignity. But this, as we have seen, was not the case with Evelyn Waugh. Or take Lord Moping: suicide by hanging has never been a graceful way of compassing one's death, but to use braces...to do it in the orangerie...and then to fail. For the last Earl of Balcairn, a dirty gas-oven — today's newspaper over yesterday's pie-crumbs.

So much for suicide. The mean circumstances of this world ensure that our passage to the next will be as humiliating as possible. There is little room for romanticism. The old frauds of antiquity who could turn a memorable phrase while falling on their swords belong to a different world. Only in time of war can men hope to emulate them without absurdity. This, of course, is one of its many attractions — an aspect of the reprieve it offers from the terrible inanition of peace. To wake daily to a world as flat as a map: what stronger incentive to suicide? 'Clocks barely moving,' Waugh writes in his diary. 'Has half an hour past? no five minutes.' [*Diaries* 722] But even war, to sustain its doubtful romance, must be fought by officers and gentlemen, and as Corporal-Major Ludovic points out, 'all gentlemen are now very old' [*OG* 186].

As a young man, taking a pleasure cruise in the Mediterranean, Waugh stopped briefly at Algiers. To his regret, he arrived just two weeks after the Foreign Legion had left their quarters in the town. 'I should have liked to see this

company of exiled chivalry — all, I like to think, suffering for
the good name of others, all of exalted and romantic origin.'
His taxi-driver is less enthusiastic:

> They got so little pay, he said, that there was nothing
> they could ever afford to do, except to stand about at
> the street corners and spit; they were for the most part
> tough, undersized young criminals of very limited intel-
> lect; he was glad to see the backs of them. [L 186]

It is some years since the dust settled on Fort Zinderneuf.
Whatever imaginative sympathy Waugh may have for the
fictional world of PC Wren, his irony effectively disables it.
A *beau geste* of that kind is no easier to accomplish than a
Roman death. In the society of the twentieth century both
of them are out of place; like any other response that suggests a romantic misconstruction of the world in which we
have to live, they can only attract Waugh's irony.

The poor showing of the Foreign Legion is not an isolated
example. In all the places where one might look for romance
Waugh firmly declines to recognize it. Towards the end of
Ninety-Two Days he lists some of the romantic fallacies that
are propagated about the explorer's life:

> For instance, *that one felt free*; on the contrary, there
> seemed no limit to the number of restrictions with
> which the 'open life' hampered one.
> Or
> *That one was untrammelled by convention*; I have
> never understood this....
> Or
> *That one eats with gay appetite and sleeps with the
> imperturbable ease of infancy.* Nonsense. [*92D* 158]

'As for sleep,' he adds, 'I scarcely had a single good night in
the open.' Myths about the brilliance of the tropical night
had left him similarly unimpressed in *Remote People*: '(...As
for the Southern Cross, which one often sees described as "a
blazing jewel", it is as dim and formless as a handful of
glow-worms)' [*RP* 137].

Critics too dull to find romance elsewhere have been pained by this sort of insensitivity. When *Ninety-Two Days* came out, the reviewer for the *Times Literary Supplement* was puzzled that Waugh should have gone to Guiana at all, since he seemed to prefer Bath. But the tone of deflation had been a feature of Waugh's travel books from the start. The title of his first one, *Labels*, is in itself an admission that the places he has visited in the Mediterranean are already the common property of the tourist. He leaves it to others to indulge a factitious sense of romance. The Sphinx, for example, he dismisses as 'an ill-proportioned composition of inconsiderable aesthetic appeal', and he is contemptuous of the gullible reactions of other travellers: 'People from the hotel went out to see it by moonlight and returned very grave and awe-struck; which only shows the mesmeric effect of publicity.' [L 102] In passing Gibraltar he refers to Thackeray's dramatic vision of it as 'an enormous lion, crouched between the Atlantic and the Mediterranean, and set there to guard the passage for its British mistress'. 'Everyone else on board,' he comments, 'was instantly struck by the felicity of this image, so I suppose that it must be due to some deficiency in my powers of observation that to me it appeared like a great slab of cheese and like nothing else.' [L 193] Etna is treated with equal brutality. Having pictured it in lyrical terms glowing pink against the pastel grey of an evening sky ('I do not think I shall ever forget the sight of Etna at sunset...'), Waugh adds: 'Nothing I have seen in Art or Nature was quite so revolting.' [L 169] The writer chooses precisely those images that are the stock-in-trade of the travel brochure and then derides them.

At Sakkara he latches onto a troop of American tourists visiting the Serapeum:

One is supposed, I know, to think of the past on these occasions; to conjure up the ruined streets of Memphis and to see in one's mind's eye the sacred procession as it wound up the avenue of sphinxes, mourning the dead bull; perhaps even to give licence to one's fancy and invent some personal romance about the lives of these garlanded hymn-singers, and to generalize sagely about

the mutability of human achievement. But I think
we can leave all that to Hollywood. [L 105]

He, by contrast, turns his attention to the tourists themselves, the coughing, limping, bruised, mosquito-bitten
company who have left the comfort of their homes in search
of the romance of Ancient Egypt. 'Funny spending all this
money,' he concludes, 'to see a hole in the sand where, three
thousand years ago, a foreign race whose motives must for
ever remain inexplicable interred the carcasses of twenty-four
bulls.'

These are just a few examples from a single book. What
room is there now for claiming that Waugh's was essentially a romantic imagination? The dominant tone seems to
be one of humorous cynicism, tinged, perhaps, with an
element of genuine disappointment. Etna, the Sphinx,
Gibraltar, the Serapeum — in reality, none of them can
quite match the romantic associations that have gathered
around its name. Even without the contamination of foolish
tourists, it is hard to see what a modern young man could
hope to make of the Sphinx by moonlight. The fashion was
against it, and Waugh was a part of the fashion. 'As for
sleep...', 'As for the Southern Cross...' — the dismissive
construction comes to have a familiar ring in travel books
of the thirties. For this post-war generation there was to be
'no nonsense of tropical romance'. 'No Nonsense' is indeed
the title of an early chapter of Peter Fleming's *Brazilian
Adventure* in which he mocks the talk of those whose notions of foreign travel have been coloured by the writings
of Rupert Brooke and Rudyard Kipling — 'As for planting
the Union Jack...'.[1]

Waugh's travel books are a reflection of this mood but not
an unthinking one. His response is essentially the same that
was analysed in the first two chapters: he detaches himself
from the scene of which he is a part and then exploits his
detachment to enjoy whatever humour the circumstances
will allow. Any disappointment is absorbed by his urbanity.

Yet it was suggested earlier that Waugh's tone of detachment

---

[1] *Brazilian Adventure*, p. 15.

might itself be seen as part of a broader commitment to an
idealized concept of style. To put it another way, the tone
that is apparently contemptuous of romanticism may conceal
a germinal romanticism of its own. The dandy and the
romantic have this in common, that both of them seek by
their attitude to mitigate the claims of everyday reality. The
romantic has two options, and these are what we shall be
examining. On the one hand, he can take the dull stuff of
routine and lend it the colours of his imagination; on the
other, he can turn his back on contemporary life and look
towards the promise of a world that is culturally or historically remote from his own — that is, in Waugh's case, either
towards the past or towards the exotic. But imaginative
indulgence of this kind has a price. In the final part of the
chapter I shall attempt to trace in Waugh's work the streng-
thening thread of opposition to this romanticism.

Waugh's revulsion, real or assumed, from Etna at sunset is a
revulsion from romantic cliché;[2] it no more proves him to be
unromantic in outlook than a contempt for verbal cliché
would prove someone to be indifferent to language. It may
have just the opposite significance. For example, set this
description of Cnossos beside Waugh's earlier remark about
the Serapeum:

> I do not think that it can be only imagination and the
> recollection of a bloodthirsty mythology which makes
> something fearful and malignant of the cramped gal-
> leries and stunted alleys, these colonnades of inverted,
> conical pillars, these rooms that are mere blind passages
> at the end of sunless staircases; this squat little throne,
> set on a landing where the paths of the palace intersect;
> it is not the seat of a law-giver nor a divan for the

[2] Particularly the form of it exemplified in popular travel books. In *Abroad* Paul
Fussell lists a string of comparable introductions — 'I shall never forget...', 'I do
not think I shall lightly forget...' etc. — including one from *Hot Countries* by
Waugh's brother Alec.

recreation of a soldier; here an ageing despot might crouch and have borne to him, along the walls of a whispering gallery, barely audible intimations of his own murder. [L 137]

He is responding here to the ruined architecture of Cnossos with just the sort of imaginative self-projection that a few pages earlier he had been holding up to ridicule — 'One is supposed, I know, to think of the past on these occasions...'. The sophisticated boredom with which he had consigned such fancies to the script-writers of Hollywood has been swept aside by an enthusiasm which is at the opposite pole. The two contradictory responses, so close together, add force to the supposition that Waugh's truculent anti-romanticism in other passages might rather indicate an emotion that has been frustrated than one to which he is genuinely impervious. 'A hole in the sand', 'the carcasses of twenty-four bulls' — the protest is too emphatic. It is the response of a romantic to the debasement of romance.

There is a recurrent tension in the books between a romantic temperament and an ironic perception of the reality on which that temperament has to work. The more powerfully one is aware of the mundanity of everyday life, the stronger will be the lure of romantic alternatives; the stronger one's allegiance to romantic alternatives, the more obstructively mundane will seem the nature of the everyday. The long littleness of life that makes a romantic perspective so appealing is exactly what makes it impossible to sustain.

In Waugh's case, both halves of the equation exercise a claim, but his irony tends to deny his romanticism the more obvious ways of expressing itself. If romanticism becomes too unsubtle, it is at once identified as cliché; the Sphinx by moonlight will not do. Romance must seek obscurer paths if it is to fly by the nets that irony puts out for it. In the end it may be harder to find romance in a tropical sunset than in the mosquito bites one gets while watching it.

Waugh's account of the Cretan ruins is not romantic in any idealizing sense; it invests the antique civilization of Minos with no unlikely splendours, no patents of nobility that raise it higher than our own. The romanticism lies simply in the intensity of the writer's absorption in what he sees. Where at Sakkara the stones had remained obstinately lifeless, confined to a world that intrudes itself at every moment in the idiocies of Waugh's fellow sightseers, here at Cnossos the winding passages are alive with whispers of a buried age. For a moment Waugh slips out of the stale world of the pleasure cruise, in which every sight has its label, and transforms the broken stones of the hillside into a theatre of bloodshed and intrigue. The Minoan fragments are briefly rescued by his imagination from the depressing round of twentieth century tourism.

And if it is not the tourists who intrude, it can be any other of the countless manifestations of our uncongenial times. They are just one instance of the crass uniformity that our age imposes. The tedium of life can only be aggravated by a modern insistence that things and people should be shaped by the gross. This is always Waugh's starting point, and to progress beyond it becomes increasingly difficult as the writer grows older and the conditions of his century bear more oppressively upon him. When he was young, the possibilities were various enough to please. If his visit to the Serapeum was empty of romance, it could at least, by its very banality, provide a source of humour. Either way it was redeemed from total dullness.

The enemy is routine. It is into the dead routine of Paul Pennyfeather's life that the anarchic action of *Decline and Fall* erupts:

> For two years he had lived within his allowance, aided by two valuable scholarships. He smoked three ounces of tobacco a week — John Cotton, Medium — and drank a pint and a half of beer a day, the half at luncheon and the pint at dinner, a meal he invariably ate in Hall. He had four friends, three of whom had been at school with him. [*DF* 11-12]

It is into the dead routine of colonial administration that Azania relapses after the anarchic action of *Black Mischief*:

> A mile above the town they stopped at the second of six identical bungalows. Each had a verandah and a garden

path; a slotted box on the gate-post for calling cards.
The Brethertons were on the verandah.[*BM* 234]

This, in different guises, is the world from which one starts
and, when the shifts of humour or romance have been ex-
hausted, the world to which one returns. With the gathered
sediment of another thirty years it has become, by the end
of *Unconditional Surrender*, almost the only world.

But *Unconditional Surrender* is the last of Waugh's novels.
The earlier books belong to another time, when sparks of
colour were less difficult to find. The passage about Cnossos
is typical of the hold a random scene or a chance encounter
could take on Waugh's imagination. In *Remote People* he
describes how, after the defeat and death of an insurgent
noble, Ras Tafari formed a troop of guards for his personal
protection. The account is frankly sensational:

Hardly had the blood congealed on Gougsa's mangled
corpse, or the bereaved empress succumbed to her
sudden chill, before orders had been issued for the
formation of this corps.[*RP* 27]

Waugh's description skirts the language of pulp fiction. It
is not untypical; throughout his career the romantic clichés
of love and battle, conquest and death were skirmishing
with the restraints of irony and decorum. Almost always
they were held in check, but the importunate voices that
torment Mr Pinfold with their trashy *Boy's Own* plots and
their fevered passages of lust and love suggest that these
clichés were subdued only by a considerable effort of artistic
control.

From first to last Waugh has an eye for the heightened
moment: Rossetti, at the end of the brilliant dinner parties
in Cheyne Walk, 'left alone in the great velvet-hung bedroom
with his own unfathomable and incommunicable despair'
[*R* 147]; or, at the other end of Waugh's career, the description in *A Little Learning* of his grandfather's nightly return
home: 'But in the evening shadows the sound of his carriage
wheels between the dense evergreens of the drive was heard
with apprehension.'[*LL* 27] Straightforward points —

Rossetti's depression, the grandfather's domestic tyranny —
are perceived as drama. Rossetti is alone on stage at the end
of the last Act; the grandfather's return is glimpsed as though
in a brief clip from the film of his son's childhood.

The heightened moment is, as past quotations suggest,
reflected in a correlative heightening of the writer's language.
The purple passage is essentially a romantic trick of style —
and its romanticism is not necessarily the less genuine for
being, on occasions, half comic. The elegy with which Waugh
marks the passing of a public school man is an early and celebrated example. Grimes, having absconded from Blackstone
gaol, is presumed by the authorities to be lost in the neigh-
bouring swamp, but Paul Pennyfeather is sceptical. His
resilient colleague was not born for death:

> engulfed in the dark mystery of Egdon Mire, he would
> rise again somewhere at some time, shaking from his
> limbs the musty integuments of the tomb. Surely he
> had followed in the Bacchic train of distant Arcady,
> and played on the reeds of myth by forgotten streams,
> and taught the childish satyrs the art of love? Had he
> not suffered unscathed the fearful dooms of all the
> offended gods, of all the histories, fire, brimstone, and
> yawning earthquakes, plague and pestilence? Had he
> not stood, like the Pompeian sentry, while the Citadels
> of the Plain fell to ruin about his ears? Had he not, like
> some grease-caked Channel-swimmer, breasted the waves
> of the Deluge? Had he not moved unseen when the
> darkness covered the waters? [DF 199]

The comic overtones here do not extinguish the romanticism
of the prose, any more than they do when the last Earl of
Balcairn goes to his fathers, or even when the blossom-
strewn waters of the Amazon close over the bald head of Dr
Messinger.

What accounts, at least in part, for the characteristic tone
of these passages is their tendency to pick up the rhythms
and sometimes the precise phrasing of the literature of the
ancient world. Echoes from the poets of Greece and Rome
give to the events of the twentieth century a resonance that

may be derisive but that also touches them with grandeur. To a degenerate race they can give the fabulous colouring of myth — even to the dying rich of Southern California:

> Here on the ultimate, sunset-shore they warm their old bodies and believe themselves alive, opening their scaly eyes two or three times a day to browse on salads and fruits. They have long forgotten the lands that gave them birth and the arts and trades they once practised. Here you find, forgetful and forgotten, men and women you supposed to be long dead, editors of defunct newspapers, playwrights and artists who were once the glory of long-demolished theatres, and round them congregate the priests of countless preposterous cults to soothe them into the cocoon-state in which they will slough their old bodies. [LOr 158]

Do these strange creatures belong to dim pre-history, to an age before our own when dozy monsters ruled the earth and browsed on leaves? Or are they, dying slowly by the seashore with their new cults and half-buried memories, the remnants of some blasted and forgotten civilization? They are, at any rate, no longer the pathetic individuals Waugh starts with; his imagination has elevated them to a more grandly representative status. The play of fantasy is typically romantic. One feels behind these creatures — descendants of Tithonus? — the pressure of popular myth. And not merely popular: 'the lands that gave them birth and the arts and trades they once practised...' — this is surely an echo from the underworld of classical antiquity; we are back in the age of heroes with the shades of those who fell before the walls of Troy.

Particularly in his early novels Waugh likes to fortify character and incident by means of discreet appeal to an epic backcloth. This may be just a title, like *Decline and Fall*, or an epic catalogue, such as the list of guests assembled for the Bollinger dinner; it need be no more than a passing reference — to Mrs Ape's car, perhaps, 'bearing the dust of three continents, against the darkening sky' [VB 9], to Salter trudging like a harassed Roman legionary towards Boot Magna, to

Rampole stepping blithely to his doom in *Put Out More Flags*. A phrase or two is enough to release the narrative from the constraints of unheroic routine. For those who have ridden with Rupert's horse or sat among the camp fires at Xanthus-side a single word can evoke images of a nobler reality. But for them alone:

> Gallipoli, Balaclava, Quebec, Lepanto, Bannockburn, Roncesvales, and Marathon — these, and the Battle in the West where Arthur fell, and a hundred such names whose trumpet-notes, even now in my sere and lawless state, called to me irresistibly across the intervening years with all the clarity and strength of boyhood, sounded in vain to Hooper. [*BR* 14-15]

There is a form of enchantment in names that is perceptible only to the romantic. By virtue of their associations, they provide a frame of reference to which experience can be assimilated and against which it can be dramatized. Once the appropriate name has been found, the constricting mould of day-to-day experience is cracked open. Even the life of a schoolboy at Lancing can take on a gleam of imaginative colour: 'We were cold, shabby and hungry in the ethos, not of free Sparta, but of some beleaguered, enervated and forgotten garrison.' [*LL* 114] At least in retrospect, the desolation has been invested with an element of the heroic.

This ability to exploit the comic or epic potential of everyday reality and thereby distort its conventional structure is a characteristic of Waugh that recurs almost as often in the biographical material about him as in his own writings. For a casual example we might refer again to Lady Dorothy Lygon's memoir in *Evelyn Waugh and his World*, where she tells of Waugh's relationship with his riding instructor, Captain Hance.

> Evelyn transposed the Captain and his family to an Olympian level at which he invented lives for them which, like the gods in ancient Greece, were still linked with the mortals below; their least pronouncement was debated and scrutinised for omens and auguries. The

Captain's name was scarcely mentioned without the mystic initials GBH — which stood for God Bless Him — being added to it and his health was frequently drunk.[3]

The story is typical: 'to him,' says Dudley Carew, 'people were perpetually playing parts in some wild extravaganza of his own imagining';[4] or as David Pryce-Jones comments of another incident, 'You were not sure if you were in the grip of his fantasy, or of your own.'[5] The private fantasy is a comic creation, but it is also an epic one. Captain Hance is elevated to Olympus by the same imagination that makes of wartime Lancing a beleaguered garrison. And for the same reason: only by a continuing campaign of subversion can reality be made endurable.

Manoeuvres of the kind we have been examining are usually protected by the writer's self-consciousness; he is aware of them as moves in a fictive game. But there are exceptions to this. Certain ways of life — more specifically, certain levels of society — could be invested by Waugh with a glamour that to some extent resisted the incursions of irony. There is no need to rehearse the points already made about his attitude to the upper classes. A glance at his description of the Bollinger dinner in *Decline and Fall* should be enough to dispel the idea that he regarded them with uncritical reverence; but there was much, even in those features of their lifestyle which he satirized, that attracted him. The contempt for middle class virtues, the frivolity, the philistinism, had an appeal for him that was magnified by the contrasting background — sober, middle class and literary — from which he came himself. But the glamour rarely survived a scrutiny of the individuals who were supposed to display it. The appeal of the aristocracy was romantic, but it did not lie primarily

---

[3] *Evelyn Waugh and his World*, ed. David Pryce-Jones, p. 50.
[4] Ibid., p. 44.
[5] Ibid., p. 4.

— or at least not for long — in the ephemeral glitter of the Bright Young People. As a foil to them in *Vile Bodies* there is the order of things represented by those who come together for the annual reception at Anchorage House, the 'great concourse of pious and honourable people' who belong to an older and less troubled generation. Humorously, but not without respect, Waugh invokes in his description of them an ideal notion, secure against individual frailties, of the traditional and proper organization of a society. Later in life he formulated it more seriously in his commentary for T. A. McInerny's *The Private Man*:

> At the head — I am not sure that McInerny would agree with me in this particular — is the fount of honour and justice; below that men and women who hold office from above and are the custodians of tradition, morality and grace; when occasion arises ready for sacrifice but protected from the infection of corruption and ambition by hereditary possession; the nourishers of the arts, the censors of manners. Below that the classes of industry and scholarship, trained from the nursery in habits of probity. Below that manual labourers proud of their skills and bound to those above them by common allegiance to the monarch. In general a man is best fitted to the tasks he has seen his father perform. [*LOr* 144]

This is recognizable at once as the clarion voice of romantic conservatism. It expresses the standard vision of an idealized world of order and civilization set in opposition to the forces of barbarism and destruction. The conservative role of the artist becomes, in Waugh's formulation of it, a romantic one as well:

> The artist's only service to the disintegrated society of today is to create little independent systems of order of his own. I foresee in the dark age opening that the scribes may play the part of the monks after the first barbarian victories. [*LOr* 33]

It is one of the complexities of Waugh's work that the

creation of these 'little independent systems of order' seems so often to involve a creative tribute to disorder. Which is more attractive to him, the order of Pennyfeather's life or the chaos that overturns it, the chaos of Azania under Seth or the order of the colonial regime that comes after? There is a fascination in the encroachments of barbarism, whatever their form. The futile dissipations of the Bright Young People, the savage customs of the Sakuyu, the ungodly rites of Whispering Glades — all of them attest the dual nature of Waugh's romanticism. Even as he states his allegiance to the order that is disintegrating, his words convey a relish for the gloomy drama which that disintegration brings in its train; the image of a monk in the Dark Ages calls to him with an appeal of its own. The seemingly contradictory attraction throughout his work of anarchy on one side, of order and decorum on the other is for the most part a product of this divided romanticism.

To some degree it is a contradiction inherent in the position of the romantic conservative. His conservatism will only keep its attraction as long as it remains a lost cause, a hopeless rearguard action fought against the inevitable process of social evolution. If his ideal were realized, then the romantic in him would at once cry out against stagnation. In fact, though, this can never happen, for the romantic conservative takes his stand not simply on retaining things as they are but on returning to them as they were. ('The Conservative Party have never put the clock back a single second,' he complained to Frances Donaldson.[6]) In so far as his commitment is directed to what is past, it will remain for ever unfulfilled, for ever, therefore, a romantic commitment. There is, as Guy Crouchback knows, 'in romance great virtue in unequal odds' [MA 174]. Against the degraded state of the present is set an older, better world to which the romantic, embattled but unsubdued, looks back with fierce longing.

This is Waugh's characteristic stance. One way or another, the conflict between civilization and barbarism is almost always conceived as a conflict between past and present,

[6] Frances Donaldson, *Evelyn Waugh: Portrait of a Country Neighbour*, p. 15.

ancient and modern. Waugh's commitment is to the past, the classics, the age of heroes. This, in some respects, is the province of a later chapter on nostalgia, but its importance to a consideration of Waugh's romanticism must not go unremarked, for it was in his idealized vision of the values and traditions of the past that he found a focus for all the romantic impulses that set him at odds with the present.

It is not surprising to discover that one of his last projects, abandoned only just before his death, was to write a book on the Crusades. His fondness for the concept of chivalry and the chivalric virtues had been evident as early as the biography of Edmund Campion. Campion was for him a hero in the mould of Sir Philip Sidney and Don John of Austria, and in writing as he does of 'the spirit of chivalry' [EC 198-9] in which the martyrs suffered, Waugh defines a particular view of martyrdom and a particular source of appeal in the figure of Campion himself.

The proposal for a book on the Crusades came from a publisher shortly after the appearance of *Sword of Honour*, and it reflects an accurate perception of that work. *Chivalry* was in fact one of the titles Waugh had suggested for the American edition of *Unconditional Surrender*. Though it is recognized from the start that Guy Crouchback's romanticism is sadly anachronistic, the author's irony is directed against his innocence, not against the ideals with which he associates himself. On the contrary, the bitterness of the irony is a measure of how close these ideals are to the sympathies of the author. It may be naive on Guy's part to suppose that the overthrow of Germany will be a victory for the values of tradition and chivalry, but this reflects no credit on those values for which it is in fact a victory. That the sword of Roger of Waybroke belongs to another age makes it no less a Sword of Honour, nor the Sword of Stalingrad any less a Sword of Dishonour.

The title of the first volume, *Men at Arms*, has a deliberately archaic flavour. It is a phrase Waugh has used on one other occasion, in *Put Out More Flags*, when Cedric Lyne appears before his son in uniform: 'For Nigel, at eight years of age, his father was a man-at-arms and a hero.' [PF 167] A 'man-at-arms' because the term has retained all the romantic

associations of which a word like 'soldier' has been deprived
by its commoner currency. Elegiac in tone, the trilogy
looks always to the past for its images of virtue. The following are three brief examples from *Officers and Gentlemen*:

1 Kilbannock's dreadful Air-Marshall has been discomfited
by the club porter:

> As the doors, which in the past two centuries had wel-
> comed grandee and card sharper, duellist and statesman,
> closed behind Air-Marshall Beech, he wondered, not for
> the first time, whether Bellamy's was all it was cracked
> up to be.[OG 15]

2 Guy, having taken on the sacred trust of Apthorpe's kit,
has called, like Roland from the gorge of Roncesvalles, for a
sign from Chatty Corner. There is no reply:

> Here it seemed he was doomed to remain forever,
> standing guard over a heap of tropical gadgets, like
> the Russian sentry he had once been told of, the Guards-
> man who was posted daily year in, year out, until the
> revolution, in the grounds of Tsarskoe Selo on the spot
> where Catherine the Great had once wished to preserve
> a wild-flower.[OG 40]

3 Finally, after the escape from Crete, Guy lies in hospital:

> Silence swelled lusciously like a ripening fig, while
> through the hospital the softly petulant north-west
> wind, which long ago delayed Helen and Menelaus on
> that strand, stirred and fluttered.[OG 226]

In each passage history is being invoked for what it has of
romance. The club's two hundred years are not a material
asset; for the author, they represent an imaginative estate of
which later members are the inheritors. The men who were
members in the past were not like those of today, average figures in an average world; they walked with a bolder step. Club
membership is a title to the company of their shades. But
Air-Marshall Beech is unimpressed, as Hooper would have been.

The Russian sentry in Tsarskoe Selo offers an image of a trivial obligation chivalrously discharged. In an increasingly unromantic war Apthorpe's kit has become a bizarre focus of romanticism. The gorge of Roncesvalles, the sentry, Guy's final approach to the Dark Tower of Chatty's lair — there is nothing very serious about these images, but they are, like the recurrent images from ancient history, points of reference which could only have suggested themselves to a romantic imagination. Moreover, in the context of a war that seems at the time to offer Guy no role other than as the guardian of Apthorpe's outrageous quantity of kit, this compound of irony and romanticism does have a function. What these images sketch out, ironically, half-humorously, but in their way convincingly, is a framework against which the incidents and obligations of daily life, even the most undignified of them, can escape total insignificance.

The appeal of the third passage is not substantially different. In a similar way it looks back to another, less constricted world with its memories of a heroic enterprise the more attractive by contrast with the unworthy performance on Crete. Even then wives could be an unpredictable asset ('Like Helen of Troy,' says Guy, explaining to Uncle Peregrine Virginia's remarriage to Mr Troy), but in the lingering rhythms of the sentence any bitterness is displaced by the languor of romance. The word 'strand' — 'rhet. or poet.', the dictionary tells us — conveys a familiar note of nostalgia for a time before that elegant word was lost in shores and beaches. Indeed, the taste for verbal archaism is in itself a form of linguistic romanticism to which Waugh is greatly drawn. There is an element of quixotry in a writer's affection for dying words and forgotten etymologies which is more than just pedantry; it has in it something of the spirit of the Russian sentry. It is, at all events, yet another muted defiance of modernity.

In the end this is what the various gestures towards the past come back to. For Waugh, as for Guy, it is against the Modern Age that the lines of battle are drawn.

The implications of this can be disconcerting. Translated into political terms, it sets Waugh in the company of the military dictators. Franco's soldiers, we are told in *Robbery*

Under Law, 'have fought under the inspiration of their past' [*RL* 269] ; they are fired by an image of Spain as it used to be in the imperial days of Philip II. Waugh is applauding kindred spirits. The disintegration of their country which, on his analysis, has driven them to rebellion has an obvious parallel in the 'disintegrated society' which is driving the artist into the role of the monks in the Dark Ages. It is an uncomfortable supposition that the two responses might be products of the same kind of romanticism. Certainly, the conception we touched on earlier of a world in which civilization is threatened by the constant encroachment of barbarism seems to lend itself to the political formulations of fascism. To have romanticized the days of the Roman Empire is a strong argument in favour of romanticizing a contemporary effort to re-establish it.

This should be demonstrable, if anywhere, in Waugh's coverage of the Italian—Abyssinian war of 1935, and indeed *Waugh in Abyssinia* was called by Rose Macaulay 'a fascist tract'. That he did in some measure romanticize what to other observers was a fairly sordid episode of Italian history is apparent in the last chapter. Its subject is the new highway being laid down by the Italians from Massawa to Addis Ababa. Waugh's eulogy of it as a triumphant symbol of civilization rises to this conclusion:

> And from Dessye new roads will be radiating to all points of the compass, and along the roads will pass the eagles of ancient Rome, as they came to our savage ancestors in France and Britain and Germany, bringing some rubbish and some mischief; a good deal of vulgar talk and some sharp misfortunes for individual opponents; but above and beyond and entirely predominating, the inestimable gifts of fine workmanship and clear judgement — the two determining qualities of the human spirit, by which alone, under God, man grows and flourishes. [*WA* 253]

Waugh admits that he is less keen on the idea of a main road in England, but assures us that 'Here in Africa it brings order and fertility.' This point of view is largely dictated by convenience. Towards the end of *Black Mischief* two Arabs saunter by the sea wall, discussing the changes brought about under the new dispensation. In Azania too, as part of the usual process of sanitizing and civilizing, the foreign rulers 'are building a black road through the hills to Debra Dowa'. But the Arabs take a gloomy view of the general result: 'Things were better in the time of Seth. It is no longer a gentleman's country.' Their disgust has some authority; the speakers are two of those 'grave, impoverished men whose genealogies extended to the time of the Prophet', and the voice of decayed aristocratic tradition is not to be dismissed lightly in Waugh's writing. Are the fine workmanship and clear judgement being brought by the eagles of ancient Rome in reality any more than the new customs-house and new bungalows that are making such a dreary place of Azania? Perhaps, but the differences are hard to identify; what primarily distinguishes the achievements of the Italians is the romantic haze through which Waugh views them.

In *Black Mischief* it was a vision of anarchy that stirred him, in *Waugh in Abyssinia* it is a vision of order. His romanticism was not essentially political; it was, like his humour, an aspect of the refusal to accept a world that was grey while he still had the resources to make it vivid. To over-simplify, the Italians in this book merely provide a convenient focus for his romanticism; they are not responsible for it. 'It was fun being pro-Italian when it was an unpopular and (I thought) losing cause,' Waugh wrote to Katharine Asquith in August 1936 [*Letters* 109]. 'I have little sympathy with these exultant fascists now.'

Even at the time it took no more than a small change in the angle of vision for the same romantic conservatism to produce a quite contradictory view of Italian policy. On the road to Dessye Waugh is briefly entertained by a local governor. It is an episode which for James Carens reveals 'the essence of Waugh's political sensibility'.[7] The governor, Dedjasmach Matafara, is a patriarchal old savage with a strong contempt for the Italians: 'They did not like the smell of

---

[7] James F. Carens, *The Satiric Art of Evelyn Waugh*, p. 135.

blood, he said; when they smelled blood they were afraid; when an Abyssinian smelled blood he became doubly brave; that was why the sword was better than the gun.' [WA 201] This, one might think, is the language of barbarism. They are the sort of sentiments that could come easily from one of the chiefs of the Wanda or Sakuyu, out of the heart of that darkness which is to be vanquished by the new Italian highways. But Waugh has been graciously entertained by the Dedjasmach; he recognizes in the old man an object of romantic virtue more potent than anything Italian:

> It had been more than a pleasant interlude; it had been a glimpse of the age-old, traditional order that still survived, gracious and sturdy, out of sight beyond the brass bands and bunting, the topees and humane humbug of Tafari's regime; of an order doomed to destruction. Whatever the outcome of the present war...Dedjasmach Matafara and all he stood for was bound to disappear. But we were pleased to have seen it and touched hands across the centuries with the court of Prester John. [WA 202]

If the Dedjasmach is to be one of the victims of the new order, then the opposition between civilization and barbarism cannot be as straightforward as it seems in the final chapter. The old patriarch is offering a perspective on events similar to that presented humorously through the two Arabs in *Black Mischief*. But it is a perspective to which Waugh does not return; the challenge is left unexamined. Both the Dedjasmach and the Italians have, in their own terms, a level of romantic appeal. Only the drab compromise of Ras Tafari has none.

Not until much later in Waugh's career did he recognize that there is a danger in this line of response, that to judge a situation by the canons of romance without concern for its moral or ideological context is to risk the sort of consequences to which Mme Kanyi points in her bitter analysis of the will to war at the end of *Unconditional Surrender*. At the time of *Waugh in Abyssinia* and in the years of crisis that followed there were few misgivings. From the realities of

middle age the coming war seemed to offer a refuge in the
pleasures of childhood and the glamour of bygone centuries.
'Pathans were Captain Truslove's business...' [*MA* 166] . Guy
Crouchback, like Charles Ryder before him, is lured to battle
by a trumpet call from the past.

Traditions of chivalry and social order are only one form
of appeal. Both Crouchback and Ryder show a devotion to
the past which extends beyond their attitude to soldiering.
Their love affair with the army was in each case preceded by
a human love affair that still dominates their outlook; for
images of emotional happiness — for romance — they must
again rely on the past.

Of all Waugh's novels *Brideshead Revisited* is the one that
ventures furthest into the conventional territory of romantic
love. Charles and Julia are brought together on a rough sea-
crossing from New York. At the height of the storm the ship
pitches them into an embrace:

> cheek against cheek, her hair blowing across my eyes;
> the dark horizon of tumbling water, flashing now with
> gold, stood still above us, then came sweeping down till
> I was staring through Julia's dark hair into a wide and
> golden sky, and she was thrown forward on my heart,
> held up by my hands on the rail, her face still pressed
> to mine. [*BR* 248]

A few days later they take the train together from London to
Brideshead:

> Julia pulled off her hat and tossed it into the rack above
> her, and shook her night-dark hair with a little sigh of
> ease — a sigh fit for the pillow, the sinking firelight and
> a bedroom window open to the stars and the whisper of
> bare trees. [*BR* 261]

This is not a style of writing we expect in Waugh — not, at

least, without the saving grace of irony. 'Her night-dark hair'
— the phrase has a Keatsian ring which twenty years earlier
would have left its author chill with embarrassment. Because
Sebastian and Julia exist as memories, the narrator can invest
them with a radiance that actuality would too probably have
denied them. The book's form as a memoir is offered in part-
excuse for its romanticism.

Once outside the charmed circle of memory, sexual relationships, for most writers the natural source of romance,
are, in the writings of Evelyn Waugh, rarely romantic. To
think of them as such is to court disillusionment. It is what
Tony Last does, first with Brenda — Lady Brenda — and
then, briefly, with Thérèse de Vitry. The Gothic dream in
which he has cast his wife as the 'ladie faire' is an illusion that
has no chance of survival in the world of reality. And when
later Tony strikes up an acquaintance with Thérèse and
presumes too far on the atmosphere of tropical romance, he
is sharply reminded of the sterner conditions of the outside
world. Her response on learning that he is already married
is abrupt and unaccommodating.

Not that Waugh had any distaste for the conventional
stage properties of romantic love. The storm at sea, the
quiet evening from the ship's rail, lights reflected across
tropical waters, night sounds, drenched hair, days of impossible summer, strawberries and wine under the tall elms
— the list of images could be continued; and he was fully
aware of their attraction. He was, however, as I stressed
at the start, an ironist as well as a romantic; and few subjects
are more vulnerable to irony than romantic love. Whatever
the appeal of these images, he uses them only in two contexts — either as the consoling stuff of memory or as an
ironic prelude to disillusionment. There are no love affairs
that end happily in Waugh.

When Kätchen enters the pages of *Scoop* with her hair
damp from the rain and a consumptive cough that publishes
her kinship with the idealized cocottes of the nineteenth
century, it is sure enough that William will fall in love with
her, but equally sure that she will disillusion him. From
Pennyfeather onwards, disappointment is the lot of all
Waugh's heroes who fall in love. William's disappointment

is largely comic, Tony's is less so, Guy Crouchback's is
scarcely comic at all; but in every case there is the same
antagonism between the conditions of romance and those of
reality. The image of Tony and Thérèse linking arms and
looking out towards the shore can be indulged only because
it is already mortgaged to the writer's irony — disillusionment
is on the way; the image of Tony and Brenda sitting at the
café and looking out towards the sea can be indulged only
because it already enjoys the protection of the past — Tony
knows it to be irrecoverable.

As these examples suggest, memories of romantic relationships are frequently entwined with memories of romantic
places. If romance blossoms more freely in the past, it also
tends to flourish abroad rather than at home. The lure of
memory is comparable to — and often combined with — the
lure of the exotic.

No part of the world demonstrates the appeal of this
fusion more powerfully than the Mediterranean. For Mr
Pinfold, as for many of his generation, it was 'that splendid
enclosure which held all the world's history and half the
happiest memories of his own life; of work and rest and
battle, of aesthetic adventure, and of young love' [GP 100].
It is to this romantic region that Scott-King looks for escape
from the austerities of post-war Britain:

> Hot oil and garlic and spilled wine; luminous pinnacles
> above a dusky wall; fireworks at night, fountains at
> noonday…the shepherd's pipe on the scented hillside —
> all that travel agent ever sought to put in a folder,
> fumed in Scott-King's mind that drab morning.[WS 203]

These are familiar images in Waugh; they have the fragrance
of a world set apart from the harsh ordinances of life as it
is lived in those northern countries beyond the reach of the
sun. Dreams of the south merge with a nostalgia that calls us
back to the paradisal landscape from which we were originally exiled. It is the romantic consummation. But this in
itself can be a problem; the images that seethe in Scott-King's
mind are overtaxed; they have already edged too far towards
the travel agent's folder. It is, in an extreme form, the problem

that Waugh had indicated by calling his first travel book
Labels; the images of the Mediterranean are too well-
thumbed to be taken up without self-consciousness; as the
property of every travel agent, their charm has inevitably
been debased. The call of the Mediterranean persists, but
only because it is also the call of 'all the world's history'.

After *Labels* there were to be no more travel books with
a Mediterranean setting. In the Preface to *When the Going
was Good* Waugh explains how he and others of his generation had set out for more distant places:

> These were the years when Mr Peter Fleming went to
> the Gobi Desert, Mr Graham Greene to the Liberian
> hinterland; Robert Byron — vital today, as of old, in
> our memories; all his exuberant zest in the opportuni-
> ties of our time now, alas! tragically and untimely
> quenched — to the ruins of Persia. We turned our backs
> on civilization. Had we known, we might have lingered
> with 'Palinurus'; had we known that all that seeming-
> solid, patiently built, gorgeously ornamented structure
> of Western life was to melt overnight like an ice-castle,
> leaving only a puddle of mud; had we known man was
> even then leaving his post. Instead, we set off on our
> various stern roads; I to the Tropics and the Arctic,
> with the belief that barbarism was a dodo to be stalked
> with a pinch of salt. The route of *Remote People* was
> easy going; the *Ninety-Two Days* were more arduous.
> We have most of us marched and made camp since then,
> gone hungry and thirsty, lived where pistols are flou-
> rished and fired. At that time it seemed an ordeal, an
> initiation to manhood. [*WGG* 8]

The tone is an interesting mixture of the elegiac and the
swashbuckling. It is hard to resist the suspicion that, like
Walter Shandy's reaction to the death of his elder son,
Waugh's rhetoric about the death of Robert Byron and the
collapse of a civilization has quite out-distanced the emotion
that gave rise to it. We do not have to know that Waugh in
reality harboured a strong dislike for Robert Byron; the
highly wrought phrases are in themselves a clear enough

indication that the writer's attention has been fully claimed by the pleasure of assimilating what has happened to the traditional language of epitaph and elegy. Whatever emotion there might have been is absorbed in verbal gesture. Waugh's response has an archaic luxuriance that marks the passage as a deliberate concession to his romanticism.

The bracing rhythm of the penultimate sentence ('marched and made camp' etc.) offers us a sparse, idealized vision of the military life. It has nothing to do with the long years of frustration and boredom recorded in *Sword of Honour*. Marching and making camp — *viginta milibus passuum confectis, castra posuerunt*; Waugh advances in the shadow of Caesar's legions. And the pistols that were flourished and fired — these, surely, cannot have been regulation weapons; one might flourish a pistol when storming redoubts or boarding Spanish ships, but hardly when being shuttled between depots and training camps in the series of futile military displacements that are the recurrent business of the war trilogy. And yet the passage is appropriate to its context, for in spite of Waugh's studied poise in the accounts he gives of his journeyings, his attitude to travel never quite lost the ardent romanticism that these sentences proclaim. Tony Last's view of himself as an explorer is half-apologetic, but his words betray an obvious relish when he talks to Thérèse de Vitry of Indian trails and untravelled country, of cutting through the bush and making woodskin canoes, of arriving, finally, under the walls of the city like the Vikings at Byzantium. His tone is that of Atwater, fantasizing about the joys of exploration in *Work Suspended*:

> Think of paddling your canoe upstream in undiscovered country, with strings of orchids overhead and parrots in the trees and great butterflies, and native servants, and hanging your hammock in the open at night and starting off in the morning with no one to worry you, living on fish and fruit — that's life... [WS 184]

Atwater and Last are doing for the life of the explorer what Waugh was doing for the life of the soldier; their words present the same grandly simplified outline, with the same preference for romantic tradition over observed reality. In both cases the fictional characters are being mocked; their illusions are precisely the ones that Waugh had gone out of his way to discredit at the end of *Ninety-Two Days*. But although he treats them with irony, he quite clearly retains a degree of sympathy with them. The flaming colours of the tropical landscape, its dizzying profusion, its strange outcrops of humanity — these aspects of the exotic could not fail to excite an imagination that craved escape from the monotony of routine. And Waugh admits as much in the opening pages of *Ninety-Two Days*. Writing of the 'fascination in distant and barbarous places', he explains that 'It is there that I find the experiences vivid enough to demand translation into literary form.' [*92D* 13] The decisive word is 'vivid': 'the dark clouds opened above him; the gutters and wet leaves sparkled in sunlight and a vast, iridescent fan of colour, arc beyond arc of splendour, spread across the heavens' [*S* 125]. This is the end of the rainy season in Ishmaelia, a characteristically dramatic reversion from storm to sunshine. One could as well have quoted descriptions of sunrise over Matodi or an abrupt thunderstorm in Debra Dowa. What stimulates Waugh's imagination are the extremes ('I to the Tropics and the Arctic'); in the vibrating life of the African landscape he finds the same elements that attract him to the vivid extremes of African politics.

Atwater's words are parody, but they mention nothing that cannot be matched from Waugh's own account of his journey in South America. What Atwater leaves out and what Waugh puts in are the other features of the explorer's life — insects, illness, fatigue, hunger, danger. It is because Waugh puts them in that his travel books strike so many readers as essays in disenchantment; he seems to be trampling the Atwater brand of romanticism underfoot. The Africa in *Remote People* is a continent of nightmare; the very title of *Ninety-Two Days* sounds, as the *Times Literary Supplement* reviewer pointed out, like a penal sentence of three months. But then Atwater's is not the only kind of romanticism. It corresponds, one might say, to the 'Etna at sunset' variety. There is also that more austere kind which can sustain itself with the mosquito bites as well as with the sunsets. We might note that in the passage quoted above Waugh includes 'gone hungry and thirsty' in his outline of the soldier's life without in any way detracting from its romanticism. To go hungry and thirsty is a proper requirement of a soldier; the image would be tarnished by ease rather than by hardship. In a similar way there are forms of hardship appropriate to the life of an explorer which only the shallowest romanticism could fail to take account of. 'The difficulty (and of course the charm) of Abyssinia is the inaccessibility of the interior,' says Waugh in *Remote People*; and the parenthesis is significant.

There is no necessary correspondence between the appeal of travel or warfare or exploration and the enjoyment they offer. To have been there at the hot gates or knee deep in the salt marsh would be a claim to romance stronger than most. The impulse is not a hedonistic one; it may be no more than a poison in the blood, a lurking discontent, responsive to a particular kind of stimulus. Even as he sits down to rehearse the ninety-two days of discomfort, danger and fatigue, Waugh notes that 'falling leaves in the autumnal sunshine remind me that it will soon be time to start out again somewhere else' [*92D* 14].

For the explorer, hardship is a measure of the authenticity of his exploration; and this is why it belongs in the picture. The role of traveller is less demanding; discomfort is inevitable, but for him what takes the place of the explorer's hardship is the murky underside of travel which the brochures leave out: the pimps and whores and swindlers, the rank flowers of boredom, the frustrations of bureaucracy, the dissolute hotels and evil-smelling streets. Everyone comes on deck for the sunrise, visits the pyramids, admires Gibraltar; what distinguishes a certain type of traveller is the curiosity that draws him to the *quartiers louches* — less for what they offer than for what they suggest.

Waugh's nocturnal expeditions in search of vice are a standard feature of the early travel books. The description in *Work Suspended* of John Plant preparing for his weekly visit to the Moulay Abdullah is closely parallel to the sort of accounts Waugh gives of his own excursions in *Labels* and *Remote People*. For Plant, the Moulay has an attraction 'which endowed its trade with something approaching glamour', and he goes on to linger affectionately over its architecture and ambience. 'There really was a memory of "the East", as adolescents imagine it, in that silent court-yard...' [WS 122].

The descriptions in Waugh's travel books have a sharper edge. The squalor is real for him; but it is transfigured by 'the intoxicating sense of vitality and actuality' [L 85]. The phrase comes from his account of Port Said, where, by contrast, the English colony maintain their distance from the Arab quarter: 'Many of them had never been there at all....They had an idea that it smelled and crawled with bugs, and that was enough for them...'. Dead to the fascinations of the exotic, as to most other things, these are nonetheless the same people of whom Waugh remarks:

> It seemed to me that the life led by these oversea business men and officials was in every way agreeable and enviable when compared with its counterpart in modern England. [L 75]

'There was, of course,' he continues, 'no nonsense of tropical romance; no indomitable jungle, no contact with raw nature...' and so on.

Waugh spurns the typical clichés, and in doing so aligns himself with the viewpoint of the Port Said business community. A part of him was predictably sympathetic towards their robust insensitivity. And yet...'no nonsense of tropical romance'?

> There was glamour in all the associations of Harar, the Arab city-state which stood first among the fruits of Ethiopian imperialism, the scene of Sir Richard Burton's *First Steps in Africa*, the market where the caravans met between coast and highlands; where Galla, Somali, and Arab interbred to produce women whose beauty was renowned throughout East Africa. There is talk of a motor-road that is to connect it with the railway, but at present it must still be approached by the tortuous hill-pass and small track along which Arthure [sic] Rimbaud had sent rifles to Menelik. [RP 92-3]

How much of this glamour would have been apparent to the Port Said businessmen?

The point made earlier is worth emphasizing: to attack the clichés of a language is not necessarily to attack the language itself. When Waugh disparages Gibraltar or mocks the dogged tourists in the Serapeum, he is doing the first — deploying a facile irony to undercut a facile romanticism. As often as not, this is merely clearing the ground for his own romanticism; after all, the difference between finding glamour in the associations of Harar and finding it in those of the Sphinx is only one of fastidiousness. Waugh's objections to the latter are really no more than a purist's distaste for vulgarization — which is why his trip to Harar retains its appeal: Rimbaud sending guns to Menelik is an image for the connoisseur, Napoleon at the pyramids is not.

The second kind of attack on romanticism is far more radical than a youthful impatience of cliché; it constitutes a challenge to the language itself. What in the early books is mere sniping at absurdities tends later to give way to a more damaging sense that romanticism can in some circumstances become a form of corruption. This is familiar ground. In each chapter the final pages have charted a similar course; the author's detachment, his humour, and his romanticism are all, from the perspective I have taken, strategies of escape, and each of them is subject to the same kind of erosion. Frequently, episodes that illustrate the process for one will do so for the others. The unfurling cigar stub which marks the passage of love between Basil and Prudence is an image that challenges romanticism as well as questioning the author's detachment. So, at the end of the novel, when Mr Youkoumian closes his café, he puts up the shutters on romance as well as on humour.

Once again *A Handful of Dust* marks an exceptional stage in the argument, for we have here a novel that on one level presents itself as a direct critique of romantic attitudes. Is Hetton Abbey a castle from Arthurian legend or, as the

guidebook claims, 'devoid of interest'? Is Brenda 'the imprisoned princess of fairy story' or a vapid adulteress? Is Tony
an explorer in the tradition of the Vikings who sailed to
Byzantium or is he the dupe of a crook doctor? From the
opening pages of the novel we are made aware of an insistent
pressure from realities that in preceding books have scarcely
impinged at all. Beaver's job — in an advertising agency —
was lost in the slump; he now has an income of only £6 a
week. The figure is exact. This is a world in which people
are concerned with economy, where they sometimes take
buses rather than taxis, where even Brenda travels third class
to save money. (It is consistent that her pretext for going to
London should be the study of economics.) No one here
would think lightly of the thousand pounds that get tossed
backwards and forwards in *Vile Bodies*. Money is at the root
of Beaver's boredom at home, Brenda's imprisonment at
Hetton, Tony's breach with her over the divorce. It is the
mainspring, in one way or another, of much of the novel's
action — a doubtful basis for romance.

Tony's attachment to Hetton is hopelessly at odds
with this reality: the place is neither modern nor functional,
and worst of all, it is uneconomic to maintain. The traditional concept of romance is out of date. 'Society' has
translated it into terms more in keeping with the new
order:

It had been an autumn of very sparse and meagre romance; only the most obvious people had parted or
come together, and Brenda was filling a want long felt
by those whose simple, vicarious pleasure it was to discuss the subject in bed over the telephone. For them her
circumstances shed peculiar glamour; for five years she
had been a legendary, almost ghostly name, the imprisoned princess of fairy story, and now that she had
emerged there was more enchantment in the occurrence
than in the mere change of habit of any other circumspect wife. Her very choice of partner gave the affair an
appropriate touch of fantasy; Beaver, the joke figure
they had all known and despised, suddenly caught up
to her among the luminous clouds of deity. [HD 57]

It is ironic that Beaver should be lodged in Galahad when he visits Hetton; his role in this updated idyll is that of Lancelot. The affair with Brenda is 'society's' tarnished parody of the romantic world in which Tony actually lives, and when he is confronted by it the dream crumbles: 'there was now no armour glittering through the forest glades, no embroidered feet on the green sward; the cream and dappled unicorns had fled...' [HD 151].

The collapse of Tony's Gothic fantasy is an admission of defeat in the face of a modern world whose conditions deny the possibility of escape into romanticism. But the problem recurs; for the degrading elements of modern life that have destroyed the dream are precisely what make it necessary. Accordingly, Tony transfers his romantic vision to Dr Messinger's South American city. In his imagination this now takes on the Gothic aspect of Hetton and becomes the focus of his dreams of another order. But Mrs Beaver has got there first. It is, as Waugh remarked, a book 'on the theme of the betrayed romantic',[8] and in his delirium Tony accepts the fulfilment of this theme:

> There is no City. Mrs Beaver has covered it with chromium plating and converted it into flats. Three guineas a week, each with a separate bathroom. Very suitable for base love. And Polly will be there. She and Mrs Beaver under the fallen battlements... [HD 207]

Polly Cockpurse and Mrs Beaver are the doyennes of the new society; their storming of Tony's City is the final recognition that no escape is possible. His fate at the hands of Mr Todd is merely a confirmation of the part that has been his from the beginning. Reading Dickens among savages is a sardonic image of what Tony has been doing anyway in his attempt to maintain Hetton within the context of contemporary society. The appraisal of romanticism is complete: Tony's fantasies can offer no permanent refuge from the world in which he has to live. In part, they are responsible for his downfall.

---

[8] Preface to the Second Uniform Edition, 1964.

And yet our sympathies are with him rather than with the forces that destroy him. By intercutting Tony's expedition through the jungle with events back in London, Waugh emphasizes the similarity of the two milieux. While the Macushi hunt bush pig, Grant-Menzies asks questions in Parliament about pig specifications; the British preoccupation with pork pies is counterpointed with the native consumption of roast pork. The identity of the two places is suggested by Tony's delirious remark that 'her Ladyship has gone to live in Brazil' — i.e. among savages. Grant-Menzies has it the wrong way round when he says to Brenda — significantly, while they are dancing at Anchorage House — 'The whole world is civilized now, isn't it...?' [HD 172] He should have said 'uncivilized'.

Waugh chose his words carefully when he described the book as 'a study of other sorts of savage at home and the civilized man's helpless plight among them' [LOr 33]. The point is surely clear: the ruined City over which Polly Cockpurse and Mrs Beaver have triumphed is not just the image of Tony's romantic dreams, it is the image of civilization. Tony is a slightly absurd figure, but he is also 'the civilized man', and his attachment to the values of civilization is inseparable from the romanticism that makes for his absurdity. To hanker after civilization at all in the world as it actually exists is to be convicted of romanticism. The book is a critique of Tony's attitudes but not necessarily, at this stage, a condemnation of them. Waugh recognizes that they are futile as a means of eluding modern social reality, but it is their failure that is regretted, not their attempt.

When *A Handful of Dust* first appeared in America, the magazine that was serializing it felt that the hero's fate was altogether too black and asked Waugh to supply a happy ending in its place.[9] Obligingly, he sent Tony Last back to England for a reconciliation with Brenda. But by

[9] This, at least, is the version given by Christopher Sykes in *Evelyn Waugh: A Biography*. In his Preface to the Second Uniform Edition of the novel Waugh himself offered the more prosaic explanation that it could not be serialized with its original ending because this had already been published separately in America as a short story called 'The Man Who Liked Dickens'.

this time Tony has caught the idiom of his society; it is he who hires one of Mrs Beaver's flats now:

> My idea is to use it when I come to London instead of my club. It will be cheaper and a great deal more convenient. But my wife may not see it in that light... in fact... [*MrL* 36]

'I *quite* understand,' replies Mrs Beaver. The implication cannot be missed. Waugh must have derived a certain enjoyment from providing his audience with its happy ending. What he has done is simply to take the triumph of barbarism one stage further: all his romanticism gone, a savage now among savages, Tony has finally succeeded in learning the law of the jungle.

Waugh's sympathy with the romantic viewpoint did not diminish in the years that followed; it was, if anything, augmented by the approach of the Second World War. *Put Out More Flags* is suffused with an exhilarating sense of heroic possibilities. But by the time of *Brideshead Revisited*, the author has returned to a position much closer to that of *A Handful of Dust*. Barbarism is everywhere triumphant. Ryder's nostalgic yearning for a lost civilization is presented with sympathy but without hope. The cigarette ends that collect in the fountain at Brideshead are part of a general process of degradation; the last refuges of nostalgia are being contaminated. Ryder's ideals about the war are long dead and his love for Julia has had to be surrendered to more imperious claims. Here and in the pessimistic satires that follow life within society seems to afford no ground for responses that have not been standardized. The modern State is upon us. There can be no question now of any perspective that seeks to make something romantic out of the conventional obligations of daily life.

And yet this is exactly what Guy Crouchback sets out to achieve at the beginning of the *Sword of Honour* trilogy. With the declaration of war his course becomes plain; he is called to arms not only by his duty as a Christian and an Englishman, but also by the appeal of what he takes to be a crusade against the Modern Age. In returning to England he

is taking his rightful place in a society that has been transfigured by romantic purpose. Life has been redeemed from
futility — 'Eight years of shame and loneliness were ended.'
[MA 12]

It is on this foundation that Guy proposes to reconstruct
his life. By a fortuitous historical accident the perspectives
of childhood seem suddenly to coincide with reality. Life
has all the possibilities that in youth one had attributed to
it; there is no need to escape or hide. Guy once used to
imagine himself 'serving the last mass for the last Pope in a
catacomb at the end of the world' [MA 16], but now the
old embattled romanticism has been revitalized; it can
become a way of living one's life rather than of escaping
from it. 'Can I go myself, sir?' Guy asks, when told that
a man is needed to lead the raid on Dakar. This really is a
world in which men like Truslove embrace danger with a
smile for the sake of their country.

Sadly, though, it turns out not to be; it turns out to
be a world in which 'priests were spies and gallant friends
proved traitors and his country was led blundering into
dishonour' [OG 240]. The effort to see the war in the
light of Boy's Own and Chums is a doomed attempt to recover
what are, after all, the unreal — or at any rate, unrealizable —
perspectives of childhood. Rugger in the mess, the 'happy
adolescence', the prep school setting — such features of life as
a Halberdier make their own comment.

It is while he is at Kut-al-Imara that Guy's illusions begin
to fade. As part of the business of shoring them up he grows
an imposing moustache and then, drawn by, amongst other
things, 'the memory of countless German Uhlans in countless
American films' [MA 105], he goes into an optician and pur-
chases a monocle. His appearance is transformed: 'The man
reflected to him had a cynical leer; he was every inch a
junker.' But the way this is phrased — 'the man reflected to
him' — suggests, what Guy himself later acknowledges, that
the face is not really his own. Examining his moustaches in
Bellamy's, he is uncertain:

True he had also seen them in the Halberdier mess, but
on faces innocent of all guile, quite beyond suspicion.

After all, he reflected, his whole uniform was a disguise,
his whole new calling a masquerade. [*MA* 124]

Guy has cast himself as a man-at-arms, an officer in the
Earl of Essex's Honourable Company of Free Halberdiers;
but a fatal awareness intervenes between himself and his
role, making of it a masquerade. He is separated from the
gallant figures with whom he seeks to identify by that self-
consciousness which divides the fallen from the unfallen.

When earlier Guy had described to Major Tickeridge his
vain attempts to get a commission, the latter 'was slightly
puzzled by the ironic note of the recitation' [*MA* 40]. It is
the old sense of irony that now exposes Guy's new identity
as romantic posturing; that quality of mind which enables
him to survive in a fallen world prohibits him from claiming
a place in the company of the innocent. The moustache
comes off:

> When it was done, Guy studied himself once more in
> the glass and recognized an old acquaintance he could
> never cut, to whom he could never hope to give the
> slip for long, the uncongenial fellow traveller who would
> accompany him through life. [*MA* 125]

The romantic mould has cracked from within. In its recognition of the internal pressures on romanticism this episode
already suggests a level of scrutiny more profound than anything in *A Handful of Dust*. The mask Guy has assumed
involves a literal refusal to face what he is. It is a perception
that cannot be gainsaid. An escape attempt has been foiled.

The strain on Guy's romanticism is increased by his growing awareness of the gap between his own view of the war
and that of practically everyone else. His indignation at the
invasion of Poland finds no echo — '"Justice?" said the old
soldiers. "Justice?"' [*MA* 25] Later, when the Finns are
beaten, no one at Kut-al-Imara seems much put out by the
disaster:

> For Guy the news quickened the sickening suspicion
> he had tried to ignore, had succeeded in ignoring more

often than not in his service in the Halberdiers; that he was engaged in a war in which courage and a just cause were quite irrelevant to the issue. [MA 142]

This is already a long way from the crusading spirit of the Prologue, but such episodes are no more than premonitory brushes with the overwhelming sense of disillusionment which is to become the dominant mood of the last two volumes. It is on Crete that Guy takes the full measure of his misconceptions. Sir Roger of Waybroke, as a man who had dedicated his arms to the service of God, was once an image for Guy of the compatibility of the ideal and the real; he is now invoked only to mark the gulf that separates them. In the middle of the débâcle Guy comes upon a village and is taken to the body of a young soldier, a Roman Catholic like himself:

> The soldier lay like an effigy on a tomb — like Sir Roger in his shadowy shrine at Santa Dulcina. Only the blue-bottles that clustered round his lips and eyes proclaimed that he was flesh. [OG 206] [10]

The bluebottles are an unchivalrous addition to the image; this is Sir Roger without romance. Later, the soldier's identity disc will be dropped into a wastepaper basket by Julia Stitch.

The scenes on Crete everywhere record the same decline. There is now no armour glittering through the forest glades; Major Hound has quickly taken on the characteristics of his name and the commanding officers of Creforce, 'the head-men of the defeated tribe' [OG 198], huddle in a cave like chimps in a zoo. Guy can only stumble between the different battle zones, 'Philoctetes without his bow. Sir Roger without his sword.' [OG 210] Alone of those left on Crete at the end, Ivor Claire seems unchanged, the face 'haggard now but calm and recollected, as he had first seen it in the Borghese Gardens'. Back in Alexandria Guy thinks of him as a prisoner of the Germans — 'that young prince of Athens sent as

[10] For further discussion of this passage see chapter 6.

sacrifice to the Cretan labyrinth' [*OG* 232]. It is the familiar trick; the old shadows of classical mythology are deployed again, this time to exalt the fate of the most romantic of all the 'happy warriors', the resourceful dandy of tradition who was, in Guy's imagination, 'quintessential England'. But on this occasion the image fails of its purpose, for Ivor is not in captivity; his men have been deserted by him. It is an order of event that not even the most elaborate metaphor can rescue for romance. A few days later comes news of the Russian alliance — for Guy the ultimate betrayal of those values on whose behalf he had set out from Italy two years earlier. His dejection prefigures the atmosphere of *Unconditional Surrender*.

In this final volume Guy moves through a world of ignoble compromise and political expediency, dominated by men like Sir Ralph Brompton, Gilpin and Lieutenant Padfield. His romantic idealism has already proved incompatible with the norms of his society and the realities of his own situation. To this extent it is like Tony Last's; but in *Unconditional Surrender* Waugh begins to tax it with something more than just a disregard for reality. In Mme Kanyi's words there is an awareness that the sort of romanticism in which Guy, and along with him the heroes of *Put Out More Flags*, had clothed their participation in the war was a vicious compensation for the futility of their own lives. The enthusiasm with which they took up arms has issued in the suffering of the ensuing years:

> Even good men thought their private honour would be satisfied by war. They could assert their manhood by killing and being killed. They would accept hardships in recompense for having been selfish and lazy. Danger justified privilege. I knew Italians — not very many perhaps — who felt this. Were there none in England? [*US* 232]

'God forgive me,' says Guy. 'I was one of them.' It is a devastating moment that catches up and judges not just Guy's early romanticism, but the author's own sympathy with it. *The Death Wish* is evidently a significant title for Ludovic's novel.

In its conclusion *Unconditional Surrender* makes a positive rejection of romance — or at least of romanticism. An element of modest but authentic romance there is, in Guy's return to the farm at Broome with his second wife. But the romance is authentic to the extent that the romanticism has been compromised. There has been an accommodation with reality. The Crouchbacks no longer occupy Broome, but they do live in its shadow; they have an heir, but he is Trimmer's son.

This is as much as can be said. In letters that he wrote at the time to Nancy Mitford and Anthony Powell Waugh himself disclaimed the idea that it was to be taken as a 'happy ending'. Things turn out 'conveniently' for Guy — not a word that gives much scope to the imagination. Domenica Plessington, whom he marries, is a world away from Virginia, the 'ghost of romance' elegized by Everard Spruce. There is nothing about her of 'the exquisite, the doomed, and the damning, with expiring voices'; she drives a tractor on the home farm. In what is surely a purposeful juxtaposition, Waugh goes on to describe her immediately after the scene with Spruce: 'From having been shy and almost excessively feminine, she was now rather boisterous, trousered and muddied and full of the rough jargon of the stock-yard.' [*US* 201] An effective antidote to Arlenesque dreams of romance.

The point is made most sharply in Guy's conversation with Kerstie about his proposal to remarry Virginia. Inferring from her previous knowledge of Guy that he is merely being chivalrous, Kerstie upbraids him for what she takes to be a piece of romantic folly. But Guy corrects her:

'Knights errant,' he said, 'used to go out looking for noble deeds. I don't think I've ever in my life done a single, positively unselfish action. I certainly haven't gone out of my way to find opportunities. Here was something most unwelcome, put into my hands; something which I believe the Americans describe as "beyond the call of duty"; not the normal behaviour of an officer and a gentleman; something they'll laugh about in Bellamy's.' [*US* 151]

It is in fact precisely the opposite of a romantic gesture, implying as it does a repudiation of the ethos to which Guy had aspired in the previous volume of the trilogy. He makes it clear that the basis of his actions has shifted from the romantic to the religious.

Again we are plotting the same course as in earlier chapters. At each stage a particular mode of response comes to be found wanting and its partial functions are superseded by the duties and consolations of Christianity. This is just what we can see happening in *Unconditional Surrender*. Mme Kanyi's words are followed by the start of a new section:

> Guy had come to the end of the crusade to which he had devoted himself on the tomb of Sir Roger. His life as a Halberdier was over. All the stamping of the barrack square and the biffing of imaginary strongholds were finding their consummation in one frustrated act of mercy.[*US* 232]

The old ideals have been absorbed into another scheme of things; romantic longings have found a religious consummation. The pattern goes back to *Brideshead*. Charles Ryder had similar longings, but his three love affairs — with Sebastian, with Julia, and with the army — brought only the disappointment which an unromantic world reserves for those who set their course by romantic lights. It is left to Julia to point out the possibility of another conclusion. His thoughts take up her theme:

> perhaps all our loves are merely hints and symbols; vagabond-language scrawled on gate-posts and paving-stones along the weary road that others have tramped before us; perhaps you and I are types and this sadness which sometimes falls between us springs from disappointment in our search, each straining through and beyond the other, snatching a glimpse now and then of the shadow which turns the corner always a pace or two ahead of us. [*BR* 288]

The language of the romantic is here merging with that of the

Romantic to suggest how easily the sequence of aspiration followed by disappointment might be transformed into the prologue to a religious tale. 'He it is that doth go with thee; he will not fail thee, nor forsake thee'; the ultimate aspiration runs no risk of disappointment. From a Christian perspective, even the ruined City of Tony Last's romanticism might be partially recoverable. Conceived as a spiritual entity, the City can perhaps outreach those who lay siege to it; 'Instead of the barbarian breaking in,' asks Helena, 'might not the City one day break out?' Perhaps if Trimmer's child were to be brought up as a Roman citizen...?

The idea is not a romantic one, but then, as Guy has discovered, romanticism is not an apt or sufficient response. It has by now been discredited both as a means of interpreting experience and as a strategy of escape. And yet, discredited or not, it continues to exert an influence — even over the religion which subsumed its functions. The intended book on the Crusades was a project of Waugh's old age.

4

Nostalgia

If, as Melville's Captain Ahab supposed, the ancestry and posterity of grief go further than the ancestry and posterity of joy, then it is not something that we generally choose to acknowledge. Our myths assure us of the contrary. Behind us lies a Golden Age, before us the millenium. Man's Christian destiny is to struggle from Paradise Lost to Paradise Regained. Whether the City to which we aspire lies in the past or the future, we exist, for the space of our adult lives, in the consciousness of dispossession. 'To have been born into a world of beauty, to die amid ugliness, is the common fate of all us exiles.' [LL 38] The image of exile that Waugh here, in his last book, associates with his own life is one that has recurred throughout his work, and close behind it is always the memory of that original exile which shut us out from Eden.

The landscape of Paradise is a familiar presence in the novels. It opens before Paul Pennyfeather as he drives into the grounds of King's Thursday:

> The temperate April sunlight fell through the budding chestnuts and revealed between their trunks green glimpses of parkland and the distant radiance of a lake. 'English spring,' thought Paul. 'In the dreaming ancestral beauty of the English country.' Surely, he thought, these great chestnuts in the morning sun stood for something enduring and serene in a world that had lost its reason and would so stand when the chaos and confusion were forgotten? And surely it was the spirit of William Morris that whispered to him in Margot Beste-Chetwynde's motor car about seed-time and harvest, the superb succession of the seasons, the harmonious

interdependence of rich and poor, of dignity, innocence, and tradition? [DF 123-4]

Underlying the ironies, there is a real attachment to this vision. And a form of it returns in *Vile Bodies*. For an idyllic interlude Adam and Nina find themselves back in a prelapsarian world when they wake under a sprig of mistletoe for the fairy-tale Christmas that precedes the outbreak of war. Life before the Fall is the burden of the first chapter of 'English Gothic' in *A Handful of Dust* and of the last chapter of 'Et in Arcadia Ego' in *Brideshead Revisited*. It is an image of the rural life that William Boot has left behind and of the days with Virginia that Guy Crouchback has left behind. Its aspect changes, but in each case it exists as a memory of past contentment to which the hero looks back from a more sombre present. The pattern of these memories and the nature of the emotion that cleaves to them are what we are now to consider.

Paradise is variously located in Waugh's books, but in the course of his travels one place more than others had fixed itself in his imagination as a source of prelapsarian imagery. Arriving in the Highlands of Kenya at the beginning of 1931, he found a landscape of extreme beauty that seemed to offer to its white inhabitants a style of life that in England had long since vanished. It is the Kenya of Guy Crouchback's early memories, the country in which he and Virginia had settled beside a mountain lake 'where the air was always brilliant and keen and the flamingos rose at dawn first white, then pink, then a whirl of shadow passing across the glowing sky [MA 18]. It is the 'equatorial Arcadia' fondly remembered by the ageing traveller of *A Tourist in Africa* as a place of refuge from the narrow tastes of the twentieth century.

In a passage in *Remote People* Waugh sets out to explain this sense of affinity with the Kenyan settlers. What attracts him, he says, is the attempt to transplant the traditional life of the English squirearchy into a country that can still accommodate it. By contrast with the cranks and criminals who colonized New England and Australia, the settlers in Kenya are

> normal, respectable Englishmen, out of sympathy with their own age, and for this reason linked to the artist in an unusual but very real way. One may regard them as Quixotic in their attempt to recreate Barsetshire on the equator, but one cannot represent them as pirates and land grabbers. [RP 183]

This analysis indicates clearly enough why nostalgia should offer a line of escape in Waugh's writing. The past against which he judges present evil is not the past of the social historian but a more or less consciously idealized version of it that can exist only in the imagination. It is not the real past that his Kenyan settlers are recreating but the fictional world of Barsetshire.

Fundamental to Waugh's response is the sense that they are out of sympathy with their time. The claim he recognizes here, as an artist, was restated over thirty years later in his interview with Julian Jebb:

> An artist must be a reactionary. He has to stand out against the tenor of the age and not go flopping along; he must offer some little opposition. Even the great Victorian artists were all anti-Victorian, despite the pressure to conform.[1]

There is, of course, no suggestion that an artist might stand out against the tenor of his age in the name of the future rather than the past, as a progressive rather than a reactionary. Waugh has no time for those whose gaze is towards Paradise Regained. 'They were all socialists,' he says of the delegates to the International Labour Congress in Mexico, 'and socialists live by hope; sometimes in one quarter of the heavens, sometimes another, the messianic dawn seems likely

[1] Julian Jebb, 'The Art of Fiction XXX: Evelyn Waugh'.

to break.' [*RL* 163] Paradise for Waugh is Paradise Lost and it is by this myth that he charts his passage.

> Man is by nature an exile, haunted, even at the height of his prosperity, by nostalgia for Eden; individually and collectively he is always in search of an oppressor who will take responsibility for his ills. [*RL* 109]

In offering here an explanation of the Mexicans' attitude to the oil company, Waugh points to the ready subterfuge by which man's sense of exile from Eden becomes a comforting sense that his ills are attributable not to himself but to a state of life that is inherently oppressive. The passage would in fact serve to explain his own nostalgia just as well as that of the Mexicans. It explains, moreover, why this emotion, apparently one of sadness, is able to function for him as a defence. Nostalgia is a form of melancholy, but it is also a justification of melancholy; the myth of decline on which it is based acts as a ratification of present discontent. It lends a spurious inevitability to the state of despair, and this in itself is consoling, for it dispels any obligation to question the emotion's validity. To scrutinize the specific causes of despair would be no less futile than distasteful, since there is nothing that can be done about them. Historical causes are registered, but they are subsumed by myth. The odious features of modern life are dramatized in a simplified form, while the complex social and political realities that account for them are disregarded in favour of a mythology of exile in which the evils of contemporary society are merely the whips and scorpions of the oppressor.

Nostalgia can thus be used as one more way of holding reality at arm's length. Like sentimentality, it indulges the emotion without analysing the object that is supposed to be responsible for it. It enables one, for example, to talk of a happier age without asking, happier for whom? And this is just what Waugh does — what, if we can believe *A Little Learning*, he was already doing as a child. 'There was nothing worth very much,' he says of the possessions of his aunts, 'but it all belonged to another age which I instinctively, even then, recognized as superior to my own.' [*LL* 51]

The allegiance to a worthier past which he saw as the principal attraction of the Kenyan settlers was to become the
defining characteristic of his own literary and public persona.

The genealogies of people, words, buildings and the like
fascinate him; the further he can reach into the past, the
better. Characters begin to appear who earn his approval
mainly by virtue of their affinities with an earlier century —
figures like Sultan Achmed in *Remote People*, 'a complete
parallel to the enlightened landed gentleman of eighteenth
century England', or the Dedjasmach of *Waugh in Abyssinia*,
or General Militiades in *Officers and Gentlemen.* In *Edmund
Campion* the old religious orders are 'sweet with the gentleness and dignity of a lost age'; in the Oxford of *Brideshead
Revisited* 'men walked and spoke as they had done in
Newman's day', and Brideshead itself, with the notable
exception of Lady Marchmain's rooms, is redolent of 'the
august, masculine atmosphere of a better age'; in a literary
review in 1954 Belloc's themes are described as 'the stuff of
common life as he knew it in a warmer age' [*LOr* 100]; in
The Ordeal of Gilbert Pinfold a decline is noted from 'the
larger hospitality of a happier age', and at the end of the war
trilogy 'Bellamy's alone retained some traces of happier
days'.

This sort of disparaging comparative becomes almost a
stylistic reflex, the automatic bristling of a defensive nostalgia. The past is everywhere exalted at the expense of the
present; it is the repository of all that was gracious and noble
and lovely. A time machine, Waugh remarks at the beginning
of *A Little Learning*, would be a desirable contrivance, but
he would only want it to go backwards:

> The future, dreariest of prospects! Were I in the saddle
> I should set the engine Slow Astern. To hover gently
> back through centuries (not more than thirty of them)
> would be the most exquisite pleasure of which I can
> conceive. [*LL* 7]

In a world in which time can only move forwards this is not
a happy inclination; the passage of every moment will inevitably take one a moment further from the ideal, adding

as it goes its tiny measure of bitterness to the pain of exile.
If Paradise is set in the past rather than the future, then the
present can only grow more oppressive. And this is what it
does, eroding without remission the fragile bridges that we
try to maintain with a past that slips further and further out
of reach.

For Waugh this process of erosion was most cruelly imaged
in the fate of the country house. It is a symbol that any discussion of his books must sooner or later take into account.
There was a sad reality behind Auden's 'New styles of architecture, a change of heart'. Waugh did not want a change of
heart; the values and traditions to which he was committed
were intimately bound up with the old styles of architecture.
More completely than anything else the country house
served as a focus for his sense of loss in the face of what he
called in *A Little Learning* 'the grim cyclorama of spoliation
which surrounded all English experience in this century'.
The country house is both the last defensive outpost against
this process and at the same time its most signal victim.
Pennyfeather is still meditating on the paradisal grounds of
King's Thursday when the house itself, transformed out of
all recognition, is brought sharply into view: 'the finest
piece of domestic Tudor in England' has fallen to Professor
Silenus. At this stage the response is more or less flippant;
it soon became embittered.

The 'specialized enthusiasm for domestic architecture'
[*WS* 145] which John Plant identifies as one of the peculiarities of his generation was an interest that Waugh shared to a
high degree. From *Decline and Fall* onwards he misses no
chance to detail the elegance and variety of those buildings
and parklands with which he endows his favoured characters.
Architecture is a habitual consideration, and its importance
is more than simply aesthetic. 'Bath,' he says, on his return
from the wild spaces of Guiana, 'with its propriety and un-
compromised grandeur, seemed to offer everything that was
most valuable in English life.' [*92D* 248] It is a note that
becomes familiar. Anchorage House, Hetton, Boot Magna,
Brideshead, Broome — they represent a way of life and a
code of values which for Waugh are what is meant by civilization. There is thus no inconsistency in seeing the approach of

the Second World War primarily as a threat to one's country house. Barbara Sothill's first thought is for Malfrey:

> it had been built more than two hundred years ago in days of victory and ostentation and lay, spread out, sumptuously at ease, splendid, defenceless and provocative; a Cleopatra among houses; across the sea, Barbara felt, a small and envious mind, a meanly ascetic mind, a creature of the conifers, was plotting the destruction of her home. [*PF* 9-10]

That Hitler's malevolence should be directed specifically against this gorgeous survival of the early eighteenth century can only make sense if we realize that, as Malcolm Bradbury puts it, for Waugh 'houses, property, and estates represent a kind of prelapsarian universe'.[2] They are, for this reason, perpetually under threat. It is impossible to talk of Waugh's country houses without at the same time talking about their decay; the idea of Eden is inextricable from the idea of the Fall. King's Thursday has already been handed over to Otto Silenus before we see it, Doubting Hall is invaded by the film makers, Hetton by Mrs Beaver and her tribe, Boot Magna is yielding to its own decay. And then the war: Plant's house is dismembered and befouled, Brideshead likewise, Margot Metroland's town house is demolished by a bomb, Broome is vacated by its hereditary owners and the contents sold up. By this time Marchmain House and Anchorage House have both made way for shops and flats. It is a uniform catalogue of decline. 'Late but ineluctable the twentieth century came seeping in' [*LL* 56] — thus Waugh glosses the eventual degeneration of his aunts' house at Midsomer Norton. He takes as his oppressor the Modern Age in all its monstrous forms.

The fate of Waugh's buildings reflects a process of corruption that is general. Even in the earliest, lightest of his books

---

[2] *Evelyn Waugh*, p. 9.

happiness is an elusive commodity that not infrequently gives place to a recurrent note of nostalgia. It is a theme that can be followed through the novels.

At the end of *Decline and Fall* Peter Beste-Chetwynde's insistent 'd'you remember?' is a refrain that looks back to a less troubling world. 'How people are disappearing, Adam,' [*VB* 187] says Agatha Runcible from her hospital bed, and then she herself disappears. Adam is one of only a handful of mourners. 'Did I tell you I went to Agatha's funeral? There was practically no one there except the Chasms and some aunts.' Much of the glamour has gone out of the London scene, as Basil too discovers on his return from Azania:

> 'What's been happening?'
> 'Almost nothing. Everyone's got very poor and it makes them duller.' [*BM* 231]

William Boot, as he steams towards Ishmaelia, thinks back to the beauties of England:

> Far away the trout were lying among the cool pebbles, nose upstream, meditative, hesitant, in the waters of his home; the barbed fly, unnaturally brilliant overhead; they were lying, blue-brown, scarred by the grill, with white-bead eyes, in chaste silver dishes. 'Fresh green of the river bank; faded terra-cotta of the dining-room wallpaper, colours of distant Canaan, of deserted Eden,' thought William — 'are they still there? Shall I ever revisit those familiar places...?' [*S* 61]

This is what we might expect — a lyrical expression of nostalgia exaggerated just enough to ensure it from the taint of too much seriousness; but then when Boot finally does get back to the waters of his home and looks out from his window across the moonlit park, there follows a curious paragraph of retrospection:

> On such a night as this, not four weeks back, the tin roofs of Jacksonburg had laid open to the sky, a

three-legged dog had awoken, started from his barrel
in Frau Dressler's garden, and all over the town, in
yards and refuse heaps, the pariahs had taken up his
cries of protest. [S 190]

And that concludes the section. Intimations of lyricism seem
to be pulling against the unattractive central image of the
passage. Why should Waugh have put it in at all? The stark
little vignette has an odd poignancy standing at the end of
the section. Is it perhaps in the nature of things that having
struggled back into Paradise we should begin to turn with
something like nostalgia to the harsher memories of life on
the east of Eden? The myth of decline is infinitely adaptable.
Once nostalgia has been taken as a mode of response, nothing
that lies securely in the past is immune from it.

In later books its focus changes. *Decline and Fall*, *Labels*,
Vile Bodies, *Scoop*, even *A Handful of Dust*, touch on the
theme of Paradise Lost primarily as a pattern that informs
individual lives; the nostalgia, such as it is, tends to take the
form of a purely personal sense of loss. But as social change
of one sort or another bears more heavily upon the author,
the decline comes to seem more general and the nostalgia
becomes correspondingly keener and more comprehensive.
The strident despair of *Brideshead Revisited* embraces practically every aspect of modern life. Hooper and Rex Mottram
divide the spoils of the twentieth century between them. 'He
was something absolutely modern and up-to-date,' Ryder
says of the latter, 'that only this ghastly age could produce.'
[BR 193] Anything that impinges on Ryder's consciousness
is likely to provide fuel for similar reflections – even the
bathroom he shares with Sebastian:

I often think of that bathroom – the water colours
dimmed by steam and the huge towel warming on the
back of the chintz armchair – and contrast it with
the uniform, clinical, little chambers, glittering with
chromium-plate and looking glass, which pass for luxury
in the modern world. [BR 149]

To an age less taxed by wartime austerities the intensity of the nostalgia can seem overwrought. Waugh realized this and acknowledged it in the Preface he wrote fifteen years later. Nonetheless, such passages do express an attitude to which Waugh was deeply and despairingly committed. The glitter of chromium and glass takes us back to the ministrations of Mrs Beaver and forward to the 'bustling hygienic Eden' of Whispering Glades.

The 'period of soya beans and Basic English' [*BR* 7] during which *Brideshead* was written may have belonged specifically to the years of the Second World War, but the decline in the quality of life which these privations exemplified was something that had been foreboded before the war and was confirmed after it. For Ryder it is imaged in the deterioration of his regiment and his own increasing age:

> There were few left in the mess now of the batch of volunteers who trained together at the outbreak of war; one way and another they were nearly all gone ...and their places were taken by conscripts...it was not as it had been.
> Here at the age of thirty-nine I began to be old. [*BR* 11]

Waugh himself was just a few months past forty when he wrote this. It is an age that we charge with significance; at no point, perhaps, does the notion of exile from Paradise seem so closely related to that of exile from childhood. 'The shades of the prison-house closed,' Waugh writes the following year in his Preface to *When the Going was Good*. Again, via Wordsworth's ode, the same parallel. What Ryder remarks upon is the gloomy coincidence that Waugh himself had experienced: the time at which life in Britain seemed most remote from the *douceur de vivre* of the pre-war years was also the time at which, with the climacteric of his fortieth birthday, the writer was made most conscious of a personal reason for looking back. One impulse to nostalgia was compounded by the other; the general decline was matched by the personal. The present world of *Brideshead Revisited*, which finds its principal reflection in the fate of the house itself, can offer nothing to temper the bitterness of Ryder's perceptions. Instead, he seeks a familiar refuge — 'These memories, which are my life — for we possess nothing certainly except the past — were always with me.' First person narrative tends inevitably to be a retrospective form, and *Brideshead Revisited* is, as its subtitle indicates, a book of memories.

How far the old world has been left behind can be seen by comparing *Brideshead* with the earlier *Put Out More Flags*. This book too was in some sense an attempt to mitigate the experience of war by referring back to the society and values of a pre-war world. To this extent it too was a product of nostalgia; it deals, as Waugh told Randolph Churchill in the dedication, 'with a race of ghosts, the survivors of the world we both knew ten years ago'. But though Waugh's imagination may 'linger fondly' among the wreckage of the twenties and Ambrose Silk may look back with longing to the days of broad trousers and high-necked jumpers, the book's overriding commitment is to the demands of the present. Its characters can turn for comfort to the past, as indeed the author himself is doing, but the action of the novel makes it clear that such nostalgia must be subordinated to the needs of the hour. This is the wartime priority, and the slightly apologetic note in the dedicatory letter confirms it.

There is no apology in *Brideshead*; the author's first loyalty has shifted firmly to the past. From here onwards the landscapes of Paradise are not simply under threat, they are already overrun. In the bleak world of post-war Grantchester the nearest Scott-King can get to any image of Paradise is the 'virtuous, chaste and reasonable community' [*WS* 198] imagined by Bellorius three centuries earlier. Neutralia offers no parallel either to the poet's utopia or to Scott-King's nostalgic vision of the lands of the south. It is 'a typical modern state' with no more to recommend it than those in which Dennis Barlow and Miles Plastic steer their subversive course. His interest in Bellorius at an end, Scott-King returns to Grantchester and settles down to entrench himself behind the decent obscurity of the learned languages. The conclusion his experience has led him to: 'I think it would be very wicked indeed to do anything to fit a boy for the modern world.' [*WS* 250] It is the sentiment of Waugh's entry in his diary the previous year: 'I thank God to find myself still a writer and at work on something as "uncontemporary" as I am.' [*Diaries* 627] [3] Mr Pinfold, with his abhorrence of everything that has happened in his own lifetime, is not far in the future.

The war trilogy, though less rancorous in tone than *Bridehead*, abates none of the latter's disgust with the workings of this century of progress. Guy's initial enthusiasm for the contemporary political cause turns out to be based on a misconception; the only enduring values are those of the past: Sir Roger, Broome, the rigid traditions of the corps. For images of happiness we have to look back to a period well before that covered in the novels. The lakeside in Kenya, the 'days of sun and sea-spray and wallowing dolphins' [*OG* 78] aboard the *Aquitania* — between these and the colourless world of wartime England there can be no intercourse save by memory. When Virginia tries to give substance to her memories through an affair with Trimmer — her former hairdresser on the *Aquitania* — she merely reinforces the point. Their romance has all the hallmarks of the world she is trying to escape. Only for a brief spell in Cape Town, the 'Interlude' of *Officers and Gentlemen*, do any of the main characters seem to get free of this atmosphere; and they do so simply because Cape Town is itself a throwback to an earlier world. Ablaze with light in a war that has plunged the rest of the world into darkness, it exists as a realized memory of life as it used to be; Ivor goes back to horses, Eddie and Bertie to chasing girls, Guy to food and drink:

'One way and another, Guy, Cape Town seems to have provided each of us with whatever he wanted.'
'Ali Baba's lamp.' [*OG* 110]

The hint of fairy-tale makes its own inescapable point.

---

[3] He was working on *Helena* at the time.

The sense of exile, the consciousness of loss, the yearning for landscapes of the past draw their poignancy from a pattern that is traced in each individual's life. It is with the loss of childhood that the shades of the prison-house begin to close, and it is in childhood that Waugh's nostalgia finds its natural goal.

The Preface to *When the Going was Good* is not the only place where we catch an echo of Wordsworth's line. Sebastian comes trailing clouds of glory when he enters the pages of *Brideshead Revisited*, and Ryder records his degeneration in appropriate language. 'But the shadows were closing round Sebastian,' he comments at the start of their last term at Oxford. It is part of a pervasive strain of imagery in the novel that associates happiness not just with the past but specifically with childhood. Sebastian appears at the beginning of the first book in dove-grey flannel and a Charvet tie, complete with wine, strawberries, and a teddy-bear. The friend, 'name of Hawkins', whom he is taking Ryder to visit is his nanny. She is the presiding genius of Brideshead — or at least of that part of it which constitutes the 'enchanted garden' — and it is to her room that Ryder returns in the novel's Epilogue. Like Sebastian's teddy-bear, she is a symbol of his attachment to his childhood. Her presence seems to ensure that nothing shall overstep the comforting bounds of the nursery. 'A pair of children the two of you,' is her complacent description, and Ryder's own account endorses it:

> It seems to me that I grew younger daily with each adult habit that I acquired....Now, that summer term with Sebastian, it seemed as though I was being given a brief spell of what I had never known, a happy childhood, and though its toys were silk shirts and liqueurs and cigars and its naughtiness high in the catalogue of grave sins, there was something of nursery freshness about us that fell little short of the joy of innocence.
> [BR 45-6]

The role of Nanny Hawkins in this nursery world had already been anticipated by her predecessors in *Scoop*. At twenty-three William Boot is still being told by Nannie Bloggs to

wash his hands and brush his hair nicely. She and Nannie
Price are the guardian spirits of Boot Magna; their existence
is vital to its appeal as a place of refuge.

That Waugh should look indulgently on this prolonged
and potentially cloying submission to childhood is perhaps
explained by the circumstances of his own early life. There
seems to be general agreement that his childhood was an
exceptionally happy one. He himself writes in *A Little
Learning* of 'the world of privacy and love' he enjoyed as a
day-boy at Heath Mount, and his early years are remembered as being 'save for a few pale shadows...an even glow
of pure happiness'. When he was four, the family moved to
a new house at North End, where, according to his bio-
grapher, his life 'was one of blissful happiness', — 'So he
described it, and so did his brother Alec.'[4] It is perhaps not
over-fanciful to see a late tribute to this happiness in the
reflections of Guy Crouchback at his father's funeral. He
looks at the falling leaves and remembers

> boisterous November days when he and his mother
> had tried to catch leaves in the avenue; each one caught
> insured a happy day? week? month? which? in his
> wholly happy childhood. [*US* 67]

The light of common day to which the adult is condemned
looks, by contrast, all the paler.

Not until one leaves childhood behind does one inherit to
the full the oppressions of a fallen world. Waugh, we might
conjecture, had some sympathy with the feelings he attributed to his friend, Ronald Knox:

> Ronald had no desire to grow up. Adolescence, for
> him, was not a process of liberation or of adventure.
> Manhood threatened him with tedious duties and grave
> decisions. His mind had flourished and matured while
> his heart was still a child's. He grew up slowly. Each
> stage of his growth imposed a burden; each enlargement
> of spirit, the loss of something fond. [*RK* 79]

---

[4] Christopher Sykes, *Evelyn Waugh: A Biography*, p. 23.

It is again the pattern of the Immortality Ode. What Waugh
regrets most is the carelessness of childhood — the privilege
of a life that is lived without responsibility. For Knox this
freedom may have been no more than a patent against
seriousness — itself no small thing in a depressingly serious
world — but for Waugh's fictional characters the possibilities
were infinitely greater. If Basil Seal can get away with so
much in *Black Mischief*, it is partly because the 'rather
childish mouth' and the 'curiously childish' expression that
are characteristic of him are the marks of someone who
still enjoys the licence of the pre-adult world. As long as
Alastair and Sonia spend their time playing happy families,
the debt-collectors cannot touch them, for these have no
place in the nursery. The claim to freedom made by the
Bright Young People of *Vile Bodies* depended, as Waugh
perceived, on a refusal to accept the high valuation traditionally put on adulthood. 'Always before,' he wrote in an
early article for the *Evening Standard*, 'it has been the
younger generation asserting the fact that they have grown
up; today the more modest claim of my generation is that
we are young.' [*LOr* 7] And so it is that, to Outrage's bewil-
derment, despite the fact that there is 'a whole civilization
to be saved and remade...all they seem to do is to play
the fool' [*VB* 131].

The degree of immunity conferred by childhood is ambi-
guously exploited in the portrait of Brenda Last. Throughout
the novel she manages to retain something of the reader's
sympathy largely because there is a vein of childish naivety
in her responses that goes some way to convincing us that
moral criticism would be inappropriate. 'Goodness,' she
remarks when censorious gossip begins to circulate about
her relationship with Beaver, 'people do think that young
men are easily come by.' [*HD* 52] And later, down on her
luck and unsupported by Jenny Abdul Akbar, '"Me? Oh,
I'm all right," said Brenda, and she thought, "It might occur
to her to sock a girl a meal once in a way."' [*HD* 180] By
phrases like this she pleads a sort of Benefit of Clergy; there
is an implicit statement that she is not to be judged by the
standards of the adult world. Any attempt at seriousness will
stand convicted in advance of pomposity. Waugh by no

means lets her escape unscathed, but a few childish habits of speech and thought afford her a remarkable degree of protection.

In *Put Out More Flags* it is the similar possibility of relapsing into the language and manners of childhood that gives the relationship between Basil and Barbara its emotional charge and kindles it with a promise of freedom. As long as Basil is really only playing pirates, anything can be permitted. The schoolroom, as we observed in another context, is an alluring refuge. It is in the words of a schoolroom game that Guy's grandmother claims Santa Dulcina and it is to the schoolroom that Guy himself returns during his period of training in the army. That his hero should be a soldier of the stamp of Ritchie-Hook is altogether fitting: 'For this remarkable warrior the image of war was not hunting or shooting; it was the wet sponge on the door, the hedgehog in the bed; or rather, he saw war itself as a prodigious booby trap.' [*MA* 72]

In other words it was schoolboy fun. And it is this point of view that brings Ritchie-Hook into some sort of alignment with the protagonists of *Put Out More Flags*. The race of ghosts was so dear to Waugh because he saw them as a generation who had clung resolutely to the frivolous and stylish notion that life was a game. In preserving this attitude, the responses of childhood are one of the principal weapons. Alastair Trumpington is 'jealous as a schoolboy' when he first sees Peter in khaki, and having joined up himself returns eagerly to the trivial round of triumphs and disappointments associated with life at school. After a hard day's training he is asked by Sonia what he has been doing:

> 'I put down smoke,' said Alastair proudly. 'The whole advance was held up until I put down smoke.'
> 'Darling, you *are* clever. I've got a tinned beefsteak and kidney pudding for dinner.' [*PF* 133]

Waugh is mocking, but he is also indulgent. The race of ghosts is a race of children and Waugh's nostalgia for them is inextricable from his nostalgia for childhood.

'Tedious duties and grave decisions' were not the only aspects of adulthood to be avoided. The relationship between Basil and Barbara offers important attractions of another kind. Before he even appears in *Put Out More Flags* Basil has been the subject of much speculation — most curiously, at the moment when Barbara and her husband are making love: 'There was a Gothic pavilion where by long habit Freddy often became amorous; he did become amorous. And all the time she thought of Basil....'[PF 17] The displacement of husband by brother at this juncture might pass unremarked, did it not recur so overtly later in the novel:

> 'I'm cleverer than Freddy. Babs, say I'm cleverer than Freddy.'
> 'I'm cleverer than Freddy. Sucks to you.'
> 'Babs, say you love me more than Freddy.'
> 'You love me more than Freddy. Double sucks.'
> 'Say I, Barbara, love you, Basil, more than him, Freddy.'
> 'I won't. I don't...Beast, you're hurting.' [PF 85]

And so on. The playfulness has a style which Doris Connolly knows exactly how to interpret:

> '...he's your boy, isn't he?' she said, turning to Barbara.
> 'He's my brother, Doris.'
> 'Ah,' she said, her pig eyes dark with the wisdom of the slums, 'but you fancy him, don't you? I saw.'
> [PF 88]

It is certainly a relationship that generates more tremors of sexuality than any other in the book, as Waugh himself was aware — 'half-incestuous' he called it in a letter to his father. And the same is true of its successor in *Basil Seal Rides Again*. Twenty years on, the amorous girl is Basil's daughter:

'Two arms embraced his neck and drew him down, an agile figure inclined over the protruberance of his starched shirt, a cheek was pressed to his and teeth tenderly nibbled the lobe if his ear.' [WS 261] The licensed intimacy of relationships in both family and nursery acts as a lightning conductor to the threat of adult sexuality.

Basil Seal Rides Again was the last piece of fiction Waugh wrote, but this sort of displacement had been practised by his characters from the start. The strain of childishness that we noted in the tone of the Bright Young People operates in one direction to dissociate sexuality from the complicated sanctions of adulthood. It is as children that Adam and Nina spend the night together at Arundel:

> 'Do you know,' she said, trembling slightly as she got into bed, 'this is the first time this has happened to me?'
> 'It's great fun,' said Adam, 'I promise you.'
> 'I'm sure it is,' said Nina seriously, 'I wasn't saying anything against it. I was only saying that it hadn't happened before...Oh, Adam....' [VB 81]

The tone persists in *Black Mischief* with Prudence and William:

> 'Lovey dovey, cat's eyes.'
> 'You got that out of a book.'
> 'Well, yes. How did you know.'
> 'I read it too. It's been all round the compound.'
> [BM 44]

They could be adults playing children or children playing adults. The ambivalence is strategic. 'Shall I do my vibrant-with-passion voice?' Prudence asks later. Whether it is Sonia and Alastair playing happy families or Kätchen exclaiming at the size of a rainbow ('Soon there will be no room in the sky for it' [S 126]), the implication is the same: sexuality is most acceptable when it can borrow the colours of childhood.

The secret of Millicent Blade's attractions in 'On Guard' is

a nose which takes the thoughts of English manhood back to
its schooldays, 'to the doughy faced urchins on whom it had
squandered its first affection, to memories of changing room
and chapel and battered straw boaters.' [WS 31] And when
later, in *Scott-King's Modern Europe*, Whitemaid is searching
for an image to express his overcharged feelings about Miss
Sveningen, it is in the same environment that he places her:

> 'Like some god-like, some unimaginably strict school
> prefect, *a dormitory monitor*,' he said in a kind of
> ecstasy. 'Think of her striding between the beds, a
> pigtail, bare feet, in her hand a threatening hairbrush.'
> [WS 218]

The slightly perverse vein of eroticism that takes the admirers
of both Millicent and Miss Sveningen back to their schooldays is one manifestation of the kind of nostalgia we have
been looking at. It is basic to a presentation of sexuality that
repeatedly sees heterosexual love in terms of a transference
from the homosexual affections of adolescence. There is
nothing idiosyncratic in this. It was an aspect of Waugh's
class and generation. Indeed, Whitemaid's fantasy originated
not with Waugh himself but with John Betjeman. ('I hope
John did not resent the parody of his erotic rhapsodies in
Scott-King,' Waugh wrote to Penelope Betjeman shortly after
the book's publication [14 July 1947; *Letters* 256].) How
widely this strain of sexual ambiguity was diffused is illustrated by contemporary fashions in female beauty. The twenties
look with its short hair and boyish figure did everything possible to blur unwelcome distinctions. 'Like two little boys' —
we remember Nancy Mitford's description of the two Evelyns
at the time of their marriage.

The residual fondness for earlier emotional patterns is
clearly articulated in another of Waugh's short stories, 'Love
in the Slump'. Here, under the pressing sense that she is
getting older, Angela Trench-Troubridge decides to marry
Tom Watch. A dull wedding gives promise of a dull future,
until Tom is rescued from the prospect of his honeymoon by
a chance encounter with an old school-fellow. The habits and
memories of an earlier time offer welcome refuge to the

reluctant bridegroom. Abandoning his bride, he finds himself next morning at the house of his acquaintance:

> It had been dinner-time when they arrived. They had drunk burgundy and port and brandy. Frankly they had drunk rather a lot. They had recalled numerous house scandals, all kinds of jolly insults to chemistry masters, escapades after dark when they had gone up to London to the '43'. What was the fellow's name? [MrL 177]

Without having discovered the answer, Tom takes off for a morning's hunting and gets lost. In the upshot, Angela manages to console herself with his friend. The woman's emotional blitheness is one mode of escape, the man's retreat into schoolboy companionship is another.

In the nature of things this companionship must be purely masculine, for the English public school allows no place to women. Ten years of security from their threatening presence are not lightly forgotten. It is nostalgia for this arrangement that sustains the male club — a sound, companionable society that is uncomplicated and right-thinking. From the stresses of wars, wives and girlfriends men can retire into their clubs and find solace with like-minded beings of their own sex.

As often as not it is moments of comradeship between men that provide the least blemished images of happiness in Waugh's novels. Bellamy's, the Halberdier mess, the isolated community of X Commando — all of them in the war trilogy are extensions of what is really a nostalgia for the protected community of school. Notably, it is Trimmer, alone of the officers of X Commando, who pines for feminine company. Notably also, when Waugh is betrayed into one of his rare lapses of tone in *Officers and Gentlemen*, it is in celebration of a moment of intense male solidarity. Tommy Blackhouse and Guy are returning from dinner with the Laird of Mugg when both are seized by a fit of laughter:

> Men who have endured danger and privation together often separate and forget one another when their ordeal is ended. Men who have loved the same woman are

blood brothers even in enmity; if they laugh together, as
Tommy and Guy laughed that night, orgiastically, they
seal their friendship on a plane rarer and loftier than
normal human intercourse. [OG 68]

Few situations could so completely breach Waugh's irony.
The ideal of staunch male comradeship has even deeper roots
than the memory of sexual humiliation.

In Waugh's case, the feeling for this sort of relationship
can perhaps more accurately be traced back to university
than to school. 'The record of my life there,' he writes of
Oxford in *A Little Learning*, 'is essentially a catalogue of
friendships.' [LL 183] And this is the aspect of it reflected
in the relationship between Charles and Sebastian in *Brideshead Revisited*. Sebastian first appears on the scene to rescue
Ryder from the 'rabble of womankind, some hundreds
strong, twittering and fluttering over the cobbles and up the
steps' who have invaded Oxford for Eights Week — 'You're·
to come away at once, out of danger.' [BR 25] The remark
is only half jocular; there is a sense in which women do constitute a danger to this society. In *A Chapter of Accidents*
Goronwy Rees gives a lengthy description of the atmosphere
he found at Oxford in the late twenties. Part of his account
is paraphrased by Martin Green:

It was a nursery life, of sexual infantilism. All had their
affections and ideas in the masculine gender...The Fall
of Man happened only to Eve. She was expelled, and
Adam was left to enjoy the garden alone with the
serpent. Men remembered Oxford in a golden glow
because only *after it* came their fall from grace into
heterosexual relationships.[5]

This conveys very plainly the extent to which Oxford's enchantment lay in the possibility of deferring for a few years
both adulthood and, more particularly, the sexual complica-
tions of adulthood. Ryder and Sebastian can experience as
adults what is basically a childhood love.

[5] *Children of the Sun*, p. 191.

Even when the doughy faced urchins and their successors at university have been left behind, the old preferences are still apparent. We have only to look at the relationships already considered — between Adam and Nina, for example, Tony and Brenda, William and Kätchen — to see the same nostalgia for a pre-sexual world. Women who cannot be children can sometimes gain acceptance by virtue of their similarity to men. It is clearly to Helena's credit that, as her father tells her, 'You look like a boy, you ride like a boy. Your tutor tells me you have a masculine mind...' [H 31] ; that a night crossing of the Channel should put her on terms of bluff good-fellowship with the ship's crew; that her reaction to gnosticism — 'It's all bosh, isn't it?' — should be formulated with such bluntness. These manly traits are passports to the author's favour. Julia Stitch's 'guttersnipe whistle' and Virginia's unfeminine sexual frankness are part of the same pattern. Characters such as these are prepared to meet men on equal terms. They play according to the same rules, in contrast to those, like Ryder's wife, who exploit the alien territory of their womanhood as a source of power. Celia, Charles comments bitterly, 'seemed to make a sacred, female rite even of sea-sickness' [BR 239] .

Only one encounter in Waugh's novels approaches this treacherous ground without irony or distaste. In Plant's love for Lucy we have the beginnings of a relationship that breaks all of Waugh's rules. She is not a child-woman like Kätchen, nor a robust tomboy like the young Helena; she has neither Julia Flyte's intelligence nor Virginia's reckless charm; as a loyal wife and an expectant mother she has, on the contrary, all the encumbrances of domesticity. When Plant falls in love with her we are on new ground. But even here the imagery is drawing us back towards familiar points of reference: 'There were no reservations in her friendship, and it was an experience for which I was little qualified, to be admitted, as it were, through a door in the wall to wander at will over that rich estate.' [WS 170] The image is one that will reappear, only slightly modified, in Brideshead Revisited to suggest the character of Ryder's friendship with Sebastian.

In Work Suspended, as in the later novel, there is already a sense that this is a world from which the adult is cut off.

'I felt too old,' Plant tells us. This was the sort of relationship he had briefly enjoyed as a schoolboy, 'when Lucy was in her cradle', but at the age of thirty-four friendship meant something different, more cautious. Perhaps what Lucy offers is in its way another invitation to the freshness of childhood. Moreover, her pregnancy, although it is on one level an assertion of womanhood, has other implications as well: 'For a term of months she was unsexed,' [WS 171] Plant notes, as he traces the start of their relationship. The paradox is one he remarks on later when he sets the progress of his love against the corresponding evolution by which Lucy herself each week 'grew heavier and slower and less apt for love'. His image for the two of them points up the ambiguity: 'Lucy and I were like characters in the stock intrigue of Renaissance comedy, where the heroine follows the hero in male attire and is wooed by him, unknowing, in the terms of rough friendship.' [WS 174] After all, the relationship may be less dissimilar from some of the others than it seemed. Though on the face of it the connection seems unlikely, Lucy has established her kinship both with the world of childhood and with the world of men.

How the affair would have developed can only be guessed, but it is hard to imagine it as a story of love fulfilled. Plant's tone is always on the verge of elegy, and already, with the birth of Lucy's child, he is aware of his waning importance. Whatever part the relationship was to have had in the completed work, it would have been for Plant, one suspects, a theme of nostalgia rather than of celebration.

For Plant, but not for Lucy. Waugh's women inspire nostalgia; they rarely feel it themselves. Even when the progress of the war has reduced Virginia to dining on imitation cheese and margarine, there is still no sense of the corrosive regret that permeates the responses of Guy: 'She was not a woman to repine. She accepted change, though she did not so express it to herself, as the evidence of life.' [US 80]

This is the other side of her emotional frivolity. Virginia's openness to life is by implication contrasted with Guy's mistrust of it, and at this point the comparison does not work to his advantage. It is not just from Virginia that the intensity of his nostalgia sets him apart. It also distances him from more frankly admired figures like Tommy Blackhouse and Major Tickeridge. At the heart of this emotion there is the taint of sickness.

———————————

To justify the word 'corrosive' we need only compare Waugh's nostalgia with that of his father. It was apparently a feeling they shared: 'My father always assumed,' Waugh tells us in *A Little Learning*, '(as I do now) that anything new was likely to be nasty.' [*LL* 115] And yet if one reads Arthur Waugh's account of his university days at Oxford in *One Man's Road*, the impression of similarity fades. The father's memories are uncorrupted by selfconsciousness. He chronicles the student's round of work and sport and high jinks with an adolescent relish that bespeaks a spirit still open to the same enthusiasms. In his undiminished loyalty to New College he proffers catalogues of long-forgotten contemporaries with a naive confidence that for his readers too he is tendering household names.

The words of his son have no such warmth. 'Hertford was a respectable but rather dreary little college,' [*LL* 158] he begins. Waugh makes it clear that Oxford was a golden period, 'a Kingdom of Cokayne', but his nostalgia is sourer than his father's, more disabused. In all the details of happiness there is a melancholy consciousness of the gap that divides past from present; the nostalgia is sharpened and made sad by a pervasive sense of the decline that has marked both himself and his university. Forty years ago the writer was a young man. He makes no attempt to recreate the happiness of this time; he merely, with consummate elegance, records it. When it comes to the catalogue of friendships, he resists the temptation to which his father had eagerly yielded. He presents instead a necrology; one by one his friends are summarized in brief, elegiac phrases: 'their names and the names of those still alive who have drifted apart, might stir wistful memories in fifty or more elderly men; no more'.

It is a nostalgia quite different in tone from that of *One Man's Road* — or for that matter from the reminiscences of

Waugh's brother Alec. Both Arthur and Alec Waugh can enjoy the memory of past happiness without conceding it any lasting power to add to the bitterness of the present; they do not repine. The result is a paradox: though their memoirs place them in an earlier, more innocent world than that of Evelyn, they were able to adjust to the demands of a changing society far more readily than he. Whatever their misgivings, they retained an openness to the conditions of the present. And yet of the three of them it is Evelyn who is our contemporary. The ironic tone of self-consciousness in *A Little Learning* sets its author apart. His was a modern sensibility in a way that theirs was not. But also, one should add, a religious sensibility. He writes from the knowledge of a fallen, sinful world, and his nostalgia is infected with that knowledge. It is corrosive because it affirms with grim consistency that the celebration of the past entails a repudiation of the present.

It is not just in the final trilogy that Waugh begins to recognize something unhealthy in this attitude. As early as *A Handful of Dust* we are invited to look critically at a character's obsession with an unreal past; behind the dreams of Arthurian romance are the relics of childhood that decorate Tony's bedroom. Later, in *Scoop*, William Boot returns gratefully to the childhood security of Boot Magna; but it is a security that can be threatened by sharper realities than the surrounding decay. For his latest contribution to *Lush Places* William draws a conventionally idyllic picture: '...*the wagons lumber in the lane under their golden glory of harvested sheaves*, he wrote; *maternal rodents pilot their furry brood through the stubble...*' [S 222]. Easy enough to let it stand as good-humoured parody, but Waugh insists on a final addition to the moonlit scene of Boot Magna: 'Outside the owls hunted maternal rodents and their furry brood.' At the end of a comfortable book it leaves a splinter of doubt in the mind.

In *Put Out More Flags* doubts are closer to the surface. The ambiguities of Basil's relationship with his sister have already been noted. Waugh is indulgent but not unreservedly so: 'Poor Basil,' reflects Ambrose, 'it's sad enough for him to be an *enfant terrible* at the age of thirty-six; but to be

regarded by the younger generation as a kind of dilapidated
Bulldog Drummond...'[PF 34]. In a book that tends on the
whole to support the reversion of the middle-aged to adolescence this is no more than a pin-prick, but it does express a
reservation — and one that is taken up with considerably
more emphasis in *Brideshead Revisited.*

This, the most nostalgic of Waugh's novels, is also the one
that subjects nostalgia to the closest scrutiny. Relationships
of the kind between Charles and Sebastian are not commended by Cara without qualification; 'I think they are very
good,' she explains, 'if they do not go on too long.' [BR 98]
The condition sounds a note of warning. It has already been
heard, in another key, from Anthony Blanche, whose role
in the novel is a brilliant concession to the possibility that an
indefinitely extended childhood might sometimes be other
than charming — even more important, that charm itself
might sometimes be other than admirable. Sebastian's preoccupation with Nanny Hawkins and Aloysius is part of this
charm; the trappings of childhood are the credentials he
brings with him from Paradise. In warning Ryder against
them, Blanche effectively forestalls the sort of criticisms
that might be forming in the reader's mind; his astringency
is there to prevent Sebastian's sweetness from cloying. It
may well succeed in this, but his reservations, once made,
cannot be ignored. There *is* a sort of charm in the whimsical
attachment to childhood, but it can also be a danger —
specifically, Blanche warns, a danger to the artist. Later we
find that Ryder has turned his art to the service of another
sort of nostalgia:

> The financial slump of the period, which left many
> painters without employment, served to enhance my
> success, which was, indeed, itself a symptom of the
> decline. When the water-holes were dry people sought
> to drink at the mirage. [BR 216]

The image of a mirage at an empty water-hole subtly endorses Blanche's subsequent judgement, which Ryder himself
accepts, that his art has been vitiated by charm.[6]

---

[6] This point is discussed in more detail in chapter 6.

For a writer as committed to nostalgia as Waugh, who is in the process of writing a book as nostalgic as *Brideshead Revisited*, this is a penetrating admission. To some extent it anticipates the later and more devastating criticism implied in the account he gives of Ludovic's novel, *The Death Wish*. It is described as one of those books by half a dozen English authors which were turning 'from the drab alleys of the thirties into the odorous gardens of a recent past transformed and illuminated by disordered memory and imagination' [*US* 188], turning, that is, in exactly the same direction as *Brideshead Revisited*. The Death Wish? To talk of something 'unhealthy' in this nostalgia was perhaps an understatement. 'Sleep innocently,' says Blanche, after his first, unheeded warning against charm. Words to a child. Near the end of the book he is still talking of charm, but to a man no longer innocent: 'It spots and kills anything it touches. It kills love; it kills art; I greatly fear, my dear Charles, it has killed *you*.' [*BR* 260] And with this contribution Blanche disappears from the novel.

In the face of this sort of evidence it seems perverse of such critics as Terry Eagleton and D. S. Savage to suggest that the ambiguity of feeling in the novel was a self-contradiction which somehow crept in against the novelist's will. Savage catches the characteristically patronizing tone in a general comment on Waugh's writing: 'Yet beneath the mask there is, somewhere in Waugh, a confused and well-meaning man — who, one feels, would speak truthfully if only he knew how — striving in a sort of anguished perplexity for self-expression.'[7] It is with the air of announcing a personal *trouvaille* that he tells us of *Brideshead Revisited* that 'the real theme is, once more, that of bondage to childhood and the impossibility of growth to adult maturity'. But this theme has not been wrested from jealous obscurity by the critic, it is one that the novelist himself quite deliberately makes manifest.

Cara's warning about such relationships as that between Charles and Sebastian is approved by more than the words of Anthony Blanche. Even at the moment when Ryder is

---

[7] 'The Innocence of Evelyn Waugh'.

most conscious of his loss, the imagery keeps a note of reservation clearly in the reader's mind:

> A door had shut, the low door in the wall I had sought and found in Oxford; open it now and I should find no enchanted garden.
> I had come to the surface, into the light of common day and the fresh sea-air, after long captivity in the sunless coral palaces and waving forests of the ocean bed....
> 'I have left behind illusion,' I said to myself. 'Henceforth I live in a world of three dimensions — with the aid of my five senses.' [*BR* 163-4]

Once again we catch an echo of Wordsworth's Immortality Ode as the clouds of glory fade into the light of common day, but the enchantment that Ryder leaves behind is not an unqualified vision of delight: the exotic lure of coral palaces and waving forests has to be set against the force of the words 'captivity' and 'sunless'; the decline into the light of common day is also a rise into the fresh sea-air. Ryder may, as he later claims, be wrong in imagining that there is ever a real world 'of three dimensions' in which one can live, but when he asserts that he has 'left behind illusion', he firmly associates the experience of the enchanted garden with the unreal City of Tony Last's romanticism and the equally unreal 'Holy Land of illusion' in which Guy Crouchback takes up arms at the beginning of the Second World War. In one sense, perhaps, these illusions are part of that 'vagabond-language' of which Ryder speaks in *Brideshead Revisited*; they are the loves which, shadow-like, prefigure an ultimate reality. But they are not themselves that reality, and to continue in them — or to encourage others to continue in them — is to foster a state of mind that is infected.

The warnings sounded in *Brideshead* are not isolated caveats, thrown in by the author merely to add sinew to what might otherwise be a rather flabby production; they are part of a continuing and increasingly critical examination of a number of the elements of nostalgia that have been the subject of this chapter. There is, for example, in the years between Ryder's worthless exhibition and Ludovic's *Death*

Wish, the tormented figure of Gilbert Pinfold — another artist whose penchant for romantic and nostalgic images threatens to contribute to his destruction.[8] In *The Loved One* the playfully perverse relationships by which characters have in the past evaded the claims of adulthood come to a grisly climax in the romance between Aimée and Mr Joyboy, honey-baby and poppa. Julia Stitch, so irresistible in *Scoop*, returns in *Officers and Gentlemen*, doubly seductive in virtue of the memories she brings with her from a happier time, but glimpsed now, just occasionally, in a more sinister light. Her social charm can be unprincipled and narcotic. The adolescent enthusiasms of *Put Out More Flags* persist into the war trilogy, but by the end of it they are being treated with weary disillusionment; the activities of Hazardous Offensive Operations, we are told, include researches into 'fortifying drugs, invisible maps, noiseless explosives, and other projects near to the heart of the healthy schoolboy' [*US* 26].

The tone is no longer indulgent; it is past time to grow out of these things. As we have seen, the limitations of extended childhood were already becoming apparent in *Brideshead*. Sebastian's idyll is fatally liable to intrusion, and since he 'counted among the intruders his own conscience and all claims of human affection, his days in Arcadia were numbered' [*BR* 123]. In time, 'like a fetish, hidden first from the missionary and at length forgotten, the toy bear, Aloysius, sat unregarded on the chest-of-drawers in Sebastian's bedroom' [*BR* 102]. Earlier, Ryder had referred to it as a 'teddy-bear'; 'toy bear' was Anthony Blanche's term. The change of phrase registers, on Ryder's part, the faintest shade of adult disdain. But more important, the image suggests what it is that finally displaces the precoccupation with childhood. The affair between Ryder and Julia founders because she sees it as an attempt to set up a rival good to God's; here, in this image of Aloysius as a heathen fetish, it is implied that the security of childhood, the nursery world that is to be found at Brideshead, might also constitute a rival good to God's.

As the Epilogue makes clear, Waugh's ultimate concern in

---

[8] See the discussion of *The Ordeal of Gilbert Pinfold* in the Conclusion.

this novel is not to indulge nostalgia but to transcend it. And he underlines his point with the emphasis of a heavy paradox. Brideshead has been vandalized and defiled; surveying the desolation, Ryder lingers in memory over the graceful world that has been destroyed; gloomily he goes off about the army's business. And then, as he enters Brigade's ante-room, the conclusion: '"You're looking unusually cheerful today," said the second-in-command.' [*BR* 331] It is a deliberately challenging note on which to end. In this last page Waugh has attempted a massive shift in his hero's perspective. For an explanation we must look to the *art nouveau* chapel which Ryder had visited a few moments earlier.

Inside, the lamp is burning again before the altar. Without reflecting on its significance, Ryder stays to say a prayer and then returns towards the camp. Everything seems to justify the unyielding bitterness of his story: 'the place was desolate and the work all brought to nothing; *Quomodo sedet sola civitas*. Vanity of vanities, all is vanity.' In the mood of the preacher he looks back with regret to what is gone. But then abruptly there intrudes a thought which reduces all this desolation to a matter of insignificance. The lament from Ecclesiastes is not the last word,

> it is not even an apt word; it is a dead word from ten years back.
> Something quite remote from anything the builders intended has come out of their work, and out of the fierce little human tragedy in which I played; something none of us thought about at the time; a small red flame — a beaten-copper lamp of deplorable design relit before the beaten-copper doors of a tabernacle; the flame which the old knights saw from their tombs, which they saw put out; that flame burns again for other soldiers, far from home, farther, in heart, than Acre or Jerusalem. It could not have been lit but for the builders and the tragedians, and there I found it this morning, burning anew among the old stones. [*BR* 331]

Whether or not we take this rhetoric to be successful, the point it makes is clear: *sub specie aeternitatis* the decline of

Brideshead is of slight importance; to exaggerate its loss is to range human values against divine. What matters is that the lamp — even a lamp of deplorable design — still burns in the chapel.

Such is the depth of nostalgia in *Brideshead* that we may find it hard to accord this ending the decisive weight that Waugh would claim for it, but in the *Sword of Honour* trilogy this problem is largely resolved in the figure of Mr Crouchback. He is a portrait of someone who was, to Guy, 'the best man, the only entirely good man, he had ever known' [*US* 65]. He is also, against every provocation, another individual who does not repine. The two points are connected:

> He was not at all what is called 'a character'. He was an innocent, affable old man who had somehow preserved his good humour — much more than that, a mysterious and tranquil joy — throughout a life which to all out-ward observation had been overloaded with misfortune. He had like many another been born in full sunlight and lived to see night fall. [*MA* 34]

One of those others must surely have been Waugh himself: 'To have been born into a world of beauty, to die amid ugliness, is the common fate of all us exiles.' Mr Crouchback shares the lot of many of Waugh's later characters, but he does so in another spirit:

> He had a further natural advantage over Guy; he was fortified by a memory which kept only the good things and rejected the ill. Despite his sorrows, he had had a fair share of joys, and these were ever fresh and acces-sible in Mr. Crouchback's mind. He never mourned the loss of Broome. He still inhabited it as he had known it in bright boyhood and in early, requited love. [*MA* 34-5]

His natural kinship is with Helena, an earlier figure whose religious faith enabled her in old age to look on with unim-paired tranquillity at the disappointments of her own life and the disintegration of that of her society.

In Mr Crouchback we find internalized the conception of

things which was more starkly put forward at the end of
Brideshead Revisited. That a character, and one who has the
author's full approval, should look on unmoved at the loss
of his ancestral home and the sale of its contents is a mark
of how far Waugh's responses have been modified by the influence of his religion. It is less than accurate to summarize
the process by saying, as Frank Kermode has done, that
'The great houses of England become by an easy transition
types of the Catholic City.'[9] In the case of both Brideshead
and Broome it is precisely the *difference* between the secular
City and the Catholic one that Waugh has gone out of his
way to stress. The houses themselves pass into other hands,
are left desolate or bare; but this is of little moment. What
remains is the light in the chapel. So it is that we are told at
the beginning of *Men at Arms*, 'And the sanctuary lamp
still burned at Broome as of old.' And again, more explicitly,
in *Unconditional Surrender*: 'all [the contents of Broome]
had come down into the front court where Guy now stood,
and had been borne away and dispersed, leaving the whole
house quite bare, except for the chapel; there the change of
ownership passed unrecorded and the lamp still burned'
[*US* 71].

Exiled from Broome, Mr Crouchback is at the mercy of
all the modern nastiness of the twentieth century. At the
Marine Hotel the daily encroachments of the Cuthberts strip
him of privilege and narrow his circumstances. But Mr
Crouchback is serenely unaware of their malevolence. Insult
and impertinence that to Mr Pinfold would have cried aloud
for vengeance quite pass him by. Mr Crouchback is an idealized figure, but that Waugh should have conceived an ideal
in this mould at all is evidence of a deepening mistrust of
the responses on which he had been accustomed to rely.

Of these, nostalgia was perhaps the most natural to him.
'Before that Year of Grace,' he wrote of Christ's birth, 'man
lived in the mists, haunted by ancestral memories of a lost
Eden, taught enigmatically by hints and portents, punished
by awful dooms. The Incarnation restored order.' [*LOr* 16]
Through the bulk of his work the Paradise that has been lost

---

[9] 'Mr Waugh's Cities', p. 171.

looms larger than that which is to be regained; it is the ancestral memories that are dominant. But this temperamental bias towards nostalgia was, in Waugh's later work, increasingly opposed to a religious sense that nostalgia was in the end a defective response which the message of Christianity must supersede. There can be no refuge in the nursery, no affection that is secure, no morality that is without ambiguity, no order that will stand for ever against chaos. All the longings which prompt nostalgia are hopeless. Like the transient accomplishments of irony and elegance and romance, they must find their consummation in the author's religion.

5

Religion

———◆———

It is only Waugh's later heroes and heroines who turn to religion. There is no divinity to watch over the careers of Basil Seal or William Boot; the generation which goes to war in *Put Out More Flags* is godless. Not until *Brideshead Revisited* does Waugh begin, as he put it in 'Fan-Fare', 'to represent man more fully, which, to me, means only one thing, man in his relation to God' [*LOr* 32]. The point is acknowledged in his diary entry for 21 May 1944: 'I think perhaps it is the first of my novels rather than the last.' [*Diaries* 566] This leaves no room for claims that the focus of his work has been religious from the start. The implication is clear: only now is his fiction beginning to turn towards God. Yet Waugh had become a Roman Catholic in 1930. Why did it take so long for him to become a Roman Catholic novelist?

An initial clue is to be found in the slightly equivocal treatment of religion that is a feature of his secondary writings. Early in *Labels* he mentions an episode at Oxford when he, amongst others, went up in an aeroplane that was offering stunt flights from Port Meadow. The experience was unnerving and he gives a humorous account of its effects on his companion, who two days later was received into the Roman Church. 'It is interesting to note,' he adds, 'that, during this aeroplane's brief visit to Oxford, three cases of conversion occurred in precisely similar circumstances.' [*L* 12] A few pages later he recounts with obvious enjoyment the discomfiture of a young priest on the train to Monaco who had returned to his *wagon-lit* after dinner to find that its other occupant was a girl just getting into bed. In consequence, he had felt obliged to spend the rest of the night standing in the corridor — 'the night air seemed to have been effective in purging him of any worldly thoughts that the encounter provoked' [L 31].

The tone of these and other passages in *Labels* is characterized by nothing more shocking than a certain genial irreverence, but when the book came out Waugh took the trouble to preface it with the following note:

> So far as this book contains any serious opinions, they are those of the dates with which it deals, eighteen months ago. Since then my views on several subjects, and particularly on Roman Catholicism, have developed and changed in many ways.

This was in 1930 and it might well have heralded an alteration in the tone of his future work. Certainly, his non-fiction writings in the thirties do give evidence of a difference in outlook. Most obviously, there is the biography of Edmund Campion, but in other works too there are signs of change: in *Remote People* an eager, almost obtrusive respect for the achievements of Christianity, in *Ninety-Two Days* the account of his miraculous salvation on the way to Bon Success, in *Waugh in Abyssinia* a reiterated emphasis on the cultural superiority not just of western civilization, but specifically of the western church.

These all indicate a change from the casual flippancy with which he surveys the Holy Places in *Labels*. But even here, in the non-fiction, the change is only partial. Waugh's sense of comedy is at odds with a sustained attitude of reverence. In the middle of an appreciative description of Swahili dances in *Remote People* he interjects, without comment: 'Missionaries look askance at the entertainments, saying that they produce a state of excitement subversive of the moral law.' [RP 163] And later, in Kenya, he observes wryly that there is no Kikuyu word for virgin — 'This, as may be imagined, has caused considerable difficulty to missionaries.' [RP 209] The sentences detract not at all from Waugh's expressed admiration for the missionaries' work, but they are not quite without an edge of mockery: the words in the first are a little too ponderous, in the

second too bland. Neither of them is allowed to survive in
When the Going was Good.

Comparable examples could be drawn from other works.
Even in the explicitly religious *Edmund Campion*, there is a
persistent vein of irony at the expense of religious subjects.
The fate of the Bishop of Lincoln and the Abbot of Westminster has already been mentioned (see above, p. 38).
Another figure is the dwarfish Duke of Anjou, whose mother
was attempting to press forward a marriage between him
and Queen Elizabeth. 'The Duke's mother, Catherine of
Medici, was impatient of religious scruples,' Waugh tells us,
'but the little fellow held out for his Mass' [EC 98-9]. Here
again one has a sense that the author's stylistic response is
to the comedy of the situation rather than to its religious
implications. 'But the little fellow held out for his Mass' —
the phrase, and the image it suggests, were too good to miss.

In his pamphlet in the series 'Contemporary Writers in a
Christian Perspective', Paul Doyle quotes a letter the author
wrote while working on *Edmund Campion*:

> I am pegging away at Campion. Hope to arrest him this
> afternoon and rack him before I leave [Belton House].
> Then I will hang, draw & quarter him at Mells. [*Letters*
> 94]

Doyle comments:

> To see humour in the painful torturing, disemboweling,
> and cutting of Edmund Campion and yet to be acutely
> aware of, and honour, the martyr's sacrifice and saintly
> motivation bespeaks a man who, in Thomas Aquinas'
> phrase, refuses to be sad in the face of spiritual good.[1]

When every allowance has been made for the Christian perspective, this still misses the point. Spiritual good has little
to do with it; at the time Waugh was refusing just as stead-
fastly to be sad in the face of spiritual evil. Indeed, he was
reluctant to be sad in the face of anything. The letter from

---

[1] *Evelyn Waugh*, p. 8.

Belton House scales no spiritual heights, it merely reflects a preference for the tones of frivolity over those of solemnity. But what it also does — and that Doyle should feel obliged to offer an explanation confirms the fact — is to highlight a degree of tension between the humorist and the committed Roman Catholic. To understand why his religion left so little mark on the early fiction, we must therefore examine the nature of this tension and then follow the stages that led to its resolution.

The account of Prendergast's painful death, set to the strains of 'O God our help in ages past', belongs to the years before Waugh's conversion, as do the blithe irreverence of *Labels* and the character of Father Rothschild in *Vile Bodies*. Had these been no more than isolated sparks of humour, they could simply have been suppressed. And to some extent this is what happened: Father Rothschild has no immediate successors, *Labels* is prefaced by an authorial disclaimer, and in general terms it is probably true that the Roman faith is henceforth treated more circumspectly than would otherwise have been the case. But such effects are largely superficial; the bases of Waugh's humour do not change. These aspects of the pre-Catholic books are not just jokes, they are the texture of a particular kind of world, which has its own defences, its own consolations, its own unreal inhabitants. To ordinary societies religion may be essential; there are, according to the formula, certain basic human needs and anxieties which nothing else can satisfy. But the world of Waugh's early novels has been created in purposeful defiance of these dreary needs and anxieties; it exists as a challenge to them. Occasionally the momentum falters, but that is the ideal. From the vile stuff of reality Waugh elicits the image of a different kind of world, exempted from those spiritual and emotional liabilities that make the consolations of religion necessary.

It was, I take it, a modification of this image that Waugh had in mind when he wrote, after *Brideshead*, of his intention 'to represent man more fully'. The religious dimension can only have a place in a fictional world where the characters aspire to fully human status, and in most of his pre-war writings, even the non-fictional ones, this condition is not fulfilled. Whether we are talking about the mutilated criminals in *Remote People* or the hanged witnesses in *Black Mischief* or the unfortunate death of Lord Tangent in *Decline and Fall*, there is no sense in which we have to do with figures who could make any human claim on us. We are watching a performance in two dimensions, like the movement of puppets in a shadow play.

But our detachment from these creatures is not unshakeable. What preserves the illusion of the puppet-show is the consistency of the author's irony. If his tone lapses, then this artificial world dissolves and we are back with the concerns and conflicts of reality. In *Edmund Campion* Waugh tells us in passing how Pius V had on one occasion turned loose a drove of harlots on the Campagna to be massacred by bandits. The episode is mentioned as an instance of the 'more severe, puritanical measures' that had distinguished Pius's reign from that of his successor. It is related with Waugh's usual urbanity and we are likely to accept it with equal composure; this is much the kind of thing that might have recommended itself to Amurath in a moment of vexation. 'A drove of harlots' is a phrase pleasingly economical in its ability to render the scene vivid at the same time as it distances it. The word 'drove' combines the visual image of the women marshalled to an unknown fate with associative overtones that coolly pick out their affinities with a herd of cattle. To call them harlots is at once precise and elegant; the word has a happy flavour of archaism that again functions both visually, in the classic image of the painted woman, and emotionally, by pushing the episode back towards the biblical contexts in which harlots are most at home. In all, it is a phrase that we read with some satisfaction; the scene is brought sharply into view, but without in any way compromising our detachment.

This is the tone that we are accustomed to; it places us in a familiar world where the response is unproblematic. But then, quite casually, Waugh goes on to refer to Pius V as a saint — not the sort of saint we might expect in this context (there was, after all, the painful case of the human sacrifices at the Bishop of Popo's consecration), but a real saint, in a world of living people. The reference is only made in parenthesis, but it is clearly intended to be taken at face value. Yet if Pius was a real saint, then the drove of harlots were real women. The tone appropriate to a world of fictional puppets contrasts outrageously with the implication that these events took place in the real world. It is a failure of irony. By calling the man a saint, Waugh obliges us to measure him as a real being, and in doing so forfeits the moral and emotional freedom of the writer whose world acknowledges its unreality.

What Waugh has done here is exactly parallel to what the editor of the *Tablet* had done three years earlier when he took up arms against *Black Mischief*. Like Don Quixote assaulting the heathen puppets, Oldmeadow came fiercely to the defence of Christianity — without, apparently, perceiving that his own world was subject to laws different from those which governed Azania. 'Two humane ladies are ridiculed;' he protests, 'in one place so indelicately that the passage cannot be described by us.'[2] He writes with an indignation which suggests that their good works might have been known to him personally. But Dame Mildred and Miss Tin are parts of a comic fantasy. To call them 'two humane ladies' because of their notional concern for animals is no more sensible than to call Lewis Carroll's Queen of Hearts an *in*human lady because she uses hedgehogs as croquet balls. And this is just the point that Waugh made in his letter of self-defence to Cardinal Bourne. ('But these, my Lord Cardinal, are wholly fictitious characters...' [*Letters* 73].) Oldmeadow's chivalry is quaint, but it mistakes the nature of Waugh's fiction.

The implications of this issue were to be touched on later by Waugh in a review of Angus Wilson's *Hemlock and After* which appeared in 1952. His comments throw light on the way his own fiction had changed:

[2] Ernest Oldmeadow, 'A Recent Novel'.

if [Wilson's] whole story is simply a flickering shadow
on a screen which, any moment, will rise on Real Life;
if there are no abiding consequences to anything [his
characters] do, if there is no heaven or hell for them —
then indeed the broadcasters are right in saying that
they are devoid of interest or meaning. [*LOr* 94]

Here, several years after the change of course announced
in 'Fan-Fare', Waugh asserts that it is only the religious
dimension that can save the novelist's world from being a
meaningless flickering of shadows. But back in 1928 his
concerns had been different; it was 'a flickering shadow'
that he took as the hero of his first novel. The 'real' Paul
Pennyfeather, 'the solid figure of an intelligent, well-educated,
well-conducted young man', has no part in *Decline and Fall*;
the character whose fortunes we follow is 'the shadow that
has flitted about this narrative under the name of Paul
Pennyfeather' [*DF* 122]. In the middle of his first novel
Waugh is making explicit the kind of world he has set out
to create — a shadow world. It may be that this would later
seem to him a worthless project for the novelist to under-
take, but there was never a doubt that it was one which
excluded any serious consideration of religion.

This was an exclusion which in life was simply not possible. When Waugh refers in 'Come Inside' to the decade after
he left Lancing, he is talking about a vision of the world
which is quite outside the recuperative powers of irony:

Those who have read my works will perhaps understand
the character of the world into which I exuberantly
launched myself. Ten years of that world sufficed to
show me that life there, or anywhere, was unintelligible
and unendurable without God. [*LOr* 148]

'The conclusion,' he adds, 'was obvious.' And it is at this
point that God, of necessity, intervenes. But in literature, as
we saw in the case of Waugh's first marriage, irony is less
easily overreached; the defences against an unintelligible
world are stronger.

In *Decline and Fall* they need to be. Prendy's Doubts were

nothing run of the mill about Cain's wife or the Old Testament miracles: 'No, it was something deeper than all that. *I couldn't understand why God had made the world at all.'* [*DF* 33] An echo of the author's own perception of things is unmistakable — and we have his suicide attempt a couple of years earlier to confirm it — but any sympathy with his character's dilemma is extinguished by Waugh's irony. Prendy's abandonment of the vicarage at Worthing is a sacrifice that cannot easily be invested with grandeur. To see this part of the book as a humorous way of broaching serious issues would be quite mistaken; rather, it is a humorous way of exorcizing them. The irony is not designed to introduce seriousness but to keep it out. And with it religion.

If hints of a graver purpose occasionally break the surface of *Vile Bodies*, they do so in spite of the dominant tone; they tend to be the points in the novel, like Father Rothschild's speech about Youth's 'fatal hunger for permanence', at which the writer's irony has momentarily given way. Such passages may be traces of an underlying earnestness, signs, in retrospect, of the later change in direction, but it would be perverse to make more of them. The amiable futility of the Bright Young People is no doubt a reflection of that world which Waugh was coming to find 'unintelligible and unendurable' without God, but the sober tones of the religious article are just what he was excluding from the novel. By the use of irony and humour he was attempting, on the contrary, to make this world, if not intelligible (which would be a boring project, anyway), at least endurable — and perhaps even attractive.

With *A Handful of Dust* we move into a different climate. The case has already been argued in the first three chapters: it is a book that deliberately puts far more strain than any previous one on the writer's habitual mechanisms of defence. Detachment is harder to maintain, humour more difficult to find, romanticism a more dangerous commitment. Though its importance is negative, religion becomes, for the first time, a subject for due consideration in one of the novels — a fact that is perhaps indicated by the title

Waugh borrowed from Eliot.[3] With its 'flavour of the major prophets' it reflects a general concern in the book with the absence of any religious consolation. The point is given some emphasis:

> Tony invariably wore a dark suit on Sundays and a stiff white collar. He went to church, where he sat in a large pitch-pine pew, put in by his great-grandfather at the time of rebuilding the house, furnished with very high crimson hassocks and a fireplace, complete with iron grate and a little poker which his father used to rattle when any point in the sermon excited his disapproval. Since his father's day a fire had not been laid there; Tony had it in mind to revive the practice next winter. On Christmas Day and Harvest Thanksgiving Tony read the lessons from the back of the brass eagle. [HD 29-30]

The routine is social rather than spiritual, but the author is fully alive to its appeal. Though it has none of the consolations of religion, Tony's Sunday is replete with those of inherited privilege and cultural tradition. It is part of a satisfying personal charade in which there are hints of Waugh himself:

> Brenda teased him whenever she caught him posing as an upright, God-fearing gentleman of the old school and Tony saw the joke, but this did not at all diminish the pleasure he derived from his weekly routine. [HD 30]

While the service goes on Tony's mind is elsewhere, preoccupied with the more material question of bathrooms and lavatories.

Not surprisingly, when his son is killed it never occurs to him that the vicar's role could be more than a social one; the man's attempts to offer comfort are merely embarrassing: 'I only wanted to see him about arrangements. He tried to be comforting. It was very painful...after all the last thing one

---

[3] The phrase is taken from a line in Part I of *The Waste Land*: 'I will show you fear in a handful of dust'.

wants to talk about at a time like this is religion.' [*HD* 115]
But the best alternatives Last himself can find are animal
snap and whisky. He is unequipped to deal with the business
as it bears on his own emotions; his reaction is centrifugal —
'It will be ghastly for that Ripon girl,' 'It's awful for Jock,'
'It's going to be so much worse for Brenda.' Concerned more
than anything for the feelings and convenience of other
people, he reveals all the virtues of his social breeding and all
its sad vacuity when unsupported by any profounder level
of response.

There are hints in the last part of the book that the City
of which he goes in search could shade easily enough into
the City of God, but it is left to Helena to develop them.
A Handful of Dust holds out no offer of Christian salvation;
but it does show how inadequate the alternatives are. Immediately after Tony's disconcerting interview with the vicar,
the novel turns to the waste land of fashionable London
where Brenda is having her fortune told by a descendant
of Madame Sosostris — from the sole of her foot. It is a scene
of grotesque, half-serious superstition. In Mrs Beaver's vulgar
substitute for religion Polly Cockpurse's house has become
the temple and the fortune-teller a new priestess. But this
modern cult is not altogether unfamiliar; if the new superstition is primarily a matter of social fashion, so also is the
Sunday routine of Tony Last. The gestures he makes towards religion take a more venerable form, but they are no
less completely defined in secular terms. His faith can provide no shelter when the illusion crumbles, because it is
itself no more than another picturesque motif in the same
Gothic dream. To be of any value, faith must be faith in
something that stands outside the general decline.

'Change and decay in all around I see,' sings Uncle
Theodore, but the following line remains unsung: 'O thou
who changest not, abide with me.' It has no place in *Scoop*,
any more than in the earlier books, yet it sounds a clear
response to those subterranean tremors of anxiety that
have been sensible in Waugh's novels ever since the epilogue
to *Decline and Fall*. Pastmaster's drunken meditation on how
things have changed is echoed at some point in each of the
succeeding novels — by Agatha Runcible, by Sonia, by Tony

and Brenda, or in *Put Out More Flags* by Angela Lyne. Only William Boot seems able to return unmarked to the same world from which he started; but then Boot Magna is itself set in a prospect of decay.

Against these intimations of unhappiness, the novelist, unaided by any god from the machine, has won a series of brilliantly precarious victories. Until *Brideshead Revisited* the 'fatal hunger for permanence' of the Bright Young People has been successfully conjured out of sight. But when change is taken to be synonymous with decline, the passage of the years must inevitably make this more difficult. Sooner or later the words of Uncle Theodore's hymn will have to be acknowledged as the only secure foundation from which to fight.

The implications of this become the prevailing theme of Waugh's writing from *Brideshead* onwards. It is notable, however, that this central image of the Church as a fixed and enduring resort in a world of change had already found its clearest expression some ten years earlier in a short story called 'Out of Depth'. Its relevance to our theme is such that it warrants separate consideration.

The story takes place in 1933, but its kernel is a dream of England in the twenty-fifth century. The country has reverted to barbarism: its buildings have fallen into ruin and its illiterate inhabitants move 'with the loping gait of savages' [*MrL* 131]. Blacks are now the dominant race. It is Waugh's vision of present trends at their calamitous point of fulfilment. Then suddenly, in the midst of this, as he begins to despair of his sanity, the hero comes upon a mission and sees outside it a black man dressed as a Dominican friar:

> Rip knew that out of strangeness, there had come into being something familiar; a shape in the chaos. Something was being done. Something was being done that Rip knew; something that twenty-five centuries had not altered; something of his own childhood which survived the age of the world. [*MrL* 136]

The black priest turns and says, 'Ite, missa est.' Rip wakes up and seeks confession.

This story contains a number of points that are worth considering. The church service Rip lights upon is a precursor of the chapel lamp that burns on through *Brideshead Revisited* and the war trilogy. The lamp is a symbol of the Church's unchanging message, and it has its verbal equivalent in the unchanging form and language of the liturgy. The century is different and the civilization Rip knows has long since foundered, but the words of the Mass remain identical. In reading the story, we understand at once why Waugh should have been dismayed by changes in the liturgy. The words of the black priest can have a meaning for Rip only because they are the same words the Church has been using since the beginning of its history.

In his essay on the Catholic Church in America Waugh took Aldous Huxley to task for suggesting that Christianity is in fact a number of separate religions, moulded by different cultures. 'Any altar-boy could tell him,' Waugh replies, 'that the "incantations" of the Mass are identical whether in Guadelupe or Gethsemani, Ky, and are comprehensible or not simply so far as one understands Latin.' [*LOr* 171] Waugh's religious conservatism was far more than another aspect of Pinfold; he saw it as an affirmation of the principles on which the Church was based. As he wrote in a letter to the editor of the *Catholic Herald*: 'I would ask [Father Sheerin] to consider that the function of the Church in every age has been conservative — to transmit undiminished and uncontaminated the creed inherited from its predecessors.' [*LOr* 187] Only thus would it be able, in the future age of barbarism, to offer an image of 'something that twenty-five centuries had not altered'.

The 'shape' which Rip sees in the chaos is another image important to Waugh's conception of Christianity; he is drawn to it both as artist and as traveller. The 'little independent systems of order' which it is the artist's job to create are a traditional analogue to the work of God.[4] In the disintegrated

---

[4] Cf. Waugh's diary entry for Easter 1964: 'When I first came into the Church I was drawn, not by splendid ceremonies but by the spectacle of the priest as a craftsman. He had an important job to do which none but he was qualified for.' [*Diaries* 792]

world of *A Handful of Dust* there is no shaping deity, and the nearest thing to a divine presence becomes, for a curious moment, Mrs Rattery, brooding like one of the Fates over her game of patience ('under her fingers order grew out of chaos; she established sequence and precedence; the symbols before her became coherent, interrelated' [*HD* 110]). But the game fails to come out. Like Tony's concern with social niceties, it is a comment on the absence of any surer ways of establishing order.

In this case the surrounding chaos has been precipitated by the death of John Andrew. More often than not in Waugh's early books it was endemic to the setting he described. A fortnight after his reception into the Church he set off for Abyssinia. The diary entry for 3 November 1930, written in Addis Ababa, begins with what was to become a characteristic image: 'Got up 7, went to Catholic church, island sanity in raving town.' [*Diaries* 332] It was later in the course of the same journey that he paid a visit, recorded in *Remote People*, to the convent of native girls at Kokonjiro — 'this little island of order and sweetness in an ocean of rank barbarity'. The contrast is one to which Waugh returns on his second trip to Central Africa in 1935. He describes in *Waugh in Abyssinia* a cattle truck of soldiers on their way to the southern front:

> all were in a delirious condition, hoarse, staring, howling for blood. In the next coach sat a dozen Italian nuns on the way to the coast; fresh faced, composed, eyes downcast, quietly telling their beads. [*WA* 164-5]

It is easy to see how this opposition between chaos and faith could become aligned with that between savagery and civilization. The idea is one that Waugh himself frequently encourages. In the early books especially, his commitment to Christianity readily takes on the colour of a disdain for alien cultures. In *Remote People* his visit to the monastery at Debra Lebanos provides the occasion for a sustained hymn to the virtues of Western Christianity at the expense of its Eastern counterparts. The Mass he attends there he finds difficult to think of as a Christian service at all, 'for it bore that secret and confused character associated with the non-Christian sects of the East'. His thoughts are taken back to the beginning of the era, when Christianity was steeped in esotericism and mystification:

> And I began to see how these obscure sanctuaries had grown, with the clarity of the Western reason, into the great open altars of Catholic Europe, where Mass is said in a flood of light, high in the sight of all, while tourists can clatter round with their Baedekers, incurious of the mystery. [RP 88-9]

Even more explicit is the cultural judgement in *Waugh in Abyssinia* when he contrasts the artistic triumphs of European Christianity in the Middle Ages with 'the artificial silk and painted petrol cans' [WA 141] of the religious festival in Addis Ababa. The view of Christianity implied in passages like this is close to the pronouncement of Hilaire Belloc that 'Europe is the faith, the faith Europe.' It is a parallel form of the kind of class snobbery with which Waugh was to be taxed after *Brideshead Revisited*. He had espoused, it was claimed, a version of Christianity that made it into the exclusive preserve of a favoured class or culture.

The cultural charge we can deal with now. Certainly, the identification of Christianity with European civilization was a tempting one. The imagery of light and space which Waugh habitually associated with his religion offers an expressive contrast to the dark enclosures that caught his imagination in Africa. (It is worth observing here that only in British colonial Africa — Kenya and the South — does Waugh seem to respond to the open spaces of this continent. In general, 'darkest Africa' is a metaphor peculiarly appropriate to his treatment of it.) Moreover, as the visit to Debra Lebanos makes clear, indigenous forms of Christianity had taken on enough of the complexion of their surroundings to look disconcertingly like barbarism.

Any view of the Christian Church in Africa which concentrates on its missionary origins will inevitably tend to see it as the gift of Europe to a benighted continent, and this is likely to become in turn a statement about the supremacy of

European civilization. But the belief that what the missionaries brought was the religion of a particular civilization was
not one to which Waugh adhered for long. The whole point
of 'Out of Depth' is to demonstrate how absolute is the
separation between the enduring message of Christianity
and the transient civilizations with which it is from time to
time associated. 'Belloc "Europe and the Faith" my foot,'
Waugh notes in the journal he kept of his visit to Goa [*Diaries*
708]. And then a day or two later, writing to his wife with
an account of his Christmas there: 'No mistletoe or holly or
yule logs or Teutonic nonsense. Simple oriental fervour
instead. I feel far closer brotherhood with these people than
in France or Dursley or Boston.' [*Letters* 388]

These are not the words of one whose faith is staked on a
claim to cultural superiority. What matter to him are the two
aspects of his religion emphasized in 'Out of Depth': that it
should be unchanging and that it should reveal in the chaos
some form of order. He looks to it, in other words, to make
life endurable and intelligible. The former on its own is not
enough; other religions can do that. For that Constantius
turns back in unregarded middle age to the Mithraism of his
youth. But Helena is impatient of its solemn obscurities; she
demands a religion that is intellectually coherent and she
finds it, we are to believe, in Christianity. While other religions shroud their mysteries in successive veils, it is the
distinction of Christianity that it seeks not to veil but to
reveal:

> as a fog, lifting, may suddenly reveal to a ship's com-
> pany that, through no skill of theirs, they have silently
> drifted into safe anchorage; to catch a glimpse of simple
> unity in a life that had seemed all vicissitude — this,
> thought Lactantius, was something to match the exu-
> berance of Pentecost. [*H* 88]

The words speak of religion both as a place of refuge and as a
promise of meaning; for Lactantius the two are indivisible.

This emphasis on the rational basis of Christianity is
crucial to Waugh's response, and yet it is balanced by an
equally vigorous strain of anti-rationalism which attaches

particular value to whatever traffic with the miraculous is admitted by his faith. Our next step will be to analyse this combination and to place Waugh's zest for the supernatural within the context of the general argument.

Helena's insistence that she should understand before she accepts is reminiscent of what we know of Waugh's own conversion. Mr Pinfold's 'calm acceptance of the propositions of his faith' reflects the state of mind described by Father D'Arcy in *Evelyn Waugh and his World*. 'Few [converts],' he writes, '...can have been so matter of fact as Evelyn Waugh,' and he goes on to mention another writer who came to him at the same time and whose principal gauge was his own experience:

> With such a criterion, it was no wonder that he did not persevere. Evelyn, on the other hand, never spoke of experience or feelings. He had come to learn and understand what he believed to be God's revelation, and this made talking with him an interesting discussion based primarily on reason. I have never myself met a convert who so strongly based his assents on truth.[5]

What may seem strange is that one who approached his faith with such calm rationality should also have set such store on its defiance of reason. 'Nothing "stands to reason" with God,' [*H* 128] says Pope Sylvester, and it is evident that this was a source of some satisfaction to Waugh. Christopher Sykes tells, for instance, of his enthusiasm for the notion of the Assumption:

> As a fundamentalist he liked the proposed doctrine because it defied rationalism, and he was delighted later, when the doctrine was defined by the Pope in 1950, that the declaration was accompanied by an encyclical

---

[5] *Evelyn Waugh and his World*, ed. David Pryce-Jones, p. 64.

letter which eschewed all thought of compromise, and
implicitly stressed that the definition was a summons to
faith irrespective of the claims of reason.[6]

Of a piece with this were Waugh's efforts to secure his
daughter's débutante ball from rain. On this and other occasions he paid a nearby convent of Poor Clares to pray for
fine weather, sending them a bonus in case of success. ('A
remarkable performance by these excellent women,' he
records in his diary, 'to whom I have sent another £3.'
[*Diaries* 764]) Admittedly, this policy seems to have been
quite effective, but it has a tinge of superstition which is at
odds with the sort of rationalism that was stressed by Father
D'Arcy.

This is one of the problems in *Helena*. The task which
the saint sets herself is ostensibly to bring an increasingly
convoluted faith back to its foundations in unadorned historical fact: 'Just at this moment when everyone's forgetting
it and chattering about the hypostatic union, there's a solid
chunk of wood waiting for them to have their silly heads
knocked against.' In the last words of the novel Waugh
makes the same point:

> Hounds are checked, hunting wild. A horn calls clear
> through the covert. Helena casts them back on the
> scent.
>   Above all the babble of her age and ours, she makes
> one blunt assertion. And there alone lies Hope. [*H* 159]

It is the image that had been used twenty years earlier when
Lady Circumference's snort of disapproval, 'the hunting-cry
of the *ancien regime*', had recalled Margot Metroland's guests
from the spell of Mrs Ape. The values of blunt commonsense
are asserted against spurious religious exaltation. This is
unexceptionable in *Vile Bodies*, but in *Helena* there is a disjunction between the aim and the means by which it is
carried out. The True Cross may point to a historical fact
but it is itself also a relic, and the veneration of relics is

[6] *Evelyn Waugh: A Biography*, p. 450.

not an aspect of Roman Catholicism well suited to an affirmation of blunt common sense. On one hand, the cross is
wanted as a piece of down-to-earth historical evidence; on
the other, it can only be found and authenticated by instances of miraculous intervention which are quite the
opposite of down-to-earth. What starts off as a challenge to
existing practices in the name of reason and understanding
begins to decline into a pietism that is as unilluminating as
the intellectual contortions it set out to counteract.

Waugh was well aware of the dangers involved in an
over-emphasis on the supernatural. Constantine provides a
satirical illustration of them. 'Everything was miraculous
that day,' he explains airily, when Helena expresses doubt
that his elaborate labarum could have been contrived on the
morning of a battle. The idiocies to which a naive form of
belief can give rise are acknowledged with an ironic humour
from which even Helena herself is not quite exempt. A
word from the major-domo attributing a dubious biblical
pedigree to the staircase outside Government House in
Jerusalem is enough to make her have the whole thing
crated up and sent back to Rome. The project shows creditable enthusiasm but doubtful taste. And there is something
of Constantine's vulgarity in her reaction to the cave of the
Nativity — 'Just the place for a basilica.' It is at about this
time that she loads up tons of 'common earth' so that she
can lay the foundations of a church in Rome on soil from
the Holy Land — again, an undertaking that the author
describes with less than perfect sympathy.

That these elements of humour should be present in this
section of the book at all does suggest a measure of detachment on Waugh's part, but when everything has been said,
a relic remains the focal point of the novel and we are obliged
to take it at Helena's valuation. An atheist is on dangerous
ground here, and before going further it is perhaps worth
quoting the opinion of Christopher Sykes, himself a Roman
Catholic: the novel's weakness throughout, he claims, 'lies
in expression of a false estimate. Unlike Islam, another down-
to-earth religion, Christianity does not depend on relics.'[7]

[7] *Evelyn Waugh: A Biography*, p. 430.

In the end, we are left with the feeling that *Helena* is pulled in two directions by two different aspects of the writer's faith. Earlier in this study a tension was noted in Waugh's writing between the ironist and the romantic, and elsewhere between a commitment to order and a contrasting delight in anarchy. It is perhaps to be expected that the conflict should find some reflection in his religion, and this clash between rationalism and a defiance of rationalism is one form of it.

In this case, however, a critic might feel with some justice that the author has not played entirely fair. Both here and in *Brideshead Revisited* the miracles are likely to strike us as a kind of special pleading that at a vital moment intervenes to spoil the balance. The decisive events are decisive simply because their miraculous nature protects them from any challenge. In the days of Seth one of the more celebrated relics at the monastery of St Mark was a wooden cross 'which had fallen from heaven quite unexpectedly one Good Friday luncheon some years back' [*BM* 173]. Suppose now that the whereabouts of the True Cross had been revealed to Helena 'quite unexpectedly one Good Friday luncheon'. Is there any more than a difference in tone between this and what actually happens? As things are, Helena is protected from this sort of irony by the religious rhetoric which surrounds the miracles. Perhaps the earlier ironies at her expense were really nothing of the kind; might they not simply be a form of pre-emptive vaccination, a literary trick to gain the reader's confidence, so that when the climactic miracles are treated without irony he will be more ready to accept the author's judgement of them? The reader is always practised upon; that is the novelist's business; but when he becomes too aware of the fact, something has gone wrong.

To Waugh himself criticism of this kind would probably have seemed at best ill-directed. Some way through *Scoop* William elaborates a colourful daydream about the heroic possibilities of his situation. He sees himself at the head of a band of Bengal Lancers and kilted Highlanders bursting open the prison doors, grappling with Benito and bearing off Kätchen in triumph to Boot Magna. It is a broad parody of the sort of romantic possibilities with which Waugh toyed, at some point or other, in most of the early novels. They are possibilities of a kind that undoubtedly attracted him, but it would never have seemed other than a gross artistic error to give them their head and let them determine the cast of the novel. The result would have been one of the undisciplined fantasies that are produced by Mr Pinfold's voices. As far as it goes, this is an argument that Waugh would have accepted, but to claim that the miraculous climax of *Brideshead Revisited* is a comparable sort of lapse would have seemed to him hopelessly obtuse. From a Christian point of view there is no element of fantasy in miracles; they are a fact of life. To show Lord Marchmain returned to the faith by a miracle can no more be called cheating than to show a sick man cured by a doctor; they are both in the order of things from which the novelist shapes his narrative. The sceptical reader can then only acknowledge that the novelist's reality is different from his own. The suspicion will remain that what the author took to be an expression of reality was in fact a surrender to fantasy as regrettable as any of the romantic flights which he had in earlier books eschewed.

There was a sense, one might argue, in which Waugh had a vested interest in miracles — and not merely because he was half-persuaded that his life had been saved by one in South America. He valued them above all as a sharp assault on our conventional notions of what is real. Miracles are refreshing supernatural evidence that the familiar stuff of everyday life is not the last word on reality. In the early books Waugh's need to escape from the tedious daily pattern was expressed by a disruptive vein of comic fantasy. Miracles were for the time being just another stage property, offering as they did a welcome licence to his imagination. The relics of St Mark's are a typical example; it would indeed be quite unexpected if a wooden cross were to fall from heaven during Good Friday luncheon. But as the element of fantasy in Waugh's novels subsided and their tone became more sober, the miraculous took on an altered role. There was no longer the same call to subvert reality by comic forays into the absurd, for religion was offering a view of it that quite changed its aspect.

The nature of this change is intimated by Ryder in the

words which first apprise us of his subsequent conversion:
'Later, too, I have come to accept claims which then, in
1923, I never troubled to examine, and to accept the supernatural as the real.' [BR 83] The idea that to see with the
eyes of religion is to see the supernatural as the real achieves
in a single leap what had previously been the object of diverse
and devious stratagems: emancipation from the suffocating
ordinariness of common reality. The miraculous is part of
the texture of daily life.

The theme which Ryder touches on is developed by Guy
Crouchback in almost the same terms. Slightly flown with
wine on the Halberdier guest night, he begins to talk religion
with the chaplain:

> 'Do you agree,' he asked earnestly, 'that the Super-
> natural Order is not something added to the Natural
> Order, like music or painting, to make everyday life
> more tolerable? It *is* everyday life. The supernatural is
> real; what we call "real" is a mere shadow, a passing
> fancy. Don't you agree, Padre?' [MA 77]

The passage opens out the implications of what Ryder had
said in *Brideshead Revisited*. Religion is offering a translation
from one form of reality into another, escape from 'what we
call "real"' into the true reality of the supernatural. What
we had thought of as the real world becomes, from the perspective of religion, a mere shadow.

The image refers us back to a previous stage of the analysis. A world of shadows was what Waugh's technique in
the early novels and travel books was designed to create.
Paul Pennyfeather, we remember, was actually described by
Waugh as a shadow flitting through the pages of *Decline and
Fall*. The point of this, according to my argument, was that
a world of shadows is proof against pain or anxiety; it can
make no claim on us; it cannot engage our feelings or trespass
on our compassion. The creation of this sort of world was the
basis of Waugh's defensive strategy, for it ratified his own
authorial detachment. Now we find him steering Christianity
in the same direction. This too offers a vision that enables us
to detach ourselves from the concerns of a world that is 'a

mere shadow'. But more than this, it does so in a way that is specifically contrasted with the superficial equivalents vouchsafed by art. Where art can effect no more than a cosmetic alteration in reality, religion, by changing its nature, can transform it. And thus, as we saw at the end of chapter 1, the precarious detachment of artistic irony is superseded by the impregnable security of the Christian's *contemptus mundi*.

In age, it seems, Waugh has attained through religion the defensive stronghold to which, by different methods, he has been aspiring since the start of his career; the important things are elsewhere, untouched by the upheavals of what we call reality. By the middle of *Officers and Gentlemen* Guy has spontaneously relegated the wartime affairs of the army to a role of subordinate importance. When he goes to make his Easter duties in Alexandria, he prefers to do so in a city church — 'Already, without deliberation, he had begun to dissociate himself from the army in matters of real concern.' It is the point that was previously noted by Sebastian in *Brideshead Revisited*. In one of their early conversations Ryder remarks that Catholics seem 'just like other people', but Sebastian contradicts him: 'they've got an entirely different outlook on life; everything they think important is different from other people'. The claims of the world recede.

Of course, the security afforded by religious detachment is sounder in theory than in practice. Mr Pinfold sees life *sub specie aeternitatis* and this simply makes it look flat as a map — without, apparently, doing much to modify its numerous vexations. The subordination of secular concerns is an ideal. What we call 'real' may be only a passing fancy but it is hard to keep this uppermost in the mind when confronted by 'a bad bottle of wine, an impertinent stranger, or a fault in syntax' [*GP* 14]. The stronghold is not impregnable at all; if any of the defences had been perfect, Waugh's life would have been happier.

Nevertheless, to a man whose persistent struggle is to offset the disappointing performance of the everyday world, a concept of religion which tends to devalue the currency of this world has obvious advantages. It can, for instance, be used to give authority to points of view or to modes of behaviour which would otherwise be unacceptable. If true reality is the supernatural, then attitudes and actions which, judged according to the natural order of things, would be repugnant or foolish, can be vindicated by appeal to a higher order that may be inscrutable, but is more truly real. The racialism of the whites in East Africa perhaps strikes us as unreasonable, but is that *necessarily* a condemnation of it? Waugh sees a loophole: 'When over a long period a great number of otherwise respectable people consistently deny the conclusions of their own reason on some particular point, it may be a disease like roulette, or it may be a revelation like the miracles of Lourdes.' [RP 191] With this breathtaking leap from racial prejudice to the miracles of Lourdes, Waugh has put himself outside the reach of argument. Rational determinants of thought and action fall away.

It is a form of special pleading that can be widely applied. To one's reading of history, for example. The evidence may suggest that Pius V was a blundering bigot, but there is no need to relinquish one's viewpoint for that. Is it not possible, after all, that in his hours before the crucifix Pius had 'learned something that was hidden from the statesmen of his time and the succeeding generations of historians; seen through and beyond the present and immediate future...?' [EC 42] There is no answer.

A resource of this kind could not but be a value to someone whose spirit of contradiction was as highly developed as Waugh's. Throughout his life he made a practice of cultivating an outrageous persona, maintaining untenable opinions, adhering to unpopular standards and, most persistently of all, sighing for an impossible world. He lost few opportunities to fly in the face of reasonable expectation. The plaque which guarded the entrance to his house — 'No Admittance On Business' — was at once a declaration of independence and a triumphant assertion of contrariety. Waugh was quite genuinely, if rather idiosyncratically, committed to another order of things. And it is in these terms that his Christianity takes up, and in the end dominates, the patterns of escape that we have examined.

The concept of his religion that emerges from Waugh's books
is closely adapted to personal requirements that earlier had
been met by other means. It is, however, quite the opposite
of a religion of convenience. Both these aspects have a bearing on our theme.

The way in which irony gave place to the possibilities of
religious detachment has already been considered. Equally
important is the extent to which Waugh's faith is expressed
in terms that make it an answer to the artist's sense of exile.
'The strong, questing will had found its object;' he writes of
Helena's conversion, 'the exile her home.' [H 90] And when
Macarius treads the road to Golgotha, his sentiments are the
same — 'It was home ground, this acre of rock, a patrimony
reclaimed.' [H 134] The incarnation, we might recall, was
seen by Waugh in his essay on the Catholic Church in America
as restoring order to a world 'haunted by ancestral memories
of a lost Eden' [LOr 167] .

What this suggests, since exile is so often conceived as exile
from childhood, is that those yearnings for the world of the
nursery which were touched on in the previous chapter
may also have a religious dimension. The shape that Rip sees
in chaos as he approaches the mission in 'Out of Depth' is
something 'of his own childhood which survived the age of
the world' [MrL 136] . It is in childhood that prayers are
first learned, and there exists between the security of religion
and the security of the nursery a close relationship. Nannies,
like other divinities, tend to offer an unchanging point of
reference in a changing world.

It is an important connection, which receives its fullest
treatment in *Brideshead Revisited*. The first we see of Nanny
Hawkins is a figure seated at an open window with a rosary
between her hands. What prevents Sebastian from taking her
to Oxford, he tells Ryder whimsically, is that she would be
all the time trying to send him to church. Later, when Julia
is talking of her past life, she says, 'I've been punished a little
for marrying Rex. You see, I can't get all that sort of thing

out of my mind, quite — Death, Judgement, Heaven, Hell, Nanny Hawkins, and the Catechism.' [BR 247] Nanny Hawkins is a natural partner in these mysteries; her presence is inseparable from a religion that struck its roots in childhood. Julia's outburst about sin emphasizes the point: it is 'A word from so long ago, from Nanny Hawkins stitching by the hearth and the nightlight burning before the Sacred Heart.' [BR 274] And afterwards, when Ryder sees her to bed,

> her pale lips moved on the pillow, but whether to wish me good night or to murmur a prayer — a jingle of the nursery that came to her now in the twilit world between sorrow and sleep: some ancient pious rhyme that had come down to Nanny Hawkins from centuries of bedtime whispering, through all the changes of language, from the days of pack-horses on the Pilgrim's Way — I did not know. [BR 278]

The passage makes a series of characteristic links which integrate the consolations of religion with those of tradition and of the nursery. It is no surprise to find Nanny Hawkins, a few pages later, talking of Sebastian in the monastery as though of a wayward child — 'I hope they look after him properly. I expect they find him a regular handful.' [BR 287] The teddy-bear was put away, like a fetish hidden from the missionary, but it has never really been left behind. In adult life the monastery will offer him the security that as a child he had found in the nursery.

It is needless to quote more examples. Nostalgia, like irony, is met by the author's religion and absorbed into it. Impulses which before had been separate, or even conflicting, can, in a modified form, become part of a coherent response to the propositions of Christianity. Romanticism is another case in point; it too is integral to Waugh's religion. The image of the convent at Kokonjiro as an island of order and sweetness is followed by this description.

> all round it for hundreds of miles lie gross jungle, bush, and forest, haunted by devils and the fear of darkness,

where human life merges into the cruel, automatic life
of the animals; here they were singing the offices just
as they had been sung in Europe when the missions were
little radiant points of learning and decency in a pagan
wilderness. [*RP* 207]

That the offices of the Church have remained unchanged is
not just a note of certainty in an uncertain world, it is a call
to romanticism in an unromantic world.

When Donat O'Donnell talks of 'a deep English romanticism'[8] as the main emotional constituent of Waugh's religion,
he points to a level of commitment that is continually making itself felt. The trip to Debra Lebanos earlier in *Remote
People* is the occasion of a brief digression which embodies
precisely this aspect of Waugh's faith. He is led to reflect on
the nature of the early Church:

I saw the Church of the first century as a dark and
hidden thing, as dark and hidden as the seed germinating
in the womb; legionaries off duty slipping furtively out
of barracks, greeting each other by signs and passwords
in a locked upper room in the side street of some Mediterranean seaport; slaves at dawn creeping from the grey
twilight into the candle-lit, smoky chapels of the cata-
combs. The priests hid their office, practising trades;
their identity was known only to initiates; they were
criminals against the law of their country. [*RP* 88]

It is not difficult in the light of this to understand why
Waugh should have been drawn to a figure like Edmund
Campion. The martyr's brief career was charged with just
this sort of drama: the hostile town, the hasty departure,
the secret Mass at dawn — such features are the life of Waugh's
biography. And it is to images of this kind that Guy Crouchback turns from his lonely station in Italy.

Often he wished that he lived in penal times when
Broome had been a solitary outpost of the Faith,

---

[8] *Maria Cross: Imaginative Patterns in a Group of Modern Catholic Writers*, p. 120.

surrounded by aliens. Sometimes he imagined himself
serving the last mass for the last Pope in a catacomb at
the end of the world. [*MA* 16]

In one form or another it is a recurrent fantasy. 'Oh for
persecution,' Waugh writes in his diary, baffled by his remoteness from sanctity.

But religion does not provide an untrammelled context for
this mode of response. The images from *Remote People*
belong to the early stages of Waugh's writing. By the time of
the *Sword of Honour* trilogy they are subject to a sharp edge
of criticism. Guy's reveries are part of the general romanticism that misleads him into a dangerous confusion of values.
He takes a political war to be a modern crusade and in
salving his wounded pride imagines himself to be serving
the cause of honour. These are attitudes of which he is gradually divested by the progress of the war. It is acknowledged
in *Unconditional Surrender* that religious faith may sometimes have to be expressed in the least stylish of gestures. The
acceptance of Trimmer's child and the half-botched attempt
to rescue the Jews constitute Waugh's most direct repudiation of religious romanticism. As far back as *A Handful of
Dust*, it was clear that Christianity, though it might accommodate romantic fantasy, was also to some extent a critique
of it. The battlements of Tony's City have fallen precisely
because its form is that of Hetton; it is the city of romanticism rather than the City of God.

The development from one to the other is the theme of
the early chapters of *Helena*. At the outset the heroine identifies herself with Helen of Troy; her quest will be a romantic
one: 'When I am educated I shall go and find the real Troy
— Helen's.' [*H* 15] And later, when Troy had been replaced
by Rome and she is going off with Constantius, she is still
the heroine of romance — '"Was it thus," she wondered,
rinsing her scaly fingers in a bucket of sea-water and drying
them in her lap, "was it thus, perhaps, that Paris brought his
stolen queen to Ilium?"' [*H* 35] But the romanticism is
already being tempered by the coarseness of the accompany-
ing image. When, on the way to Nish, she studies the road
'so smoothly metalled, so straight, so devious, that led to

Nish, to Rome, and whither beyond', the turn of her
thoughts is no longer purely romantic; the intimation that
her road might lead to a City which lies beyond even Rome
is a passing glance towards a journey that is spiritual.

Before they reach Ratisbon, she asks Constantius about
the wall that marks the boundary of the civilized world. His
reply is a heartfelt affirmation of romantic conservatism:

> Think of it, mile upon mile, from snow to desert, a
> single great girdle round the civilized world; inside,
> peace, decency, the law, the altars of the Gods, indus-
> try, the arts, order; outside, wild beasts and savages,
> forest and swamp, bloody mumbo-jumbo, men like
> wolf-packs; and along the wall the armed might of the
> Empire, sleepless, holding the line. Doesn't it make you
> see what The City means? [H 39]

This is the language that Waugh himself might have used in
another context; it is the language he did use in such books
as *Remote People* and *Robbery Under Law*. Civilization
is figured as a city under constant threat which can be
preserved from the irruption of barbarism only by uncompromising vigilance. This has always been Waugh's vision,
and in the main it continues to be; but just here it is ques-
tioned. Helena is reluctant to accept that this must always
be the case. Will Rome never go beyond the wall,

> into the wild lands? Beyond the Germans, beyond the
> Ethiopians, beyond the Picts, perhaps beyond the ocean
> there may be more people and still more, until, perhaps,
> you might travel through them all and find yourself
> back in The City again. Instead of the barbarian break-
> in, might The City one day break out? [H 39]

This is a crucial speech, for it marks the point at which the
romantic ideal of The City is displaced by the religious one.
The new vision is not without its own romanticism, but the
emotion has been modified; the old image of embattlement
must now be adjusted to a concept of The City in which even
Trimmer's son might have a place.

There is no room in *Unconditional Surrender* for the sort of crusading romanticism with which Guy had taken up arms at the start of the war, but it would be false to suggest that Waugh's faith has simply made terms with an unromantic world. The portrait of Guy's father would be enough to discredit this idea. A sober, almost colourless figure, Mr Crouchback has nothing striking to recommend him to us. His life has been without public drama and his sufferings have not been heroic. Waugh emphasizes his apparent ordinariness. For a religious hero he is as strange a successor to Edmund Campion as one could imagine. And this is the point. A man like Campion who could stand with Sir Philip Sidney and Don John of Austria had need of supernatural grace to be a Christian hero, but he was already a romantic one. In Mr Crouchback it is impossible to separate the two; the romantic and the religious elements are identical. Devoid of heroic attributes, he is luminous with a deep religious romanticism. There is nothing he can do or say that does not reflect his sanctity.

After his funeral Guy goes into the front court at Broome and notes that despite all the vicissitudes to which both house and family have been subject, the lamp in the chapel is still burning. The image is one that takes us back through *Brideshead Revisited* to that earlier image in *Remote People* of the 'little radiant points of learning and decency' that were brought into being by the first Christian missions in Europe. The tone has changed, all sorts of qualification have had to be taken into account, but a basic romanticism survives, still directing our attention away from the grim 'realities' of the world around us, still, however soberly, finding expression in the same religious image.

The continued burning of the lamp is a symbol of God's providence, but it is also a testament to the continuance of men's faith. This, on a human level, is its affirmation. In spite of all that works to undermine belief, men go on believing. The light in the chapel is what is left when families have been dispersed, relationships destroyed, and great houses have fallen into decline. When everything that can be said to the disadvantage or discredit of religion has been said, that is what remains: the endurance of the Faith.

But if this image of fidelity is important to Waugh, it is so
because the disadvantages are real to him. One reason why
the miracles in *Brideshead Revisited* and *Helena* tend to jar
on us is that they smack of an evasiveness that is uncharac-
teristic; they seem to be claiming exemption from just the
sort of scrutiny that Waugh is at other times rigorous in
applying. When Guy Crouchback determines, like Moses,
to lead the Jews up out of captivity, there are no answering
miracles. He is Moses with cuckold's horns, and the sea does
not divide. That God should choose not to intervene is
noted by Waugh.

He did not, any more than Milton, conceive of his religion
as a faith necessarily congenial to average human standards.
Ryder is clearly right in his intuition that it is Catholicism
that stands between him and Sebastian; he may also be right
when he says to Brideshead, 'It seems to me that without
your religion Sebastian would have the chance to be a happy
and healthy man.' [*BR* 140] But 'happy' and 'healthy' refer
to values that are human rather than divine. Sebastian's
religion imposes standards of judgement that transcend the
human ones, and when the two are in conflict, it is the
former that must command allegiance. A. E. Dyson's com-
plaint that 'the notion of a God who sets an absolute wedge
between the best in human love, and Himself, is in no way
challenged by Julia',[9] makes perfect sense in human terms;
we have every right to feel outraged. But this is not, as
Dyson's criticism implies, something that Waugh fails to
recognize; it is central to the conception of Christianity
that he presents in the novel. The demands of religion may
not be attractive, they may indeed run counter to what is
attractive — to the claims of both social charm and human
affection — but they are none the less absolute.

The person of Brideshead is a powerful representation of
the difficulties this can involve. Alone among the principal
characters, he displays a commitment to his religion that is
unswerving; yet he, of all of them, is most lacking in charm.
'He's all twisted inside,' Sebastian explains when Brideshead
first appears. 'He wanted to be a priest, you know.' [*BR* 85]

[9] 'Evelyn Waugh and the Mysteriously Disappearing Hero'.

Time and again his social and moral awkwardness is thrust upon us. It is not just that he collects matchboxes, talks without wit, and marries a woman like Beryl Muspratt; there is behind all this a rebarbative rigidity of principle which, however offensive it may be, is the product of his religion. He shocks the reader as much as the narrator by his calmly expressed hope that Sebastian be suffering from dipsomania rather than just a wilful fondness for drink. The latter, it is true, would be a sin, whereas the former is no more than a misfortune, but Ryder is likely to carry the reader with him when he replies: 'D'you know, Bridey, if I ever felt for a moment like becoming a Catholic, I should only have to talk to you for five minutes to be cured.' [BR 158-9] It as though Brideshead's religion blocks out a whole area of human sensibility. He is, for example, quite unable to understand why Ryder or Julia should be upset by his bland refusal, on the grounds that the two of them are living in sin, to bring Beryl on a visit to the house.

There is a comparable scene in *Men at Arms* when Guy, having discovered that the laws of the Church still entitle him to sex with Virginia, eagerly sets out to take advantage of the fact. Her reaction might have been predicted by anyone but Guy himself:

> 'It's absolutely disgusting. It's worse than anything Augustus or Mr Troy could ever dream of. Can't you see, you pig, you?'
> 'No,' said Guy in deep, innocent sincerity. 'No, I don't see.' [MA 132-3]

Virginia has to explain:

> 'I thought you'd taken a fancy for me again and wanted a bit of fun for the sake of old times. I thought you'd chosen me specially, and by God you had. Because I was the only woman in the whole world your priests would let you go to bed with. That was my attraction. You wet, smug, obscene, pompous, sexless lunatic pig.' [MA 132-3]

The condemnation leaves Guy floundering; he had been doing no more than abide by the dictates of his religion. That Waugh should be willing to subject him to a humiliation of this kind, and for this reason, is a daring stroke of honesty.

Near the beginning of *Officers and Gentlemen*, the Cuthberts, perplexed by Mr Crouchback's unselfishness, can only explain it by concluding that 'Somehow his mind seems to work different than yours and mine.' [*OG* 38] This is as it should be: Mr Crouchback is a Christian. But one of Waugh's strengths is his refusal to claim that this difference is always a comfortable one; Brideshead's insensitivity and Guy's obtuseness with Virginia spring from the same difference.

Waugh does not generally load the dice in favour of Catholicism. The only other Catholic officer at Kut-al-Imara is Hemp, 'the Trimmer of the Depot'; the priest to whom Guy confesses in *Officers and Gentlemen* turns out to be a traitor; in *Men at Arms* the Catholic priest at the Halberdiers' local church is an unappetizing graduate from Maynooth, interested only in his capitation grant. Catholics are given no monopoly of virtue, and Catholicism itself is in no way presented as a convenient option. It may be true that Waugh's religion fulfils certain escapist needs, but it has none of the blandness of conventional religious escapism. The existence of Hell, for example, far from being a stumbling block, was a doctrine he accepted with enthusiasm.[10] From the start he was unafraid to subject the external forms of his religion to a degree of irony, and he obstinately declined to pass over those features which, by purely human criteria, might render it repulsive. Dyson is probably in agreement with the majority of non-Catholic readers in finding something distasteful about a God who so intransigently demands the sacrifice of human love.[11] But in taking this as a ground for criticism, he is, I think, making the same mistake as those who criticize *Mansfield Park* for the way in which Mary Crawford is displaced by Fanny Price. Jane Austen was as sensitive as Waugh to the attractions of wit, grace and style; like him, she gave them their full value in the novel, but then, like him, she subordinated them

[10] Cf. Christopher Sykes, *Evelyn Waugh: A Biography*, p. 440.
[11] 'Evelyn Waugh and the Mysteriously Disappearing Hero'.

ruthlessly to the demands of a higher principle. Both writers
are fully aware how unattractive are certain aspects of what
they recommend and how attractive are the corresponding
aspects of what they sacrifice. It is a measure of their moral
toughness that they do little to disguise the inclemency of
their commitment.

To take the argument further would be misleading. The
externals of Waugh's religion are tested by his irony and its
principles by his sense of social and emotional style. This
much is true, and in neither case is the result entirely one-
sided: the outward forms can give rise to absurdity, the dogmas
to ugliness and inhumanity. Having said this, however, we
must at once admit that by far the most searching questions
go in the other direction; it is Waugh's irony and his sense of
style that are tested by his religion. This is a theme that has
already been taken up in the first two chapters, but its implications are not confined to the effect this process had on the
tone of Waugh's novels or the sources of their humour. The
influence of his religion entailed readjustments of a far more
radical kind. These must be the subject of the final section.

To the reader whose image of Waugh has been formed on the
popular notion of a blimpish figure bristling with prejudices
of race and class, the story we considered earlier will have
had at least one unexpected feature: the priest whose words
bring comfort to Rip amid the chaos is black. Waugh is
simultaneously manipulating two levels of response here.
On one hand, the substitution of blacks for whites as the
dominant race is perceived as a monstrous inversion, the
shockingness of which depends on an unquestioned assumption of white superiority. On the other hand, this assumption,
along with any other sort of social value, melts into nothing
before the transcendent reality of shared religious faith. The
climax of the story undermines exactly the prejudices which
have been made use of in the approach to it. Black man or
white — Waugh's Catholicism demolishes the secular norms
that makes such distinctions seem important.

In view of the frequency with which he is decried as a
racist, the point is worth stressing. It could be supported
from elsewhere. A few years later, in *Robbery Under Law*, he
was affirming the equality before God of the native Indians
at the great shrine of Guadalupe. 'All the limitless variety of
the Church seemed to be represented there,' he says with
evident approval. 'No doubt there were also "members of
the *genus puplex*" [12] but it did not seem the least important.'
[*RL* 234-5] Ash Wednesday in New Orleans was another
occasion on which Waugh found himself among a promis-
cuous crowd of worshippers. At the Jesuit church across the
road from his hotel there was a 'continuous, dense crowd of
all colours and conditions':

> all that day, all over that light-hearted city, one en-
> countered the little black smudge on the forehead
> which sealed us members of a great brotherhood who
> can both rejoice and recognize the limits of rejoicing.
> [*LOr* 171-3]

It is in the same essay, 'The American Epoch in the Catholic Church', that he speaks of the inspiration afforded by 'the
heroic fidelity of the negro Catholics', concluding his tribute
with the words, 'honour must never be neglected to those
thousands of coloured Catholics who so accurately traced
their Master's road amid insult and injury.' The inhabitants
of Azania were not the only blacks who had a place in
Waugh's scheme of things. This is a different language from
that of the early novels and its generous tone is the gift of
his religion. As he grew older, the erosion of this particular
prejudice became more complete. The reader of *A Tourist
in Africa* finds himself listening to a voice of tolerant disenchantment. There is no question of being scandalized by
apartheid, but no question either of treating it with anything
but disdain.

Thirty years earlier Waugh had noted in his diary a visit to
the Savoy theatre where he saw the last two acts of Robeson's

---

[12] This is a contemptuous echo of a phrase used by T. Philip Terry in his *Guide
to Mexico*. Waugh scouts his distaste for the Indian pilgrims.

Othello. 'Hopeless production,' he comments, 'but I like his great black booby face. It seemed to make all that silly stuff with the handkerchief quite convincing.' [*Diaries* 311] Even when he made the entry, Waugh was probably well enough aware of Robeson's stature, but the maintaining of a certain tone — especially at this time, just after the breakup of his marraige — was more important than the recording of an accurate judgement. No such necessity is felt in *A Tourist in Africa*. 'What a part for Mr Paul Robeson could be written of his doom,' he remarks of Lobengula, having just compared him to the great figures of Shakespearean tragedy. The comment is purely respectful.

Of all Waugh's works this journal of his last visit to Africa gives the impression of being the closest to whatever lay behind the Pinfold persona. Perhaps this was one of the reasons why Waugh, according to Christopher Sykes, regarded it with shame. The strategies of defence which are the subject of this study seem to have been set aside. It is a book that lacks the enamelled finish of most of Waugh's writing; his guard seems temporarily to have dropped.

The extent of the change is indicated by his response to those who speak of the Europeans as having 'pacified' Africa: 'and a generation which has seen the Nazi regime in the heart of Europe had best stand silent when civilized and uncivilized nations are contrasted' [*TA* 151]. The old certainty of racial and cultural superiority has been deeply undermined. Waugh now stands silent where earlier he would have been sharply partisan. And his reason for this must give us pause. The rise of the Nazi regime is apparently not something from which his generation can totally dissociate itself. Though they fought against it, the menace was for all that a product of their own civilization. The silence that Waugh enjoins is an admission, not of guilt, or even complicity, but of implication; it is, in other words, a recognition of ties which would previously have been denied.

This tone and the attitudes it expresses can be largely credited to the transforming influence of Waugh's religion. It would never have occurred to Constantius to think of the wall as other than an absolute dividing line. Within it are the members of The City, on the far side the barbarians. It takes

Helena to perceive that in the end everyone might belong to the same community: 'I meant,' she explains to Constantius, 'couldn't the wall be at the limits of the world and all men, civilized and barbarian, have a share in The City?' Though she is not yet a Christian, she is here expressing a Christian conception of The City.

It is not the sort of outlook that is generally attributed to Waugh. If there is an accusation levelled at him more frequently than that of racism, it is the charge of class snobbery. Far from seeing in his religion any attenuation of this trait, critics have tended to find just the reverse — a direct expression of it. A standard version of this criticism was aired by Charles Rolo in a foolish article for *Atlantic Monthly*. The Catholicism in Waugh's fiction, he asserts, 'is so inextricably bound up with worship of the ancient British nobility...that the Church is made to appear a particularly exclusive club rather than a broad spiritual force'.[13] The theme became tedious to Waugh. Six years later, in a letter to *Encounter*, rebuking Frank Kermode for a similar imputation, he quoted the passage from *Helena* that describes her reaction to the Roman mob. It is worth setting down in full:

'*Odi profanum volgus et arceo*.' That was an echo from the old empty world. There was no hate in her now and nothing round her was quite profane. She could not dispense with her guard but she mitigated their roughness, and always her heart was beyond them, over their big shoulders, in the crowd. When she heard Mass at the Lateran basilica — as she often did in preference to her private chapel — she went without ostentation and stood simply in the congregation. She was in Rome as a pilgrim and she was surrounded by friends. There was no way of telling them. There was nothing in their faces. A Thracian or a Teuton might stop a fellow countryman in the streets, embrace him and speak of home in his own language. Not so Helena and the Christians. The intimate family circle of which she was a member bore no mark of kinship. The barrow-man grilling his garlic

---

[13] 'Evelyn Waugh: The Best and the Worst'.

sausages in the gutter, the fuller behind his reeking
public pots, the lawyer or the lawyer's clerk, might
each and all be one with the Empress Dowager in the
Mystical Body. And the abounding heathen might in
any hour become one with them. There was no mob,
only a vast multitude of souls, clothed in a vast variety
of body, milling about in the Holy City, in the See of
Peter. [*H* 92-3]

To someone more reflective than Mr Rolo such an uncompromising statement might have seemed worth pausing over.
So far from being confined to a particular group, Waugh's
concept of the Christian community is quite explicitly inclu-
sive of all kinds and conditions of men, and the point is made
still more emphatic by contrasting this with the old ideas of
exclusivity which the new order has replaced. As the passages
already quoted from *Robbery Under Law* and 'The American
Epoch in the Catholic Church' confirm, there was nothing
random about these sentiments in *Helena*; Waugh had considered the implications of his religion and he was prepared
to accept them.

This is not, of course, to imply that Waugh's is in any sense
a socialist Christianity. The distinction between society and
the Mystical Body is fundamental to his thinking. To say
'equal before God' is not to say 'equal before man'. Within
the structure of a society that is properly hierarchical differences of class exist and are valued; uniformity, as Waugh
emphasizes in *The Loved One*, is the hallmark of sterility
and death. But in the context of Roman Catholicism these
differences of category sink into insignificance; the common
man ceases to be an object of revilement and becomes an
equal participant in the community of the Church.

This argument can only explain so much. The fact remains
that though Helena may have enjoyed mingling with the
crowd, Waugh himself did not. There were times – Ash
Wednesday in New Orleans, perhaps, or Christmas in Goa –
when he too could experience his heroine's feeling of exulta-
tion in Christian brotherhood, but on the whole his preference
would have been for the private chapel rather than the
Lateran basilica. (Indeed, he was intriguing to get his own

private chapel in the year the book was published.[14]) Mr
Pinfold places himself unyieldingly on the side of the old
order that Helena feels to have been superseded:

> And at the very time when the leaders of his Church
> were exhorting their people to emerge from the cata-
> combs into the forum, to make their influence felt in
> democratic politics and to regard worship as a corporate
> rather than a private act, Mr Pinfold burrowed ever
> deeper into the rock. Away from his parish he sought
> the least frequented Mass; at home he held aloof from
> the multifarious organizations which have sprung into
> being at the summons of the hierarchy to redeem the
> times. [GP 13]

And Guy Crouchback. 'Even in his religion,' we are told,
'he felt no brotherhood....He never went to communion
on Sundays, slipping into Church, instead, very early on
weekdays when few others were about.' [MA 16] The conclusion must surely be that while Helena's attitude may
represent an ideal, the responses of Pinfold and Crouchback
come closer to the author's own experience. 'I postponed my
own veneration,' Waugh notes of his visit to the shrine of St
Francis Xavier, 'until I could make it more privately.'
[Diaries 705]
    In one sense Waugh's willingness to put forward an ideal
that is so patently at odds with his own disposition is another
instance of that fairness which was referred to earlier. He was
aware of the demands of his Faith and aware, too, of how far
he fell short of meeting them; but no tenderness towards his
own feelings led him to minimize the gap. There is a scene in
Men at Arms when Guy intervenes in a dispute between
Halberdier Glass and a Goanese steward[15] on board the
troopship at Liverpool. As evidence of his Christianity, the
Goanese produces a gold medal he wears round his neck.

[14] Cf. letter to Nancy Mitford, 15 April 1950 [Letters 323].
[15] That the steward should be Goanese is given particular relevance by Waugh's
response to the Christmas he spent in Goa. (Cf. the letter to Laura Waugh quoted
above, p. 153).

Guy's heart suddenly opened towards him. Here was his own kin. He yearned to show the medal he wore, Gervase's souvenir from Lourdes. There were men who would have done exactly that, better men than he; who would perhaps have said 'Snap' and drawn a true laugh from the sullen Halberdier and so have made true peace between them. [*MA* 219]

But instead Guy gives the man two half-crowns, 'and the Goanese turned and went on his way rejoicing a little, but not as a fellow man at peace; merely as a servant unexpectedly over-tipped'. This is just another small failure to add to Guy's list, but it is specifically a failure to acknowledge fellowship in religion, and Guy recognizes it as such.

To have a religious ideal always before one and always to be conscious of how far one falls short of it is a constant invitation to doubt and self-questioning. On the night of the Ensa show at the Halberdier barracks Guy lies in bed reviewing the various failures of the day — his conclusion: 'There was much to repent and repair.' [*MA* 57] The phrase is striking for what it suggests about Guy as a hero. The nightly examination of conscience which he was taught to make in his youth could hardly be further from Waugh's accustomed stance of 'never apologize, never explain'; yet this is a character in whom the author has clearly invested much of himself. The Pinfold persona must be treated with caution; 'hard, bright, and antiquated as a cuirass', it is only a partial representation of the figure behind it. What it conceals is the process of self-questioning that began with John Plant and culminates in the portrayal of Guy Crouchback.

Occasionally a hairline split will show in the Pinfold defences. Waugh's diary entry for 29 July 1947 records events with untypical hesitancy. It was the day of a ball given by Daphne Bath:

After dinner the men shout at one another over the brandy. I do not shout but am I becoming supercilious? to my host? to an American journalist named Forbes? Guilt is beginning as my memory grows feeble....I sat with people — Debo, Venetia, who else? — for long

periods. Were they bored by me? I kissed people — Liz
and Liza, Angie and Clarissa, Daphne and Kitty; who
else? Did they like it? I became captious of people I
did not know. Were my strictures well received? [*Diaries*
683-4]

There is much in the same tone. The questions are presented
as an intellectual puzzle, but they have the ring of something
considerably more personal.

Other episodes in the later part of Waugh's life confirm
this. There is, for example, the story Christopher Sykes tells
of Waugh's sudden fear that he had behaved badly to a BBC
man to whom he had given a signed copy of one of his books
— 'How did I know that he wanted it? He may think I'm a
very bad writer indeed. I acted presumptuously. When he gets
back to Bristol he'll tell his fellow-electricians that he met a
conceited beast who fancied himself as the local squire and
behaved in an odiously patronizing way to him.'[16] Another
incident mentioned by Sykes, and also recorded in the diary,
is the rumour he got wind of that the Governor of Trinidad
and his wife had found him tedious during his stay with
them. Four years afterwards he could still be troubled by
the thought: 'I went to bed at 9 o'clock,' he writes to Ann
Fleming, 'and brooded about Buchan-Hepburn finding me a
bore. I have not been the same since that revelation.' [*Letters*
636] Again it seems that Waugh had reacted with exaggerated sensitivity.

These matters are trivial, but the questions they raise are
the same ones that were posed, more aggressively, by Pinfold's
voices. Cumulatively they suggest a vein of self-doubt that is
in contrast to the much publicized facade with which Waugh
confronted the world. And this self-doubt is in the end a
product of his religion — more precisely, of the gap between
the religious ideal he acknowledged and the kind of person he
knew himself to be. Anyone who can conceive of Mr Crouchback and yet portray himself as Mr Pinfold will have much to
repent and repair.

Part of Waugh's reparation is, I take it, contained in

[16] *Evelyn Waugh: A Biography*, p. 586.

Unconditional Surrender. In his recension of the trilogy
Waugh deprives Guy of the children which in the earlier
version had been the issue of his second marriage. The point
of this, according to Laura Waugh,[17] was to make it quite
clear that his marriage to Domenica Plessington was moti-
vated purely by generosity towards the child of Trimmer and
Virginia. This may well involve problems of its own; it is
unlikely to make Guy seem more attractive to us. It does,
none the less, stand as a powerful affirmation of those sentiments which had been expressed by Helena eleven years
earlier: The City has opened its gates to the barbarian. In
Unconditional Surrender her words are for the first time
given substance. There is not much joy left, but nor is there
much rancour. In this one area, Waugh's fiction has fallen
into step with his non-fiction.

Behind it, however, there is still a concept of escape. In
1945 Waugh had been told of the plight of Moray McLaren,
a Catholic writer, who for the last five years of the war had
been Head of Polish Region Political Intelligence Dept.
Like Guy Crouchback, and indeed like Waugh himself, he
had been obliged, in Sykes's words, 'to watch and to act as
an agent in what he took to be the betrayal of principles,
and the betrayal of people who had received solemn British
promises of support'.[18] At the end of the war he suffered
something akin to a nervous breakdown, abandoning his
religion and seeking refuge in drink. Waugh set out to help
him back to his career as a writer and was succesful. But the
first priority was McLaren's religion. Sykes puts it thus,
revealingly: '[Waugh's] immediate object was to rekindle
his faith, the only possible form of rescue, he insisted, from
the deadly sin of despair.'[19]

It is the same conviction that underpins the final volume
of *Sword of Honour.* Throughout the trilogy Guy has been
shown embracing specious antidotes to reality. His seclusion
in Italy, his love affair with the army, his romanticism about
the war, his nostalgia for the past — they lead only to the

---

[17] Cf. Gene D. Phillips, *Evelyn Waugh's Officers, Gentlemen and Rogues: The Fact behind his Fiction*, p. 137.
[18] *Evelyn Waugh: A Biography*, p. 390.
[19] Ibid., p. 391.

Death Wish of *Unconditional Surrender*. In his acceptance of
Trimmer's child and his efforts to save the Jews in Jugoslavia,
Guy finally assumes the burden of his Faith. And with it the
consolations. The despair from which this rescues him is a
temptation that, more than any other, beset Waugh himself.
When the *Sunday Times* featured a series of articles on 'The
Seven Deadly Sins', he chose to write on 'Sloth':

> Man is made for joy in the love of God, a love which he
> expresses in service. If he deliberately turns away from
> that joy, he is denying the purpose of his existence.
> The malice of Sloth lies not merely in the neglect of
> duty (though that can be a symptom of it) but in the
> refusal of joy. It is allied to despair.

This is the sin that lay in Waugh's road. The shifts by which
he has tried from the start to hold reality at bay are in
essence stratagems to avoid despair. Despair of life is despair
of the love of God. The conclusion is inevitable and it has
already been drawn: from that deadly sin, faith is the only
possible form of rescue.

6

'Experience Totally Transformed'

I must try to justify the hypothesis that was my starting point. Although the patterns I have traced in Waugh's writing exist independently of any argument about his motivation, it was nonetheless an argument of this kind that prompted my interest in them. I have assumed throughout a particular relationship between Waugh's life and his work. On what evidence?

A year or two before he died, Waugh gave an interview to Kenneth Allsop. 'I suppose,' he said towards the end of it, 'when one has ceased having experiences, one can draw upon one's gifts and spin yarns artificially.'[1] It is evidently a course he would take up with reluctance; his fiction, he implies, grows more naturally with its roots in personal experience. When war broke out in 1939, not the least of his reasons for wishing to be on active service rather than behind a desk was the stimulus it would afford him as a writer, and when, after four years, his enthusiasm had waned, he expressed his disaffection in similar terms: 'I want to get to work again. I do not want any more experiences in life. I have quite enough bottled and carefully laid in the cellar, some still ripening, most ready for drinking, a little beginning to lose its body.' [*Diaries* 548] The notion of experience as a precious and expendable commodity is one to which Waugh returns. What enriches Dennis Barlow at the end of *The Loved One* is 'the artist's load, a great, shapeless chunk of experience' [*LO* 127]; and a few years later the urgent business that draws Mr Pinfold away from his current story is 'a hamper to be unpacked of fresh, rich experience — perishable goods' [*GP* 157].

[1] Kenneth Allsop, 'Pinfold at Home'.

Experience, then, was for Waugh the writer's capital, and he was resourceful in making use of his own. There are areas of his life which a diligent reader can follow through three or four different incarnations. It is a life that falls readily into periods, boldly distinguished from one another by the vigour with which Waugh played his adopted roles. Anthony Powell writes of him as 'in his way, an extraordinarily uncomplicated man'. This simplicity was particularly evident, according to Powell, in his attitude to social life: 'He really did believe in entities like a "great nobleman", "poor scholar", "literary man of modest means".'[2] It was in terms of such entities that Waugh identified himself. The traditional roles of socialite, traveller, man-at-arms, country gentleman, imposed certain theatrical obligations which he did his best to fulfil.

Each of these roles corresponds to a stage in his life, and each of them is refracted through various literary forms. The activities of the Bright Young People, for example, were the stuff of contemporary gossip columns as well as the basic material for *Vile Bodies*; on one level they were part of the daily life Waugh recorded in his diary, on another they were the subject of a good deal of his early journalism. Similarly, if we turn to his experiences in Africa, there is a recognizable trail to be followed from the diary to the travel books to the novels. And again, when we come to the war trilogy, the relationship between fiction and reality can be more than conjectural; here too we have the evidence of Waugh's journal as well as the accounts of several of those who served with him.

There is, in other words, a considerable amount of documentary material about the sources of Waugh's novels — though he himself was often reluctant to admit as much. 'Pure fiction,' he insists in the prefatory note to *Officers and Gentlemen*. The story, we must understand, is 'of experience totally transformed'. More elliptically, he had made the same point in the author's note to *Brideshead Revisited*: 'I am not I: thou art not he or she: they are not they.' And yet they clearly are they and equally clearly *Officers and Gentlemen*

[2] *Messengers of Day*, p. 20.

is not, by any normal definition, 'pure fiction'.

The space that lies between a writer's life and his work is a no man's land in which the psychoanalyst is likely to achieve more than the literary critic; it is mined with uncertainties. In Waugh's case, however, the sort of documentation I have mentioned at least reduces the purely speculative element in any attempt to bridge the gap. As long as we can point to the evidence of intermediary stages between the experience and its embodiment in fiction, we are not moving entirely in a void.

The range of possible material is wide. *Decline and Fall* opens with a meeting of what is obviously a fictional version of the Bullingdon Club, *Unconditional Surrender* closes with a commando reunion in what is no less obviously a fictional version of White's Club. Between the two there is not a novel that is not studded with personal reminiscences. Sometimes it is no more than a name: Philbrick, Cruttwell, Blount, Hooper, Apthorpe and the like — names remembered from the school notice-board or the college lodge and later pressed into service. More often it will be an incident — the encounter with a madman in South America,[3] the haphazard delivery of telegrams in Abyssinia, the scene at a friend's death-bed during the war.[4] It might be a place — a hotel in London, a German guest house in Addis Ababa,[5] a burial ground in California — or a person, like Diana Cooper or Mrs Graham.[6] Sometimes it was a whole section of his life that found its way into the fiction, as in the case of his years at Oxford or in the army. The list of echoes and parallels could be indefinitely drawn out. A reading of the diaries, letters and

[3] Cf. the description of Mr Christie in *Ninety-Two Days* and Mr Todd in *A Handful of Dust*.
[4] Hubert Duggan's death-bed scene (1943) inspired Lord Marchmain's in *Brideshead Revisited*.
[5] Cf. the Deutsches Haus where Waugh stayed when he was reporting the Italian–Abyssinian war and the Pension Dressler in *Scoop*.
[6] The mother of Waugh's friend Alastair Graham was a source for Lady Circumference in *Decline and Fall*.

travel books throws up page after page of comparable references. To catalogue them all would be very dull. What follow
are no more than the handful that seem most readily to lend
themselves to my argument.

From the start Waugh viewed his experience with an
artist's eye. 'For eighteen happy months I taught the young,'
[*LOr* 28] he wrote in a survey of his early life for *Nash's
Pall Mall Magazine.* He actually taught the young for something like twenty-seven months and, as far as one can tell,
they were anything but happy. He was a schoolmaster first
at Arnold House, then at Aston Clinton, finally for a term
in Notting Hill. 'I have been too sad & weary to write anything,'[7] he tells Acton after a few weeks at Arnold House.
And at the beginning of the second term his tone is unchanged: 'I think that my finances have never been so desperate or my spirits so depressed.' [*Diaries* 211] This is one
of many notes in his diary that express a similar mood. The
entries that mark his early days at Aston Clinton are not
unfairly resumed by Christopher Sykes as a 'long monotonous
record of drunkenness and drunken quarrels, of vomitings,
hangovers, and so on...'.[8]

Altogether it was a messy sort of reality. In the elegant
self-portrait that he was in the process of sketching it could
have no place. Waugh simply tidied it up, as he would have
done if he had been writing a piece of fiction — as he did
again when he came to write his autobiography. In *A Little
Learning* it is the period at Aston Clinton that is implicitly
ignored, and for much the same reasons. After describing
the suicide attempt, he concludes with the words: 'Then
I climbed the sharp hill that led to all the years ahead.'
[*LL* 220] It creates a satisfying image: on the threshold of
manhood the young Waugh tears up his suicide note and
turns to meet the demands of a new life. Just so, in the
cemetery of Père Lachaise, Balzac's hero, Rastignac, had
shed the last tear of his youth and turned to face the lights
of the city. The sentence breathes a resolution tempered by

---

[7] Letter written in February 1925 [*Letters* 22]. The reference is to letter-writing,
not to literary composition.
[8] *Evelyn Waugh: A Biography*, p. 101.

the elegiac perspective of old age. There would be struggles and set-backs, but the young man who has emerged from this baptism of despair is steeled to survive them. He is fulfilling a classic pattern. In this handsome conclusion Waugh has pardonably re-ordered the ensuing months of his life. If the climbing of the hill is to be symbol as well as narrative, then the prospect from the top can hardly include drunken days at Aston Clinton and a depressing term at the Notting Hill crammer. Considerations of aesthetic propriety have shifted his account a small but perceptible distance away from autobiography towards fiction.

It is noteworthy that this, the period of Waugh's blackest depression, should also be the period that generated the funniest episodes of *Decline and Fall*. Many of the details Waugh caught up and translated into his novel have no doubt passed unrecorded, but the diaries and the autobiography do afford us a glimpse of the material on which his fantasy worked. It is instructive to compare the figure of Young as he appeared in Waugh's diary with his later incarnation as Captain Grimes. Waugh notes his presence at the beginning of the summer term, 1925, and mentions a few days later that he has been negotiating 'with the man Young' to buy a revolver — presumably with thoughts of suicide already in his mind. Only two references in this part of the diary give any further information. On 14 May: 'Young, the new usher, is monotonously pederastic and talks only of the beauty of sleeping boys.' [*Diaries* 211] Then on 3 July:

> Young and I went out and made ourselves drunk and he confessed all his previous career. He was expelled from Wellington, sent down from Oxford, and forced to resign his commission in the army. He has left four schools precipitately, three in the middle of the term through his being taken in sodomy and one through his being drunk six nights in succession. And yet he goes on getting better and better jobs without difficulty. It was all very like Bruce and the spider. [*Diaries* 213]

Several months later Young makes a brief reappearance while Waugh is at Aston Clinton. Having mentioned his arrival on

26 March, Waugh records on All Fools Day 1926: 'Young of Denbighshire came down and was rather a bore — drunk all the time. He seduced a garage boy in the hedge.' [*Diaries* 250]

The salient features of Captain Grimes are plainly recognizable, but Waugh's response is less than enthusiastic. Though the revelations are acknowledged in the diary to be one of the things that have happened 'to comfort me a little', they have none of the comic radiance that informs the world of *Decline and Fall*. As Waugh puts it in *A Little Learning*: 'The catalogue was diverting rather than consoling.' [*LL* 219-20]

The Grimes who appears in the autobiography is an intermediate figure. He has been shorn of his less marketable characteristics; there is no suggestion here of a man who could conceivably be thought of as boring:

> Every disgrace had fallen on this irrepressible man; at school, at the university, in the army, and later in his dedicated task as schoolmaster; disgraces such as, one was told, make a man change his name and fly the kingdom; scandals so dark that they remained secrets at the scenes of his crimes. Headmasters were loath to admit that they had ever harboured such a villain and passed him on silently and swiftly. Grimes always emerged serenely triumphant. [*LL* 219]

Grimes is still, in this description, trailing some of the clouds of glory that marked him out in *Decline and Fall* as one of the immortals. Waugh's rhetoric urges him towards the borders of myth. This is a character quite different from the man who figures in the diaries; the stray references have been worked up into a humorous vignette that also functions as a counterpoint to the concluding description of the suicide attempt.

To say that the Grimes of *A Little Learning* has been worked upon is not to claim that his original in the diaries is somehow the true Grimes. How 'boring' did Waugh really find him, this man who had casually seduced a garage boy in the hedge? The word itself should put us on our guard.[9] Here too Grimes — or rather, Waugh's response to him — is being 'presented'. The diarist has modified his experience in characteristic style, accommodating it to what is in fact a fictional pose.

In the nature of things neither a diary nor an auto-biography can carry this process as far as a book that is avowedly a work of fiction. Grimes as he is reborn in *Decline and Fall* can have more than mortal powers. Con-siderably seedier than his original, he nonetheless trans-figures his setting. It is clear at once that in a world in which Grimes exists nothing can truly be serious. In this he is like Apthorpe, with the difference that at this stage the vein of fantasy is resilient enough to survive. What is recorded in the diaries as no more than a pleasant evening ('I promptly gave in my notice to the Banks family and made Gordon and Young and myself agreeably drunk at the Queen's Hotel' [*Diaries* 212]) becomes, with the sub-stitution of Grimes and Prendergast for the two ushers, an evening of inconsequential but inspiriting comedy, which culminates in Grimes's effort to juggle 'with a whacking great bottle and a lump of ice and two knives' [*DF* 104].

Absolved from the constraints of reality, the fictional character, unlike his counterpart, can be more than just 'diverting'. It is notable that when he disappears at the end of Part One his fake suicide should be a replica of Waugh's own unsuccessful venture a few years earlier. The sad, theatrical attempt has been turned to laughter. In 'the Agony of Captain Grimes' the devils have been exorcized. An improbable scapegoat, Grimes carries the burden lightly. Here, at least, is 'experience totally transformed'; the old despair has been resolved in a disreputable assertion of comic vitality. Reshaped by the writer's imagination, the drab world of the student schoolmaster has become a comic world, his distresses part of its comedy. *Decline and Fall* stands at the beginning of Waugh's fiction as an artful and attractive defiance of reality.

In his next novel, *Vile Bodies*, Waugh takes up those

---

[9] Cf. the earlier discussion of Waugh's use of it, pp. 10-12.

aspects of the social world of the twenties that are already slightly surreal and elevates them into total absurdity. Archie Schwert's Savage party not only ends up in 10 Downing Street but also results in the fall of the government; Lady Metroland's star guest becomes the focus of a scandal that involves everyone from the Archbishop of Canterbury to the Maharajah of Pukkapore; finally, the whole scene dissolves into a war which leaves Adam on the biggest battlefield of human history.

The battlefield, the party, the star guest have a clear origin in the social memory of the period. Even the later party in the captive dirigible owes its outlines to the whimsical habits of the time. In the year that *Vile Bodies* was published the *Daily Sketch*, in 'Echoes of the Town', carried a report of one such party held by the Bright Young People on 17 July. Parties of this kind were already fantasies; Waugh effects his transformation by releasing them from their moorings in reality. His denial that there was any model for Shepheard's Hotel exploits this element of unreality with bland disingenuousness:

> In order to avoid trouble I made it the most fantastic hotel I could devise. I filled it with an impossible clientèle, I invented an impossible proprietress. I gave it a fictitious address, I described its management as so eccentric and incompetent that no hotel could be run on their lines for a week without coming into the police or the bankruptcy court. Here at least, I thought, I was safely in the realm of pure imagination. [*LOr* 14]

All this is true; the hotel in *Vile Bodies* is fantastic, impossible, unrealistic. But the details which make it so are a comic embroidery beneath which the lines of the original are unmistakable. Waugh was of course aware of this and he could assert with equal truth in his 1965 Preface to the novel that it contained 'a pretty accurate description of Mrs Rosa Lewis and her Cavendish Hotel, just on the brink of their decline but still famous'. Shepheard's is both 'the most fantastic hotel I could devise' and at the same time 'a pretty accurate description'. The two conflicting statements reflect the ambiguous relationship between the experience and its fictional representation; reality is preserved but in a form that enjoys freedom from the sort of constraints that in life can be relied on to make it irksome or unremarkable.

The travel books are full of observations that are later transplanted to more fertile ground. The state of the road leading out to the British Legation in Addis Ababa, which Waugh merely noted in *Remote People*, becomes for Sir Samson Courteney the ground of a heart-breaking diplomatic saga that produces in the end only a heap of stones at the roadside, 'the monument to his single ineffective excursion into statesmanship' [*BM* 50]. It was on this trip, too, that Waugh first had close experience of the vagaries of his fellow journalists. The sort of strictures he makes on the reporting of Haile Selassie's coronation are taken up in greater detail when he goes back five years later to cover the Italian–Abyssinian war. These are the observations that come to life some time afterwards in his fiction. One of his colleagues, he tells us, 'waged a pretty little war in his hotel bedroom with flags and a large-scale map' [*WA* 212]. The hint is not thrown away; later Sir Jocelyn Hitchcock will practise a similar economy. The details noted in the travel books are only a shadow of the enhanced absurdities of *Scoop*. Corker, Wenlock Jakes, Sir Jocelyn and the rest have their origins in the real world of imaginative and highly paid foreign correspondents, but, like the proprietress of Shepheard's Hotel, they themselves exist in a world that has been shaped to the larger requirements of comic fantasy.

It is in the same manner that the character of Julia Stitch has emerged from the outlines of Diana Cooper. Again, her first appearance bears the stamp of a real incident. She is introduced in bed, abstractedly directing the affairs of the household, her face encased in clay. The germ of the episode can be found in Waugh's diaries. 'Message to call on Diana;' he noted in 1936, 'found her with face expressionless in mud mask.' [*Diaries* 391] The visit was not of great moment but the clay mask made enough impression to be worth recording. As an image that already existed on the edge of surrealism, it had a value to which the writer was sensitive. It was by means of such shreds of fantasy, wrested from the predictable texture of everyday life, that Waugh could pass most easily into the less fettered world of fiction.

Comic fantasy was not the only possibility. There were other forms of fantasy and other ways of shaping experience to his inclination. A reading of juvenile pieces such as 'The Balance' or 'Antony, Who Sought Things That Were Lost' supports the contention that Waugh's initial inspiration was as much romantic as comic. There is nothing to be gained by retracing the ground covered in the chapters on romanticism and nostalgia, but it is worth pausing for a moment over the nature of the evidence presented in them.

The relationship between Waugh's flights of romanticism or nostalgia and the actual experiences they idealize is an elusive one. The essence of these emotions is intangible. Waugh's years at Oxford acquired in memory a golden haze which, precisely because it is so subjective, defies any attempt to relate it to verifiable circumstances. We cannot turn back to the Oxford of the early twenties and say, 'Just here and here he shades the truth; this friendship was more flawed than he remembers, that summer afternoon less bright.' We can only say that as soon as he begins to write of this period, he strikes a note which celebrates landscapes that are imaginary rather than real. 'Oxford,' says Ryder in his opening apostrophe, ' — submerged now and obliterated, irrecoverable as Lyonnesse, so quickly have the waters come flooding in — ' [BR 23]. And again in A Little Learning, 'The town was still isolated among streams and meadows. The surrounding woods and hills were those the Scholar Gypsy haunted...' [LL 162]. It is in the invocation of Lyonnesse and the Scholar Gypsy that we sense the glide towards fiction. The place and its people are still there, indistinguishable in form from their originals, but they have been transfigured by the operation of nostalgia.

Perhaps the clearest evidence we can get of this process comes from a letter written to Waugh by Pansy Lamb shortly after the appearance of Brideshead Revisited. It accuses him of distorting the world he wrote about in that book. Passages from the letter are quoted, with slight variations, in Sykes's biography and also in the edition of Waugh's letters by Mark Amory. I quote from both of them:

> you cannot make me nostalgic about the world I knew in the 1920s. And yet it was the same world as you describe, or at any rate impinged on it. I was a debutante in 1922, & though neither smart nor rich went to three dances in historic houses... & may have seen Julia Flyte. Yet, even in retrospect it all seems very dull. Most of the girls were drab & dowdy & the men even more so....Nobody was brilliant, beautiful, rich & owner of a wonderful home though some were one or the other. Most were respectable, well-to-do, narrow minded with ideals no way differing from Hooper's except that their basic ration was larger....Oxford too, were Harold Acton and Co really as brilliant as that, or were there wonderful characters I never met?...You see English Society of the 20s as something baroque and magnificent on its last legs....I fled from it because it seemed prosperous, bourgeois and practical and I believe it still is....[10]

This is a notable sidelight on what Waugh has done in *Brideshead*. And we seem to find a confirmation of it in the memoirs of Anthony Powell. Even in later life, he says, when Waugh had gained some acquaintance with fashionable circles, he hung on to the imaginary vision of them he had created in his early fiction — 'he was on the whole not much interested in their contradictions and paradoxes. He wished the *beau monde* to remain in the image he had formed.'[11]

Was, then, the world of the Flyte family no more than a romantic fiction, in its way as remote from reality as Llanabba Castle? 'Most of the girls were drab & dowdy & the men even more so.' The London season of which Julia was the cynosure and which was spoken of as 'the most brilliant season since

[10] Christopher Sykes, *Evelyn Waugh: A Biography*, p. 342; *Letters* 199.
[11] *Messengers of Day*, p. 21.

the war' must have acquired its brilliancy from people other than those encountered by Pansy Lamb. Is it possible that finding in Mayfair the same essential elements of drabness and dowdiness that had surrounded him in Arnold House, Waugh simply shifted the ground of his defence to a different sort of fantasy — from the comic to the romantic?

Before moving on to the later work, we must mark the omission from the discussion of *A Handful of Dust*. Of all Waugh's novels it is probably the one that remained closest to the experience which had given rise to it — 'written in his blood'[12] was Harold Acton's description. Yet for just that reason it stands apart from my line of argument. *A Handful of Dust* is a more painful book than the others because in it Waugh has declined to commit himself fully to any of the defensive responses with which we are concerned. The experience has been turned into fiction, but for once the transformation is designed to explore the pain rather than to escape it.

At first glance the same might seem to be true of the war trilogy. If we read the account of the débâcle on Crete or of the steady erosion of principle that is anatomized in *Unconditional Surrender*, we are left with no sense that the disappointment has been palliated or deflected. On the contrary, the fictional form that these events have been given picks out for us the depressing patterns that underlie their confusion. An episode from the fall of Crete will serve to illustrate something of Waugh's method. This is how he records it in his memorandum on Layforce:

> In the square a peasant girl came and pulled at my sleeve; she was in tears. I followed her to the church, where in the yard was a British soldier on a stretcher. Flies were all over his mouth and he was dead. There was another girl by him also in tears. I think they had been looking after him. There was also a bearded peasant who shrugged and made signs that might have been meant to describe the ascent of a balloon, but which told me what I could already see. Again with signs, I told them to bury him. [*Diaries* 504]

[12] *More Memoirs of an Aesthete*, p. 318.

Now the same incident from *Officers and Gentlemen*:

> There a young girl, ruddy, bare-footed and in tears, approached him frankly and took him by the sleeve. He showed her his empty bottle, but she shook her head, made little inarticulate noises and drew him resolutely towards a small yard on the edge of the village, which had once held live-stock but was now deserted except by a second, similar girl, a sister perhaps, and a young English soldier who lay on a stretcher motionless. The girls pointed helplessly towards this figure. Guy could not help. The young man was dead, undamaged it seemed. He lay as though at rest. The few corpses which Guy had seen in Crete had sprawled awkwardly. This soldier lay like an effigy on a tomb — like Sir Roger in his shadowy shrine at Santa Dulcina. Only the bluebottles that clustered round his lips and eyes proclaimed that he was flesh....It remained one of the countless unexplained incidents of war. Meanwhile, lacking words the three of them stood by the body, stiff and mute as figures in a sculptured Deposition. [*OG* 206]

The ground is too stony to bury him — 'Later, perhaps, the enemy would scavenge the island and tip this body with others into a common pit and the boy's family would get no news of him and wait and hope month after month, year after year.' He removes one of the boy's identity discs, leaving the other on the body. 'Guy stood. The bluebottles returned to the peaceful young face. Guy saluted and passed on.'

It is at once apparent that no attempt is being made in the fictional version to dissipate the emotional force of the scene. Waugh emphasizes the girl's distress, the soldier's youth, the fruitless anxiety of his family. The body, ravaged by flies, will go with other anonymous corpses into a common pit.

It is a cluttered passage, not Waugh at his best; but whatever we think of the relative effectiveness of the two descriptions, these are points which could only have been introduced to increase the pathos of the scene. The author's claim to have worked a complete transformation on his material is legitimate, but it is evidently not the same kind of transformation as we have been considering. There is, perhaps, a hint of the old romanticism in that last paragraph. The short, dignified sentences carry their dignity a little too self-consciously. To salute and pass on is so very much what one should do that anyone who does it (and in just those words) cannot but be open to suspicion. The point need not be stressed, for Waugh's presentation of the incident has been determined in the main by a purpose that is clearly anti-romantic. This is attested not only by the realism of the description, but also, more subtly, by two of the details that Waugh has added to it: the comparison with Sir Roger and the mention of the identity disc. The first implies a bitter comment on Guy's early notion of the war as a crusade, the second looks forward to the moment at the end of the novel when the glamorous Mrs Stitch will drop the disc into a wastepaper basket in the belief that she is helping to obscure the treachery of the glamorous Ivor Claire. It is a moment that damages her partly because Waugh has already troubled to direct our attention to the waiting family.

So far the author's treatment of this episode seems merely to have thrown into relief those aspects of it which are most painful. Far from softening its outlines, the transformation has made them harsher. But the introduction of Sir Roger and the mention of the identity disc are not entirely negative. It is the identity disc which tells Guy that the soldier is a Roman Catholic. There is no mention of this in the memorandum, but here it prompts Guy to a short prayer for 'the faithful departed'. Sir Roger, too, though he may be a reminder of the gulf between political realities and religious ideals, is also a reminder that those ideals do exist. Waugh's image of the three of them as figures in a sculptured Deposition sustains the impression that however dismal the occurrence, it is something that exists within the structure of Christianity. These references give it a context in the work of fiction which, despite the mention of a church, is quite absent from the bare account in the memorandum. To this extent they function in the same way as Waugh's repeated references to the unfolding of the Christian year. Throughout the trilogy military and political events are constantly being set within the framework of the Christian calendar. Guy's performance of his duties as an officer is counterpointed with the performance of his duties as a Christian, and in so far as the two diverge it is clear that his primary allegiance is to the latter. What we are being given is an alternative perspective; it does not diminish the bitterness of what happens, but it does affirm that these happenings are only a partial truth. There is a context within which their significance dwindles.

In this sense the episode we have quoted is a model of Waugh's procedure in the trilogy. His own experiences are taken over with what are often only minor changes, but they are set against a Christian framework which mitigates their attendant desolation. The most important single element in the trilogy that has no direct counterpart in Waugh's experience is the thread of narrative which concerns Guy's father. He probably did have an original of sorts in the person of Harry Scrope, the head of one of England's oldest Catholic families, but the part he plays in the trilogy is Waugh's invention. In so far as Mr Crouchback is the focus of the work's religious theme, his role has a decisive effect on our interpretation of the events related. Here again we are concerned with a mode of transformation that has little in common with the fantasy of the early novels. The real change that Waugh's experiences undergo in *Sword of Honour* is a change in meaning.

The religious perspective which comes to dominate his writing tends, as we have seen, to render obsolete the earlier lines of defence. This is one reason for his willingness to treat later material with more realism. There is less need to adapt it to strategies of escape.

It is a development reflected in the changes Waugh made when he revised his earlier work. The first and most extensive piece of revision was for the publication in 1946 of *When the Going was Good*. Turning from the travel books to this one volume abridgement, we find that a striking number of the passages I selected for quotation in earlier chapters have been excised. This is not usually because the sections of which they were a part have been left out; as a rule, the passages have been individually suppressed. Possible reasons for this are worth investigating.

In *Labels* certain longish sections have been cut altogether, such as the author's disquisition on Gaudi and his visits to Ragusa and Cattaro. Given the demands of making an abridgement, this is understandable. More interesting are the cuts which have evidently been made as a matter of taste. The accounts of brothel-going, for example, are noticeably more restrained. I referred in chapter 1 to Waugh's description of the entertainments on offer at the Maison Dorée; these are no longer specified. There is no mention now of the fact that some of the cheaper girls at Port Said were attractive, or that the Sudanese dancer in Cairo (inspirer of Whisky-Soda?) was naked under her frock. 'After dinner, inevitably, we sought out the houses of ill-fame,' Waugh informs us in *Labels*; it is another sentence that does not reappear in *When the Going was Good*. Equally often it is Waugh's summary remarks in disparagement of foreign cultures that disappear. Thus, we do not read in the later volume that Mohammedans drink, that the Egyptian attitude to their antiquities is avaricious, that the Mena House is an appalling hotel, that the magic of the Sphinx is no more than a confidence trick.

The same pattern continues in the two chapters of *When the Going was Good* that are taken from *Remote People*. Again Waugh is exercising unwonted diplomacy. Slighting remarks — about European colonists, say, or the wives of British officials — are often cut out altogether. Most thoughtful of all, having originally written of the Government Rest House at Bukama, 'It is unfurnished and, presumably, infested with spirillum tick,' [*RP* 230] he reproduces the sentence now without its adverb — a delicate attention, one would like to think, to local sensibilities. For our present purposes, the most notable omissions are three passages, all of which were quoted above (see chapters 3 and 4): the first disputing the brilliance of the night-time constellations over Africa, the second alluding to the blood on Gougsa's corpse, and the third making a lengthy apology for the Kenyan settlers. Each of these passages is a casualty of the revision.

Comparison is less useful in the case of *Ninety-Two Days*

and *Waugh in Abyssinia*, since the author's abridgement is far more extensive; together they make up only a little over a third of *When the Going was Good*. The instances from the other two books, however, are an indication of the way Waugh's mind was working. The passages I referred to in earlier chapters — the dance at the Maison Dorée, the Sphinx, the recurrent lure of the red light districts, the three examples from *Remote People* — were all quoted because they seemed to typify a certain kind of response on the part of the author. They were evidence that could be grasped of his romanticism, his detachment, his nostalgia — points, in other words, at which he could be caught in a particular attitude. It is in this that they are related to the other kind of omission I have emphasized: the passages where Waugh is at his most abrasive. These too have the effect of freezing him in a certain attitude. Like rough projections on a smooth surface, they afford the reader a purchase.

When he wrote these books, Waugh was still developing a satisfactory persona through which to mediate his experiences. The romanticism, the arrogance, the slightly facile sophistication were what gave the material its shape; they were the modes of response by which it was subdued and made part of the writer's world. The process of abridgement does not change this shape but it does point up by omission some of the ways in which he felt it to have been outgrown.

With the war behind him the author is a middle-aged man — experienced, successful, disillusioned. The more strident notes in his pre-war travel books are an embarrassment to him; they represent the scaffolding of what is now a largely obsolete framework of responses. It is the same perception that leads him several years later to set about modifying what has come to seem 'distasteful' in the clamorous nostalgia of *Brideshead Revisited*. As one line of defence gave way to another, so the dominant principle of transformation changed.

The process, of course, has none of the neatness which this suggests; a writer does not slough his skin like a snake. The

strong opinions of the travel books were toned down because they had served their turn, not because Waugh was
yielding to a general access of moderation. On the contrary,
his views, as he grew older, became more extreme, his public
pronouncements more uncompromising. The harshness of
many of these recorded utterances makes a contrast with
the subtler tones of his imaginative work that repays
examination.

Outrageous opinions are in part an aspect of Waugh's
habitual role-playing. For the social sentiments of someone
like Mr Pinfold to have been anything but grossly illiberal
would have been a chink in the armour; they are counters in
a tactical game. Early in 1945 Waugh noted in his diary:
'By choosing preposterous objects as possessions I keep them
at arm's length.' [*Diaries* 610] And the same might be said of
preposterous opinions. Asked on one occasion why he had
never voted in a Parliamentary election, Waugh replied that
he would not presume to advise his sovereign on her choice
of ministers. The answer is characteristic of his tendency to
exaggerate a sincere opinion — in this case about the hierarchical nature of society — until it becomes an absurdity. The
advantage to the speaker is that his real degree of commitment thereby remains elusive. By presenting opinions in
caricature, he evades the gloomy responsibilities of seriousness; defending them is a game rather than an obligation. The
outrageousness which seems initially to be aggressive turns
out to be another strategy of defence; the preposterousness
of the opinions serves as a shield behind which the speaker
can maintain his detachment.

But this function is only necessary in the context of
non-fiction, where the writer is vulnerable because ostensibly speaking in his own person. In the novels the air is
freer. One instance has already been touched on: the cold
judgements of the *Spectator* article are suffused with a
much warmer light in the fictional world of *Vile Bodies*.
Another article that was mentioned earlier was the piece
for the *Daily Mail* in which Waugh denied having any model
for Shepheard's Hotel. He goes on to speak of the 'heroine'
of *Vile Bodies*, meaning, it appears, Agatha Runcible rather
than Nina:

She was a young lady of crazy and rather dissolute habits. No one, I should have thought, would see herself in that character without shame. But nearly all the young women of my acquaintance, and many whom I have not had the delight of meeting, claim with apparent gratitude and pride that they were the originals of that sordid character. [*LOr* 14]

As a description of Agatha Runcible (or for that matter of Nina Blount), 'that sordid character' is roughly on a par with Oldmeadow's 'two humane ladies' for the animal lovers in *Black Mischief*. Waugh's strictures suggest a reading of the novel that has primly translated it into a sermon on youthful depravity. He seems to be displaying the kind of blank failure of sympathy which is usually thought of as the prerogative of churchmen and literary critics. Compare, for example, these remarks of F. Lapicque about Lady Circumference:

Lady Circumference se charge tout particulièrement d'illustrer la bêtise, la prétension et la vulgarité des gens parés de titres nobiliaires. Et il est clair qu'aux yeux de l'auteur, une noblesse symbolisée par des êtres aussi creux que cette femme, chez qui le rang ne correspond plus à aucune supériorité d'intelligence ou d'éducation, prépare sa démission et sa perte.[13]

It's true, of course, as is Waugh's description of Agatha Runcible. But where Lapicque's absurdity is unconscious, Waugh's is part of a deliberate game. He is enjoying his own self-righteousness in a way that transforms the opinion expressed into what is almost a comic prop. In both passages we are being drawn — inadvertently by Lapicque, intentionally by Waugh — towards the chosen ground of Waugh's fiction.

[13] 'It is Lady Circumference who, more than anyone else, illustrates the stupidity, pretentiousness and vulgarity of those who are bedecked with aristocratic titles. And it is clear that in the view of the author, a nobility symbolized by people as hollow as this woman, who has no superiority either of intelligence or education to correspond to her rank, is paving the way to its own capitulation and ruin.' ('La Satire dans l'oeuvre d'Evelyn Waugh')

To approach *Vile Bodies* or *Decline and Fall* with such earnestness is to generate a form of the comic confusion that results from the application of wholly inappropriate standards. It is from the same perspective that Monsieur Ballon tries to interpret the activities of the British Legation in Azania — 'The old fox, Sir Courteney, is playing a deep game.' Waugh's comments in this passage are only a step away from those of Sir Joseph Mannering on Basil Seal.

But here we must pause. Although Waugh is playing with the opinion he puts forward in this essay, it is not therefore justifiable to dismiss it. His condemnation of Agatha Runcible is inappropriate as applied to the character in *Vile Bodies*, but it may yet be a sincere opinion about the sort of person on whom that character is based. The essay is another instance of writing that occupies a middle ground between fiction and reality. The moral rigour of the *Spectator* article is still Waugh's point of departure, but it has been attenuated by the fiction writer's delight in constructing a persona. The indignant novelist, bemused by the reception of his latest work, is already half-way towards being another of Waugh's minor characters.

In the passage from reality to fiction it is not so much the author's moral seriousness that evaporates as his moral rigidity. Views which have an iron inflexibility in his non-fiction can often shiver and disintegrate in the prismatic world of the novels. This is not just because the novels are too unserious to accommodate them. Even those, like *A Handful of Dust* and *Unconditional Surrender*, in which the humour is most subdued can serve to illustrate the point. Brenda Last, for example, continually eludes the sort of simple judgements which her role seems to invite. To speak, as D. S. Savage does, of her 'utter worthlessness' [14] is to respond to her as a type rather than as a specific character. In the process of bringing her to life Waugh has complicated and to some extent disabled the straightforward moral condemnation to which she would be liable as a frivolous adulteress who has brought ruin on her husband.

It is as though Waugh has exploited the latitude of fiction

[14] 'The Innocence of Evelyn Waugh'.

to humanize his moral judgements. Virginia's search for an abortion in *Unconditional Surrender* is an incident that has already been mentioned. Waugh's readiness to give credit to the 'high incorrigible candour' with which she goes about it bespeaks a fairness that is less often manifested in his non-fiction. It is the sympathy of the novelist that Virginia engages — in defiance of the moralist, whose judgement is summed up in Waugh's description of her to Julian Jebb as 'dissolute'.[15] This is a pertinent echo of his comment on Agatha Runcible. The later remark has a more serious context, but it reveals exactly the same distance between the imaginative writer and the moralist. Nowhere is this more evident that in the running comparison between Virginia and the wife of Ian Kilbannock — 'the one so prodigal, the other so circumspect and sparing' [*US* 47]. Kerstie Kilbannock has all the domestic virtues and even a measure of unselfish kindness; she would stand high in the priest's good offices. And yet as we read *Unconditional Surrender*, it is impossible not to feel that for the author these virtues are all but undone by the streak of illiberal calculation that runs through them. 'All the pretty objects in their house had been bargains' — from the start, the economy is noted with a certain sourness. However 'dissolute' she may be, there is, by contrast, nothing mean-spirited about Virginia. Lavish of what lies in her gift, she errs in the opposite direction; and finally, it seems, this may be preferable. Perhaps, after all, the prodigality that conduces to sin may be more sympathetic than the parsimony that conduces to virtue. But this is the judgement of the story-teller, not of the moralist.

What is at issue here is a point that has been raised in a number of different contexts in this study. It can be summarized by a quotation from David Lodge: 'The artist in Waugh seizes with glee upon what the educated Catholic gentleman most deplores.'[16] Lodge's words point directly to the aspect of Waugh's fiction we have been considering. As soon as he starts to write, the opinions of the Catholic gentleman are under pressure from the sensibilities of the

---

[15] 'The Art of Fiction XXX: Evelyn Waugh'.
[16] *Evelyn Waugh*, p. 9.

artist. This is true not merely of the novels; even in Waugh's non-fiction there is, as we have seen, a continual edging towards fiction, which can be equally subversive. Immediately Waugh addresses a subject, the pull of fictional models begins to make itself felt.

There is a moment in *Scoop* when William, having discovered the existence of a Russian agent in Ishmaelia, wakes Corker in high excitement to pass on the news. Unfortunately, Shumble has already invented a story about a Russian agent, which has been scotched by the other reporters. Corker explains to William what this means:

> Russian agents are off the menu, old boy. It's a bad break for Shumble, I grant you. He got on to a good thing without knowing — and the false beard was a very pretty touch. His story was better than yours all round, and we killed it. Do turn out the light. [*S* 101-2]

The fact that one story is true and the other false is not even a side-issue. Corker's assessment of their relative merits is purely aesthetic. It is, in its way, an artistic view of journalism. He and the others are objects of satire in *Scoop*, but this time the author is satirizing something closer to his heart than usual. Compare what Corker says with an early entry in Waugh's diary:

> The other evening I bought a bottle of Dow's 1908 port. Dean [a colleague at Arnold House] mixed his with lime juice and soda and when I offered him sugar too said that he preferred it 'dry'. This story is not really quite true but I have recounted it in so many letters that I have begun to believe it. [*Diaries* 211]

The bit about preferring it 'dry', Corker might have remarked, was a very pretty touch. The story is too good not to set down and if, on this occasion, a moment of compunction forces Waugh to admit that it is not wholly true, there is no guarantee that he was always so scrupulous. What of the note he makes in his diary at Lancing [*Diaries* 141] to the effect that Tom Driberg had surprised Roxburgh with one of the boys on his knee in a darkened room? Driberg himself, who might have been expected to have a sharpish memory for such things, had no recollection of the incident. It seems quite likely that a fantasy about what could, or even ought to, have happened has simply been recorded in the diary as something that did happen. Its general propriety — if that is not an unfortunate term — has given it the status of an honorary event. The good diarist's first duty, it could be argued, is to produce a good diary.

As an endless series of anecdotes about him proclaim, adherence to the literal truth was not Waugh's highest priority. Even in his journalism, he was not entirely free from the tendencies he satirized in others. The *Tablet* under Oldmeadow's editorship is an unreliable guide to his work, but it is still worth noting the criticisms of bias that were levelled against his reporting of the Italian—Abyssinian war. 'Time after time,' Oldmeadow writes,

> he has increased prejudice against Abyssinia by padding out his meagre messages with stories which he himself admits to be 'unconfirmed' or 'of doubtful authenticity'. In one case he put it into the reader's mind that the Abyssinians may have killed Italian prisoners; and, in another case, that an Italian airman who fell from a 'plane was perhaps murdered, instead of being rescued and cared for.[17]

This is thin evidence, but it would be rash to discount it. Waugh's easy way with the truth was not always as disinterested as in the case of his story about Roxburgh. When he had a point to make, his presentation of the facts could be markedly selective. Indeed, it seems that in his report at the end of the war on religious toleration in Jugoslavia he was rather more than selective. In order to strengthen his case for Allied interference, he not only slanted the evidence but at one point actually doctored it.

This slightly uncandid way of going to work could also affect his involvement in the religious controversy which

---

[17] 'News and Notes'.

overshadowed his old age. When Father Ryan wrote an article for *Commonweal* in support of changes in the liturgy, Waugh was not above composing a reply that significantly distorted what his opponent had written. The specific instances are listed by J. M. Cameron in another article for *Commonweal*.[18] If they make rather melancholy reading, it is perhaps because the offence in which Waugh has been found out seems a particularly inglorious one. That he should have cared deeply enough about something to expose himself so blatantly makes him, for a rare moment, look vulnerable. The level of ingenuity is not high: Father Ryan writes that the Canon contains 'an obscure and puzzling list of Roman worthies', Waugh presents it as a statement that the Canon *is* 'an obscure and puzzling list of Roman worthies'. And so it continues. This is the artist reduced to working on his hands and knees. There is a sort of pathos in such unhandy shifts to guard his faith. But to what defence can he resort, when the religion which is his ultimate defence is being undermined?

These trivial misrepresentations are dead branches of what was once a sturdier growth. The journalists of *Scoop* are not an isolated group in Waugh's writing; falsification of one sort or another was an abiding concern. In book after book he returns to the ways in which, by distortion or false report or just a change in tone, the nature of an experience can be transformed, so that what was familiar seems unfamiliar, what was cowardly seems heroic, what was colourless seems infused with colour. The novels themselves not only illustrate this process, they also make it their subject. Though *Scoop* is the obvious example, there is not a novel between *Vile Bodies* and the war trilogy (indeed, scarcely a book of any kind) that does not at some stage take up the theme. Newspaper reports — garbled, sensationalized or invented — are one of Waugh's enduring interests. Enough examples have been quoted in earlier chapters. From the moment that Adam takes over as Mr Chatterbox there is an evident fascination with the journalist's alchemical powers: the social world of the Quests, the 'barbaric splendour' of Azania,

18 'A Post-Waugh Insight'.

the fascist troops at Laku — these and other figments of the imagination are all monuments to his art.

During the war it tended to be the mechanisms of propaganda and counter-espionage that supplied the author with the substance of these transformations. In *Put Out More Flags* Basil Seal can turn Ambrose's work of art into a Nazi tract and in the trilogy Kilbannock manages to convert Trimmer's incompetent raid on France into an epic of military heroism. The artless movements of Guy Crouchback are meanwhile reinterpreted in accordance with the sweet and sinister design of Grace Groundling Marchpole.

Sometimes the theme appears at one remove. Is Hetton Abbey the house that is seen by Tony Last or by the writer of the guide book? Or take the opening paragraph of *Helena*:

> Once, very long ago, before ever the flowers were named which struggled and fluttered below the rain-swept walls, there sat at an upper window a princess and a slave reading a story which even then was old: or, rather, to be entirely prosaic, on the wet afternoon of the Nones of May in the year (as it was computed later) of Our Lord 273, in the city of Colchester, Helena, red-haired, youngest daughter of Coel, Paramount Chief of the Trinovantes, gazed into the rain while her tutor read the Iliad of Homer in a Latin paraphrase. [*H* 13]

Side by side, the language of legend and the language of factual reality give to the same scene a wholly different complexion. Waugh's shift from one mode into the other offers a playful image of a story whose essence is that it should be at once both fabulous and prosaic. Its nature is perceived in the transforming play of words.

As often as not, this preoccupation leaves only a superficial mark on the books — a brief reference, as it might be, to the distorted accounts of Charles Ryder's trip to Central America. Except in *Scoop*, the question of reporting and mis-reporting never becomes a focal point in the novels; and yet it is at the centre of Waugh's work. The art of journalism as it is practised by his characters is a coarsened image of his own trade as a novelist; but more than this, it provides a literary paradigm of all the other sorts of metamorphosis that are the staple of his writing.

What are the elements of his experience that most obviously caught Waugh's imagination? Arnold House, one feels, was a coincidental source of *Decline and Fall*; had he been employed in a bookshop, he could well have written a similar sort of novel with a different setting. Other kinds of experience fired his imagination more directly — his visits to the barbarous places of Africa and South America, his occasional brushes with the film world, his two assignments as a foreign correspondent, his discovery of the cemetery at Forest Lawn. These are some of them, and there is one feature that they share: they were all, in Waugh's perception of them, studies in different kinds of transformation.

Savages interested him not as a cultural phenomenon in themselves but in so far as they distorted or displaced what properly belonged in another culture — clothes, customs, ideas, political systems, mechanical inventions. Similarly, what attracts him to the film makers, whether in *Vile Bodies*, *The Loved One*, or 'Excursion in Reality', is their freedom to translate whatever material they start with into a reflection of their own caprice. The life of Wesley or a play by Shakespeare can as easily be modified as Miss del Pablo's nose and nationality. What first absorbs both Dennis and his creator in the arts of Whispering Glades are those processes by which the departed Loved Ones are transformed under Mr Joyboy's hand into things of beauty. To reshape the hideously disfigured body of Sir Francis and impart to it the Radiant Childhood Smile is a delicate operation. But such metamorphoses are in the run of daily life for the morticians. A few weeks earlier a loved one had been delivered to their care after a month in the ocean: they fixed him up, as the hostess informs Dennis, 'so he looked like it was his wedding day'.

This is an order of achievement that deeply appeals to Waugh. 'He is a true artist,' says Aimée of Mr Joyboy. 'I can say no more.' [*LO* 48] The author is drawn to Whispering Glades by a kernel of truth in this grotesque claim. It is not by chance that the dreamer's vision has been realized on the edge of Hollywood. The magical transformations which are

his stock-in-trade have a perverse affinity with those of the
dream-factory at Megalopolitan; the fate of Sir Francis is
not altogether dissimilar from that of Miss del Pablo. It is
in these contexts where the face of reality can be adroitly
reworked that Waugh finds 'the experiences vivid enough
to demand translation into literary form'. The quotation
is taken from the beginning of Ninety-Two Days. He was
writing then about 'the borderlands of conflicting cultures
and states of development, where ideas, uprooted from
their traditions, become oddly changed in transplantation'
[92D 13]. It is precisely the same imaginative stimulus
that he finds in these other strands of his experience.

They are all areas in which conventional reality is liable
to a sudden, surreal face-lift, but amongst them it is the
world of journalism that most nearly touches the world
of fiction, for the journalist, like the novelist, effects his
transformations with words.

Deprived of hard news during the Abyssinian war, correspondents began to feature in their dispatches a mysterious
force of Yemen Arabs, who were reported to have put
themselves in the Emperor's service. Waugh recalls how their
status was established: 'There was in fact a number of venerable old traders from the Yemen, dotted about the bazaar
quarter. If two of them sat down together for a cup of
coffee it was described as a military consultation.' [WA 123]
This is an uncomplicated trick, but for just that reason it
illustrates with perfect clarity the sort of transaction which
has been the subject of the present chapter. When reality
fails to meet the journalists' requirements, it is simply nudged
into a more amenable condition; between a friendly cup of
coffee and a military consultation there is only a modest gap
for the imagination to bridge. Waugh points satirically to
the moment at which truth expands into fiction.

But is 'truth' the appropriate term? As a satirist, Waugh
too has an axe to grind. By describing the Arabs as old
and venerable, by referring to them as 'dotted' around the
bazaar, he has created a deliberate antithesis to any notion
of concerted military activity. This may, of course, be entirely accurate: perhaps all of them were old, venerable, and
unconcerned with politics. On the other hand, it could be

that where the journalists have added colour, Waugh has withdrawn it. It seems possible that he is here doing for the sake of satire exactly what he accuses the reporters of having done for the sake of sensation. He, like them, one may suspect, has slightly modified the original scene, but in the opposite direction; the demands of satire can be as pressing as those of journalism.

It is a sense of this relationship with the contrivances of the artist that sustains Waugh's interest in journalism. The cup of coffee that becomes a military consultation is an apt image for the process whereby a humdrum reality can be touched into colour at the urging of the imagination. 'When the water-holes were dry,' Ryder tells us, 'people sought to drink at the mirage.' [BR 216] What he does as an artist is to create the mirage; in a dry land he can produce the illusion of water. However crudely, this is what the journalist is doing as well; his lies, as Waugh presents them, serve a similar end. The motives are different, the degree of skill is different, the product is vastly different, but both the artist and the journalist start from the same proposition: reality is malleable. Their business is to turn this fact to advantage.

But it cannot be done without risk. The charge that Waugh sometimes doctored his evidence in the non-fictional writings is in effect an accusation that he was using words to distort rather than to communicate the truth. Ryder's image of the mirage and the water-hole points to the possibility that an analogous charge could be made against the novelist. The artist's medium, Ryder seems to suggest, can act as the distorting haze through which the dry water-hole appears as an oasis. In other words, we turn to art for an illusion of that well-being which reality cannot afford us. But what then is the difference between art and escapist fantasy? Is it not rightly the function of art to dissipate the haze? Should we not turn to it for a keener perception of reality rather than for a retreat into unreality? The germ of this criticism is there in Ryder's own image, and Anthony Blanche makes it explicit when he whispers to Ryder at the exhibition: 'My dear, let us not expose your little imposture before these good, plain people' [BR 257]. What Ryder is presenting as art is in fact a fraud. Like Gauguin and Rimbaud, he has gone to the tropics, but his art is an emasculation of what he found there — 'Where, my dear Charles, did you find this sumptuous greenery? The corner of a hothouse at T-t-trent or T-t-tring?' In the end, it is 'simple, creamy English charm, playing tigers'. The attack is directed against a form of art that opts for the pleasing mirage in preference to the dusty reality. Though the art in question is Ryder's, Waugh himself, as he must have known, shares some of his hero's vulnerability.

It is a criticism that has lain in wait at every turn of our argument. The theme of these chapters has been escape; Waugh's writings, I have suggested, are in one important sense a defiance of reality and an evasion of it. In so far as this is the case, it must be their tendency to move in exactly the direction which Blanche criticized. Even when the artist is painting tigers rather than country houses, they will never be the fearful beasts of reality. This is not just because they will have become comic beasts or romantic beasts or beasts of the Revelation, but because essential elements of their bestiality will have been left out. In studying the ways in which the writer's material is assimilated to various kinds of escapist response, we have so far said little about those aspects of it which are casualties of the process. Inevitably there are forms of censorship. The effects of humour, romance and so forth depend on saying things in a certain way, but they also depend on declining to say other things at all. They depend, that is, on the author's reticence.

Whatever kind of vision he wants to present will have to be protected by areas of silence. If an adolescent attempt at suicide is to be described with proper urbanity, then it will not do to dwell too curiously on the emotional state that prompted it. If the achievements of a dictator are to be set in a properly heroic light, then it will not do to examine too closely the rhetoric of his followers or the fate of those who oppose them. To admit, as the author does at the end of *Waugh in Abyssinia*, that there will be 'a good deal of vulgar talk and some sharp misfortunes for individual opponents' is to step as close as one may to the viciousness and suffering that are the dark side of the dictator's star. A few words more, an example or two of the 'sharp misfortunes', and the romantic light would begin to fade. So the author keeps silent; we shall not know all that he could have told us.

To see what happens when the previously unstated realities are sketched in, we have only to look at the spare, romantic image of military life given in the Preface to *When the Going was Good* ('We have most of us marched and made camp since then, gone hungry and thirsty, lived where pistols are flourished and fired' — see above, p. 89) and then turn from that to the description of military life as it is lived in the war trilogy.

The Preface was written in 1945. If we go back a few years, the difference in tone is more marked still. Readers of *Life* magazine in 1941 might have been surprised to know that the commando raid on Bardia, here recalled for them with modest but manly pride by Captain Waugh, was later to be the source of his descriptions of the fiasco at Dakar in *Men at Arms* and the raid by Trimmer into occupied France. 'A good commando fighter,' the magazine informs us in its gloss on Waugh's article, 'known jokingly as a "Churchill Marine", should have the imagination of a mystery writer, the cunning of a burglar, the endurance of an Olympic athlete and the patriotism of a hero.' Far from being an embarrassment to Waugh, this is just the sort of language that he himself takes up in his account of the raid. The troop leaders, he says, picked every man individually:

> The qualities they were seeking were simply the qualities of any good soldier — physical strength and endurance, fighting spirit, knowledge of his weapons, enterprise. There was nothing peculiar about our men. They were simply the best types of the regiments from which they came.[19]

There follows his account of a signally incompetent raid on the coast of Libya, which concludes with the assurance that

---

[19] 'Commando Raid on Bardia'.

'we had made all our objectives'. In fact, they had found the town deserted, lost a party of men who went to the wrong beach, and finally been obliged to blow up one of their own boats which had run aground. Their only contact with the enemy came when a couple of motorcycles drove past them down the road:

> Everyone near had a shot at them with Tommy guns and grenades but they somehow got through. They were not an easy target. It was very lucky really that they did escape for it was through them that the enemy learned, as we particularly wanted them to learn, that a landing was taking place.

Very lucky really, since they *particularly* wanted the enemy to learn. The adverbs are taking too much strain for comfort. Trimmer and Kilbannock would have been on home ground here.

So would Ivor Claire. Earlier in the article Waugh had described himself arriving at the commando mess in Scotland: 'I found a young troop leader wearing a military tunic and corduroy trousers. He was reclining in a comfortable chair, a large cigar in his mouth. Then I noticed above the pocket of his coat the ribbon of the Military Cross, and later when I saw him with his troop I realized that his men would follow him anywhere.' This engaging figure is the original of Claire as he first appears to Guy on the Isle of Mugg. Of course his men would follow him anywhere. The question of whether he would lead them anywhere was not one that could be asked in November 1941; not, probably, one that Waugh would have wanted to ask. It was a time for discretion in his treatment of officers and gentlemen.

In the end, the only line of defence which does not rely on the artificial protection of the author's reticence is his religion. And this is one reason why it is the most secure. Instead of excluding everything that might make it look ridiculous or impotent or unattractive, Waugh forcefully acknowledges these things: his religion is not immune from absurdity; in a world of hate and waste it does little to banish human suffering; its demands are often rigorous and uncongenial. Sharp misfortunes can fall on its adherents as easily as on its opponents, and Waugh does not blink them by in a phrase; the accounts are fully drawn up. His religion may be unappealing, but, on this count at least, it is also unassailable.

The weaknesses of Waugh's position are elsewhere, in those other sanctuaries which can be maintained only by the author's tact. There, I have suggested, he must pass over in silence aspects of reality which would otherwise unmake his fiction. And it is along these lines that Waugh's status as an artist can most damagingly be challenged. When Sonia tells Basil towards the end of *Black Mischief* that people have got duller and poorer, she does try to offer a vague explanation: 'There was a general election and a crisis — something about gold standard.' [*BM* 231] It is one of the moments in Waugh's early fiction when real and unpleasant events can be felt pressing lightly against the fabric of the comic world; the scene provides a brief intimation of sadder realities. But this is as far as it goes. To have said more would have been to fracture the mood of comedy. Whatever details Sonia's words conceal must remain unpublished. The question we are left with is how far this necessity detracts from Waugh's achievement as a novelist.

In an essay on P. G. Wodehouse, Stephen Medcalf refers in passing to Waugh's characteristic irony — 'a classic, suave, even creamy surface covering *accidie* and terror'.[20] By chance he has selected just the epithet that was used by Anthony Blanche to describe Ryder's paintings. For Blanche, though, the creamy surface is all that his friend's art can attain, whereas in Waugh's case, according to Medcalf, this surface is only a covering over the abyss. It is the difference between creamy English charm playing tigers and tigers playing creamy English charm. The argument is a convenient one: Waugh's urbane response to horror and distress need no longer be taken for a mark of insensibility; it has become an exacting and watchfully defended barricade against despair.

This has been more or less the tenor of my own argument, but it perhaps furnishes the critic with rather too opportune

[20] 'The Innocence of P. G. Wodehouse'.

a vindication of Waugh's attitudes. What of the charge that
this despair against which he girds himself owes less to any
deeper feelings than to the selfish boredom of a man un-
mindful of his own good fortune? In an essay already
referred to, D. S. Savage makes the standard accusation:
'Ironic detachment from the futile whirligig of human
affairs is hardly an adequate or promising attitude for a
serious writer, even for a serious comic writer, for the richest,
humour is bred from fullness and not paucity of life.'[21] It is
an argument pursued in similar terms by A. E. Dyson in his
later article for *Critical Quarterly*. Waugh's irony, he notes,
is used 'to evade humanity', and he goes on to attack the
ideal of defensive withdrawal that he takes to be the position
set out in *The Ordeal of Gilbert Pinfold*. His principal objection is that 'it does not make for great art, which presupposes,
indeed, the rejection of just such an attitude, in favour of
exactly the costly identification with suffering humanity here
refused'.[22]

This is close to the point made by Savage. Together they
amount to the charge that Waugh, like Ryder, has settled for
an art that is without substance. Under the creamy surface
there is nothing but the artist's impoverished sensibility. If
Sonia refrains from going into the details of national crisis,
it is not from some Conradian instinct that the result would
be 'too dark — too dark altogether', but simply because the
details themselves are, for her and for Waugh, inherently
boring. At this level Waugh's indifference to 'suffering
humanity' can surely not be denied. Dyson and Savage are
right: the reality behind Sonia's words is as remote from
Black Mischief as is the reality of the General Strike from
Brideshead Revisited or of the Abyssinian war from *Scoop*.
It is true that we shall not find 'fullness of life' in most of
Waugh's novels: his comic world is not Shakespearean; it
is a more partial and precarious construction which subsists
by evading potential tragedy, not by attempting to resolve it.
To this extent it is minor art.

But there are two points to be made here. True, Waugh's

---

[21] 'The Innocence of Evelyn Waugh'.
[22] 'Evelyn Waugh and the Mysteriously Disappearing Hero'.

comic vision is preserved at the cost of ignoring those realities that would undermine it, but there is nothing new in this; much the same might also be said of the moral vision of the great nineteenth-century novelists. How but by suppressing discordant evidence could their novels continue to affirm a causal link between morality and happiness? There can be moral fantasies as well as comic ones, and though they are no doubt more respectable, we cannot therefore assume that they are less evasive.

Nor — and this is the second point — that their evasiveness is fundamentally more serious. For Waugh, too, escapism was a serious business. He did not have a highly developed social conscience and his writings breathe no very urgent concern for 'suffering humanity' — they may even, some of them, strike us as lacking in humanity altogether. They are in many cases light, easy to read, unmarked by sorrow — everything, in fact, that a frivolous book is supposed to be.

And yet the earlier comparison with Conrad is not entirely fatuous. This is what Bertrand Russell wrote of him in *Portraits from Memory*: 'I felt, though I do not know whether he would have accepted such an image, that he thought of civilized and morally tolerable human life as a dangerous walk on a thin crust of barely cooled lava which at any moment might break and let the unwary sink into fiery depths.' Waugh might have deprecated the metaphor, but he would have understood the sentiment. At the end of *Robbery Under Law* he formulates a version of it himself:

> Civilization has no force of its own beyond what is given it from within.... Barbarism is never finally de-feated; given propitious circumstances, men and women who seem quite orderly, will commit every conceivable atrocity. The danger does not come merely from habitual hooligans; we are all potential recruits for anarchy. [*RL* 278-9]

It is not quite fortuitous that if we turn from *Black Mischief* to look for other examples of cannibalism in English fiction, our first stopping place is Conrad.

There is, after all, an abyss beneath the writer's urbanity, but it is not the gulf of social misery seen by the humanitarian. It has the outlines of the pit of Hell. What underlies the polished surface of Waugh's writings is the steady conviction of man's limitless capacity for evil. We shall overburden these delicate books if we labour the point; it is just this that Waugh has refrained from doing. His pessimism imparts no warmer touch of humanity to the novels, but it gives to their studied poise a tense significance: below are fiery depths.

And not just the depths of man's general capacity for wickedness; one circle, at least, has the character of a more personal menace. Medcalf was right to link terror and *accidie*. Boredom for Waugh was not a trivial threat. How could it be when sloth was requited with damnation? *Accidie*, we remember, was the definition that Waugh himself had fixed on for this sin — one of the few, he insists, that merit the extremity of divine punishment. With such ease can boredom assume the spiritual dimension of sin. For Waugh it had the aspect of a private road to Hell. His escape attempts were not lightly undertaken.

But nor were they undertaken solemnly. I wish only to claim for them a kind of literary seriousness that has its own validity. The nature of this seriousness will be explored in the Conclusion when we turn to *The Ordeal of Gilbert Pinfold*. The book records a brief period in Waugh's life when the crust of lava broke open. The horrors that lie beneath are real.

Had he exposed them to view more often, Waugh's academic standing would no doubt be higher. Of all the arts literature has been the most subject to critical demands for moral purpose and philosophical profundity, and among literary genres the novel has been particularly resourceful in satisfying them. It is unsurprising that by the yardstick which critics such as Dyson and Savage apply Waugh's novels should fare badly. The author himself would have appealed to different standards. He states them in the opening paragraph of *The Ordeal of Gilbert Pinfold*:

It may happen in the next hundred years that the English novelists of the present day will come to be valued as we now value the artists and craftsmen of the late eighteenth century. The originators, the exuberant men, are extinct and in their place subsists and modestly flourishes a generation notable for elegance and variety of contrivance. It may well happen that there are lean years ahead in which our posterity will look back hungrily to this period, when there was so much will and so much ability to please.

His claims for his art are not grandiose but they are exact. It is beside the artists and craftsmen of the late eighteenth century that he ranges himself, not beside the novelists of the nineteenth and early twentieth centuries. In doing so he directs our attention to just those works of art which most gracefully elude the portentous demand for 'costly identification with suffering humanity'. Such words would fall heavily on a scene by Fragonard or a shepherdess from Dresden. Waugh's novels are a deliberate attempt to step away from reality. The processes by which this step is taken are the stages of an escape; we have looked at them here under the heading of 'transformations'. No stretch of ingenuity can translate these agile movements into the stuff of moral philosophy. We must content ourselves with the rarer gifts of elegance and variety of contrivance. It is not a slight thing to have used language precisely and with respect. For 'suffering humanity' it may, in the end, be the most important thing.

Conclusion

The proprieties of academic discourse exercise a grim coercion. This is not the book I intended to write; its emphasis has shifted inexorably towards those sorts of complexity where literary criticism can best find nourishment. My starting point was a momentary misreading of a phrase from 'Fan-Fare'. 'I wanted to be a man of the world,' Waugh had written, 'and I took to writing as I might have taken to archaeology or diplomacy or any other profession as a means of coming to terms with the world.' [LOr 31] It should have been clear from the context what Waugh meant by the last few words; they correspond to some such phrase as 'making one's way in the world'. But having once misinterpreted them, I could not escape the notion that, whatever its conscious import, this phrase might after all be able to support the meaning I had attributed to it. Perhaps Waugh had indeed used his writing not simply to make his way in the world but also to come to terms with it, in the sense of reaching some sort of accommodation with it.

It is a common endeavour — and one that Waugh himself well understood — to modulate the harsher notes of daily life by more or less subtle essays in distortion. A man may be impotent to change events, but he can sometimes change their aspect; with skill they can be brought to terms: they can be aestheticized or ironized, mythologized, romanticized or sanctified, shaped and reshaped, according as his imagination and the velleities of his temper direct. Literature is the natural medium of such strategies. They are voices in which the novelist can speak, masks he can put on, modes of perception he can adopt. Waugh himself was reluctant to discuss his writing. This talk of masks and voices would probably

have seemed distasteful to him; but to deny that they are a
fit subject for discussion is not to deny their existence. Even
if we did not have the story of Gilbert Pinfold, the presence
of Atwater and Apthorpe in his work would be evidence
enough.

Arthur Atwater is a shiftless, seedy character whose identity flickers into different shapes from one moment to the
next; John Plant is a respectable writer whose life is as orderly
as his novels. How are we to explain the unlikely alliance that
grows between them? Atwater seems destined to play an
increasing part in Plant's life. 'Why don't you come and live
with me,' Plant says at the end of their last conversation. 'I've
got a house in the country, plenty of room. Stay as long as
you like. Die there.' The final words impart an ominous note
to his invitation; Plant's chosen genre, as we know, is the
murder story. That Atwater should be the man who killed
Plant's father has already marked their relationship with a
curious mixture of complicity and antagonism. A bond exists
between them which Plant is obliged to recognize but which
the irony of his tone is striving to resist. Then the fragment
breaks off and we are left to speculate in the dark.

Or perhaps not altogether in the dark. When Cyril Connolly
reviewed *Men at Arms*, he inadvertently substituted Atwater's
name for Apthorpe's. It was an error that drew from Waugh
the acknowledgement that 'there was a strong affinity'
between the two characters. He does not expand the point,
but we can guess at the similarities he had in mind. Guy's
comrade-in-arms is another elusive figure. As Guy himself
points out, the nuggets of Apthorpe that come to light tend,
under assay, to fade like faery gold. Both he and Atwater are
charlatans, yet neither of them can be defined by the word.
The identity they claim for themselves is not entirely fraudu-
lent, yet it continually reveals aspects of fraud. In each case
they develop an ambiguous but close relationship with the
novel's sober protagonist. There are hints that it is a relationship of ego and alter ego. In the course of *Men at Arms*
Apthorpe gradually absorbs more and more of Guy's commitment to his life as a soldier until it seems that Guy can only
be released from thrall by his friend's death. And this he
helps to bring about.

The same sort of pattern, I think, would probably have emerged from the earlier book. In their respective relationships with Plant and Crouchback, Atwater and Apthorpe embody a recognition by the author of impulses that cannot be comprehended within the persona of conventional novelist or unassuming Catholic gentleman. 'Gloriously over-Technicoloured' is how Guy thinks of Apthorpe. It is revealing that, by contrast, Guy himself should most commonly be criticized by readers for seeming somewhat grey. Apthorpe takes on all the imaginative extravagance which the character of the hero precludes. He and Atwater come into being as projections of the novelist's daemon. This implausible, slightly threatening relationship between the hero and his anti-type was as near as Waugh came in his fiction to a disclosure of the intimate tensions by which the writer lives.

It was an artistic indulgence that he seems to have regretted. His contempt for *Men at Arms* was disproportionate to its faults and derived, it may be, from a measure of concern at the way in which the relationship between Guy and Apthorpe had developed. If the events of his voyage to Ceylon had not supervened, there would surely have been no return to this theme. Apthorpe had given Waugh an awkward time; he had, so Nancy Mitford was told, taken 'the bit between his teeth'. It is a remark which suggests an unaccustomed loss of control on Waugh's part. But Apthorpe's recalcitrance was only a prelude to the real mutiny. Within two years of the publication of *Men at Arms* Waugh is confronted by a far more desperate attack.

For twenty-five years the author-magician has employed a perilous magic to reshape his world. The arts he practises have been the subject of this study. In *The Ordeal of Gilbert Pinfold* he faces their consequences. It is the book in which accounts are rendered for all the imaginative strategies that have sustained him as a novelist. An analysis of it must constitute the last stage of our argument.

To Mr Pinfold the doctor's explanation of his experience is

unconvincing. 'A perfectly simple case of poisoning'? He has survived a more personal challenge than this; he has won a victory. That he should now celebrate it by turning the episode into a book is entirely appropriate, for the nature of his experience has been directly related to his craft as a writer. Throughout the ordeal his tormentors remain disembodied. Existing only as words in the air, they are a depraved product of that alliance between language and imagination which, in another form, is the basis of the novelist's art. Waugh himself had noted the connection: 'the word made manifest' was how he described the voices in his interview for the *Paris Review*[1] — a striking phrase from one who saw his business as a novelist primarily in terms of the manipulation of words. It was in the same interview that he said: 'I regard writing not as an investigation of character, but as an exercise in the use of language, and with this I am obsessed.' The fantasies that beset Mr Pinfold and the novels that have sustained him are sprung from a common root in this obsession with words.

Behind much of what Waugh wrote, behind much that has been quoted in previous chapters, is the compelling perception that fragments of life can sometimes be rescued from tedium by a trick of words.

Middle-aged and middle-class, the SS *Caliban* is a ship quite untouched with romance — boring, in fact — but the writer can subtly augment its promises. 'The SS *Caliban*, Captain Steerforth master, was middle-aged and middle-class.' [*GP* 34] Captain Steerforth's name and rank, introduced after the name of the ship, deftly evoke the atmosphere of narratives from an earlier century. The parenthetic phrase is a bracing reminder of traditions now debased; its associations, vaguely stirring in their antiquity, reach back to the naval exploits of a more heroic age and partially redeem the ship from its nonentity. By a couple of words the scale of Mr Pinfold's world has been enlarged; a rift has opened in the pall of twentieth century mediocrity, through which can be seen the glint of possible adventure.

This is no more than the habitual device used by Mr

---

[1] Julian Jebb, 'The Art of Fiction XXX'.

Pinfold's creator to relieve the pressure of monotony, but on this occasion the breach in his surroundings gives passage not simply to the animating quirks of fantasy but to imaginative forces which, though they do indeed relieve the monotony ('It was the most exciting thing, really, that ever happened to me' [*GP* 154]), do so with a malevolent energy that threatens to destroy the mind that gave them birth. The sorcerer finds himself in the position of the sorcerer's apprentice. It is a reversal of role underlined by the Shakespearean parallels from *King Lear* and *The Tempest*: the father becomes the sport of his children, the king becomes a clown, Prospero is caught in the toils of Caliban. These are all inversions that mirror the one central transformation out of which the book is constructed.

The character of this transformation is suggested by the contrasting titles of chapters 1 and 2, 'Portrait of the artist in middle-age' and 'Collapse of elderly party'. It is more than the jump from middle to old age; between the two Mr Pinfold loses his status as an artist. From being in the first title both artist and artist's model, he becomes in the second merely an object of mild facetiousness. The delicate balance between the writer and his social persona has been upset.

Already in the opening chapter it was clear that the relationship between them was not free from strain:

> It was his modesty which needed protection and for
> this purpose, but without design, he gradually assumed
> the character of burlesque. He was neither a scholar nor
> a regular soldier; the part for which he cast himself was
> a combination of eccentric don and testy colonel and he
> acted it strenuously, before his children at Lychpole and
> his cronies in London, until it came to dominate his
> whole outward personality. [*GP* 15]

The contradiction between what he is and what he makes himself out to be is explicit; he exists for the world less as a novelist than as a character from a novel, more specifically from one of his own novels. The details we are given of him suggest a deliberate process of construction, an accretion of mannerisms that makes out of the personality an artefact which to some extent stands detached from the 'real' self. The analogy with Mr Pinfold's attitude towards his writings is pertinent: 'He regarded his books as objects which he had made, things quite external to himself to be used and judged by others.' [GP 9] His personality, like his novels, is a work of polished, resilient craftsmanship, 'as hard, bright, and antiquated as a cuirass' [GP 15]. Archaism is relished as a style not just by the man but also by the artist, so that the felicities of the writer's prose lend an implicit sanction to the foibles of the writer's persona. Mr Pinfold eschews the telephone, and the word 'eschew', fastidiously chosen to suggest fastidiousness, is, for the reader, a statement about the artist as well as about the public image: the manner of describing Pinfold's conservatism acts at the same time as a partial endorsement of it.

He is presented with a studied solemnity which keeps him always on the edge of absurdity, reminding us of the engaging, slightly ridiculous figures, encountered in remote places and recorded in the travel books, whose sense of their own dignity, humoured by a tolerant author, demanded, as does Mr Pinfold's, a constant formality of address. Time and again in describing his hero's ordeal Waugh shifts the language into a register slightly above what seems appropriate to the situation. 'And now his mind became much overcast,' [GP 26] we are told, as Pinfold declines into a drugged, alcoholic stupor. Odysseus sick for home? Aeneas on the walls of Carthage? Such genial whispers of the epic might, like the title of the book itself, be an invitation to mockery; but they are not that, quite. What stands between Mr Pinfold and absurdity is his art. The old-fashioned eccentricities of the public man, his formality and punctiliousness, his conservatism, have their chaster analogues in the prose style of the artist. And as artist Pinfold is in command. The middle-aged writer may have constructed for himself an absurd persona, but he remains distinct from it by virtue of the fact that he *is* a writer. The balance in the opening chapter is finely judged; Mr Pinfold is both painter and portrait, a creator of absurdity and an absurd creation. As artist he is the creator, whose artefacts, including his own public image, are under control; as elderly party in a state of collapse he is the creation, a character who finds himself the butt of fantastic absurdities, no longer, apparently, of his own imagining. From being a writer of novels he has become a character in one. This is Mr Pinfold's ordeal.

The wayward powers of the imagination have turned against their master. Formerly an ally in the life-long campaign against boredom, they have now slipped the artist's leash and taken on a life of their own. It is the collapse of a crucial tension between the anarchic impulses of the writer's imagination and the restraints imposed upon these impulses by the conditions of his art and the stringencies of his temper. Mr Pinfold's art, his religion and his character all bear the stamp of a common response: his books are so designed as to provide no access to his personality, his public character is a cuirass, and of his religion we are told, 'Mr Pinfold burrowed ever deeper into the rock' [GP 13].

It is the language of defence; the phrases betray a cast of mind stickling and reserved, alien in its disciplines to the freakish play of the imagination. Out of the conflict the artist has established an equilibrium, and it is this which breaks down aboard the *Caliban*. Mr Pinfold, writer and Roman Catholic, can neither write nor pray. Cut off from the ordering principles of both his art and his religion, he is at the mercy of those powers which previously he had wielded for his own protection. The imagination, used in earlier times to distance a bad world or quicken a dead one, now ranges the byways of the past, gleaning random scraps from which to construct its plots and accusations. The artist's progeny, his usual skilfully composed, modestly successful novel, is changed to a brood of vicious children, bent on tormenting him with fictions as cruel as any of his own. The creator is challenged by a revolt of the Angels. What follows is a dubious battle from which Pinfold obtains brief respite in the Church of St Michael, winning final victory only with his return to Christendom.

Critical approaches to the ordeal have tended, understandably, to focus on the precise nature of the charges brought against Mr Pinfold in this conflict. But the emphasis is misplaced, and Pinfold himself suggests why: 'I mean to say, if I wanted to draw up an indictment of myself I could make a far blacker and more plausible case than they did. I can't understand.' [GP 155] J. B. Priestley was quick to unperplex him. With a misleading air of discernment he presented his own version of Pinfold's faults, summarizing the case against him thus: 'Because the voices talked a lot of rubbish, making the most ridiculous accusations, he is ignoring the underlying truth uniting them all, the idea that he is not what he thinks he is, that he is busy deceiving both himself and other people.'[2]

Priestley, however, has shifted the direction of the charges; Mr Pinfold is not accused of being other than he thinks he is or of deceiving himself. The implication, on the contrary, is that he is well aware of the deceit he is practising — this, indeed, is the foundation of the charges. But what sort of challenge can an attack along these lines present to the man who wrote the first two chapters? Pinfold's bafflement is surely justified. In the opening portrait the charge of inauthenticity is recognized and taken into account more economically and more conclusively than in any of the subsequent fantasies on the *Caliban*.

The randomness of these fantasies is a temptation to critical ingenuity. The hints of religious allegory are only one option among many. There is also Pinfold's identification of himself with King Lear. By emphasizing the paternal bond, it gives a certain piquancy to his relationships with the young people, particularly with Goneril and Margaret — 'a sort of Cordelia'. The threat of a younger, aggressively sexual generation on one hand, and on the other the incestuous prompting of a father's heart, might both be grist to the psychoanalyst's mill.

Then there are the echoes from Mr Pinfold's past. The laughter of the Bright Young People stirs him to envy. The catchphrase from *Vile Bodies* quite explicitly takes us back to an earlier decade and an earlier book, to a society of which Pinfold was himself a part and which is now heard dancing happily to the rhythm of a political torture. Intimations of guilt to add to those of envy? Student follies from an even more distant past jostle with distorted episodes of snobbery

---

[2] 'What was Wrong with Pinfold'.

and intolerance, compounding both the guilt and the envy and penetrating them with a dull awareness of the time that has passed. Hints of sexual repression are scattered through the narrative. There is a subdued nostalgia in the memories of love and battle in the Mediterranean. All these are aspects of Pinfold, and of Waugh, elements of the writer that have been exploited or evaded or transformed in the course of his writings. Now they rise up to haunt him. The real assault is on his habits of imagination, not of morality.

Waugh, as we have seen, is a writer whose imagination has always been stimulated by the borderlands where civilization and savagery meet, where the sublime shades into the ridiculous, sanity into lunacy, sadness into hilarity. From these uncertainties, out of the clash of opposite categories, is born the absurd. Its life is a continuing flirtation with insanity, and for Mr Pinfold, underlying all the insults and accusations, there is the threat that madness, courted assiduously for so long and so expertly held at bay, might at last have absorbed him into his own fictional world. This is the peril to which the imaginative powers on which he must rely in his 'dangerous trade' expose him.

The beginning of chapter 4 marks a decisive stage in his experience. Up to that point his hallucinations have suggested no element of persecution; the scenes of which he has been an appalled witness have had no obvious reference to himself. But with the broadcast of Clutton-Cornforth he is brought under personal attack for the first time:

The basic qualities of a Pinfold novel seldom vary and may be enumerated thus: conventionality of plot, falseness of characterization, morbid sentimentality, gross and hackneyed farce alternating with grosser and more hackneyed melodrama; cloying religiosity...an adventitious and offensive sensuality that is clearly introduced for commercial motives. All this is presented in a style which, when it varies from the trite, lapses into positive illiteracy. [GP 62-3]

If we take Pinfold's novels to be anything like those of his creator, then these criticisms present at best a wild distortion of anything that could be called fair comment. There are, however, lurking in *Gilbert Pinfold*, the plots of several novels to which the strictures of Clutton-Cornforth could be applied with some justice. They are the gaudy plots which Mr Pinfold's imagination constructs when freed from the artist's control. Consider a few examples: the cloying religiosity of the interview between Billy and the chaplain ('That is God knocking at the door of your soul,' [*GP* 39] etc.), the morbid sentimentality of the father's relationship with Margaret ('You'll not be my little Mimi ever again, any more after tonight and I'll not forget it' [*GP* 114]), the adventitious and offensive sensuality of the Captain's relationship with Goneril or Pinfold's with Margaret, the conventionality of plot and characterization that mark the 'International Incident', and carry with them a corresponding triteness of style ('"I knew I could trust you," said the Captain. "You're all men who've seen service. I am proud to have you under my command. The yellow-bellies will be locked in their cabins."' [*GP* 93-4])

What rise to the surface of Mr Pinfold's mind are images from Hollywood and the station bookstall: the mutiny on the Man of War, the scene of torture in the Captain's cabin, 'which might have come straight from the kind of pseudo-American thriller he most abhorred' [*GP* 58], the incident off Gibraltar with its echoes of the War of Jenkins Ear and the Private of the Buffs, the intricate ramifications of Angel's conspiracy, 'more modern and horrific than anything in the classic fictions of murder' [*GP* 128]. Spiced with violence, perverse eroticism and unrestrained romanticism, these plots display precisely the qualities that the artist whose portrait we are given in the first chapter must be imagined to have most rigorously suppressed.

Which is not to say that they were the qualities he found least attractive. Clutton-Cornforth charges him with just those delinquencies to which he would have been most inclined, had he not exercised the discipline of his art to keep them under restraint. What the accusations point to are those impulses that Pinfold has spent his career resisting. We glimpse the world of Evelyn Waugh as it might have been represented had romanticism been unchecked by irony, delight in anarchy by a concern with form, disgust with his fellow men by a kindling of religious charity — had he been unable, that is, either to write or pray. This is no tormented, subconscious indictment of the various sorts of censorship and repression practised by Mr Pinfold, it is a vindication of them. Without them the writer is vulnerable to exactly those powers on which he relies as an artist, especially if, like Mr Pinfold, he relies on them not just in his art, but also in his life.

The writer's trade is dangerous because fiction is itself a two-edged weapon. A world that can be made habitable by fantasy can as easily be made uninhabitable by it. This is what happens to Pinfold, and he unwittingly connives at the process of transformation. Deprived of the artistry which distinguishes the writer from the public figure, Pinfold can only find his responses within the range afforded by his image of eccentric don and testy colonel, an image which, as victim rather than creator, he is unable at the time to see with any irony. He makes himself party to the novelettish plots thrown up by a mischievous imagination, and does so with a certain relish. He plays the man of action ('He would fell the first with his blackthorn, then change this weapon for the malacca cane' [GP 73]), the commanding officer ('He would "throw the whole book" at them' [GP 80]), the Truslove figure ('he would go to the sacrifice a garlanded hero' [GP 97]). Given the outlines of the incident off Gibraltar, he immediately fleshes it out with appropriate sentiments:

> Captain Steerforth was now fully restored to Mr Pinfold's confidence. He saw him as a simple sailor obliged to make a momentous decision....Mr Pinfold wished he could stand beside him on the bridge, exhort him to defiance, run the ship under the Spanish guns into the wide, free inland sea where all the antique heroes of history and legend had sailed to glory. [GP 88]

The very mechanism used in the past to invest his world with the brilliance which it lacked now serves to fortify those illusions that are harrying him into insanity.

It is only when he has conceived of the persecutions as an

elaborate series of fictions, orchestrated by Angel, that the voices go on the defensive. By recognizing as fictions the situations in which the voices try to make him participate, Pinfold implicitly denies his role as a character in them. The 'Rules' which his voices enjoin on him are those of fictional consistency. As artist he would normally be the one to impose these 'Rules', as character he is subject to them. By perceiving that the world of the voices is a fictional world, and by asserting his independence of it in going to the Captain and writing to his wife, he checks their ascendancy. The point is most concisely made in his reading of *Westward Ho!* Like Mr Pinfold's experiences aboard the *Caliban*, it involves love and intrigue, conflict with Spain and adventure at sea; but it is all, explicitly, a world of fiction. And this world Pinfold remorselessly destroys, 'making gibberish of the text, reading alternate lines, alternate words, reading backwards, until they pleaded for respite'.

Significantly, it is from this point onwards that his feelings about the voices undergo a change. 'He was becoming like the mother of fractious children who has learned to go about her business with a mind closed to their utterances.' His response to their continued challenges points up the difference, '"Oh God," said Mr Pinfold, "How you bore me!"' The echoes of Hamlet, Lear and Prospero have died along with those of Nelson and Truslove. He is again the Pinfold of the first chapter, whose most potent enemy is boredom. The voices have become part of the humdrum world which he finds flat as a map. Their fantasies no longer engage him. When Angel makes a final attempt to treat with him, Mr Pinfold's reply is an uncompromising rejection of the sort of debased fictions in which he had previously been embroiled: 'Don't call me "Gilbert" and don't talk like a film gangster.' [*GP* 151] But although he has detached himself from the fantastic scenes imagined in the earlier stages of his ordeal, Mr Pinfold is still ensnared by illusion. He is no longer a victim, but neither is he yet 'Pinfold Regained', the artist of the opening chapter. The voices are still real to him, and his theory of 'The Box' holds him in their unreal world. To accept Angel's offer of a permanent truce in exchange for his silence would have been to accept as reality a fiction not created by his conscious mind. He must break the 'Rules' a final time, reaffirming his allegiance to the real world by submitting his fantasies to outside investigation. When he does so, the voices of the *Caliban* fade as completely as the fabric of Prospero's vision.

The creator has regained control of his creatures. In honour of his victory he celebrates a triumph — *The Ordeal of Gilbert Pinfold*; and the conclusion of the book makes it clear that we should take this account to be written by Mr Pinfold himself. The middle-aged artist is an artist once more, and the weapons which Pinfold the invalid had been without — pre-eminently that of ironic detachment — are now deployed by Pinfold the writer to translate a nightmarish bout of insanity into a conversation piece. The threatening voices repeat their words under his direction and a proper distance is re-established between the artist and the elderly party.

The resulting narrative is an object lesson in Waugh's method. To turn the stuff of horror stories into the groundwork of comedy has been his lifetime's study. It is a project that at different stages of his career has been sustained by all those aspects of his writing that have been the subject of this book.

For a concluding model of how the transformation is effected we might turn to the end of chapter 5, where the process assumes the neatness of paradigm. It is the moment of Pinfold's severest test. Having climbed to the main deck, he finds no sign of the Spanish Corvette; instead of the babbling voices he has imagined, there is silence. He is 'the only troubled thing in a world at peace', and for a moment the indifference and immensity of the darkness suggest an engulfing threat more terrible in its impersonality than any persecution.

He had been dauntless a minute before in the face of his enemies. Now he was struck with real fear, something totally different from the superficial alarms he had once or twice known in moments of danger, something he had quite often read about and dismissed as overwriting. He was possessed from outside himself with atavistic panic. 'O let me not be mad, not mad, sweet heaven,' he cried. [*GP* 98]

The horror of the situation is real, but Pinfold, carrying atavism a step further, has borrowed his response to it from King Lear. The image has been stylized. The writing transmits the fact that Pinfold was afraid, while distancing the experience of his fear. When Pinfold as victim gives to his voices names from Shakespeare's play, he affirms their reality; when as artist he uses words from the same play to express his hero's fear, he does exactly the reverse. With a familiar movement of the pen he substitutes the literary for the lived.

Such are the arts by which he has endured. *The Ordeal of Gilbert Pinfold* is both a tribute to them and a warning; it is at once a demonstration of artistic mastery and a revelation of how precarious that mastery is. Neither language nor imagination is a certain refuge. At Mr Pinfold's triumph there is, as tradition demands, a mocking slave who stands always beside him in his chariot reminding him of mortality.

After this Waugh's writing changed. Still to come were *Ronald Knox*, *A Tourist in Africa*, *Unconditional Surrender*, *A Little Learning*. Superficially diverse, they nonetheless form a recognizable group. The voices we hear in them are more subdued, their tone more uniform. There are moments of colour and intensity in these books, but they tend to be just the moments that put us in mind of Waugh as he used to be. If we look for the author of *Edmund Campion* in *Ronald Knox*, it is in the pages on Bishop Valpy French that we find him. But the dry wind and the desert villages, the austere and isolated figure of the man himself have stirred an imaginative zest in the writing which is alien to the temper of the rest of the book. It is not that these works of Waugh's last decade are a lesser achievement than his early ones; they are an achievement of a different kind. They are, we might say, the least daemonic of his writings.

The various aspects of Waugh's work that have been our

study are still discernible, but they no longer have the same
strategic role to play. No longer are they bearing the burden
of the author's defence. In the Introduction I quoted one of
the last passages Waugh wrote, the description of his attempted suicide, and used it to unravel a number of the threads
I wanted to follow — the responses that were aesthetic,
ironic, romantic and so forth. It was a convenient argument
but a little disingenuous. What my analysis ignored was the
fact that it was by this time quite unnecessary for Waugh to
employ any strategies to set the episode at a distance; the
passage of forty years had already done that for him. When
Grimes makes his comparable exit in *Decline and Fall*, the
distance Waugh achieves is a deliberate triumph over the
actual nearness of the event; in *A Little Learning* it is no
more than an accurate reflection of its remoteness. There
are indeed elements of comedy, elements of nostalgia, elements of romanticism; the voices are all there, the lines of
defence are all drawn up. But they are not now being used
for a defensive purpose. The detached, half-mocking, half-
nostalgic view of the affair is an adequate representation of
how, across a gap of forty years, Waugh actually sees it.

So perhaps, after all, the account is, in its fashion, an
honest one. True, there are details the author suppresses
and emotions he makes no attempt to realize, but then it
is the autobiography of a man reticent about his private
life; it makes no pretence to be anything else. If it forgoes
the self-analysis of *The Ordeal of Gilbert Pinfold*, it also
forgoes the defensive mask which that analysis looks behind.
The experiences in it are sometimes distorted, but not in the
interests of producing a falsified image of the author.

The punctilious, melancholy man whose bitterness flickers
through his resignation is a recognizable presence in this
book, as in others of the same period. It is the personality
that leaves its stamp on *A Tourist in Africa* and *Ronald
Knox*, and it is not, I am tempted to claim, just another
screen. The cuirass has been lowered. It is perhaps significant
that of the four books Waugh published after *The Ordeal of
Gilbert Pinfold* three of them should have been works of
non-fiction.

And the fourth? After a lifetime of fictional warfare

Waugh ends with a novel called *Unconditional Surrender*. As
the various illusions to which Guy is committed crumble, we
realize it to be, amongst other things, a surrender to reality —
on the part of the author as well as the hero. For over three
decades Waugh has artfully withstood the assaults of the
outside world. He has set himself apart from them, transformed them into comedy, transformed them into romance,
turned away from them to earlier and happier times. But
finally it is the last and most secure of his defences that has
rendered the citadel: the adoption of Trimmer's son is the
price exacted by his Christianity. Until now the City has
been protected by the Wall, but the Wall, as Helena had
already perceived, has no place in a Christian conception of
the City. In turning for defence to his religion, the writer is
obliged to lower his own defences.

Of all Waugh's novels this final one puts least between its
author and the unfriendly world. Guy abandons his castle
in another country and returns with Trimmer's son to the
Lesser House at Broome. It is a surrender, but also, perhaps,
a kind of triumph. To say that Guy has come to terms with
the world would be a way of putting it. Whether it would
mean anything to say the same of Waugh himself, I do not
know.

Bibliography

THE WORKS OF EVELYN WAUGH

This is a chronological list of the first editions. Page references in the text are those of the standard Penguin editions of all the fictional works (the Penguin Modern Classic for *LO*) and of *WGG*. Short stories unpublished by Penguin are referred to in the Chapman and Hall edition of *Mr L*. References are to the first editions of all other works, except: *EC* (Oxford University Press, 1979), *LL* (Sidgwick and Jackson, 1973), *R* (Duckworth, 1969).

'Antony, Who Sought Things That Were Lost', *The Oxford Broom*, no. 3, June 1923

'The Balance: A Yarn of the Good Old Days of Broad Trousers and High Necked Jumpers', *Georgian Stories 1926*, ed. Alec Waugh, London: 1926

Rossetti, His Life and Works, London: Duckworth, 1928

Decline and Fall, An Illustrated Novelette, London: Chapman and Hall, 1928

Vile Bodies, London: Chapman and Hall, 1930

Labels, A Mediterranean Journal, London: Duckworth, 1930

Remote People, London: Duckworth, 1931

Black Mischief, London: Chapman and Hall, 1932

Ninety-Two Days, The Account of a Tropical Journey through British Guiana and Part of Brazil, London: Duckworth, 1934

A Handful of Dust, London: Chapman and Hall, 1934

Edmund Campion: Jesuit and Martyr, London: Longman, Green and Co., 1935

Mr Loveday's Little Outing and Other Sad Stories, London: Chapman and Hall, 1936

Waugh in Abyssinia, London: Longman, Green and Co., 1936

Scoop, A Novel about Journalists, London: Chapman and Hall, 1938

Robbery Under Law, The Mexican Object-Lesson, London: Chapman and Hall, 1939

Put Out More Flags, London: Chapman and Hall, 1942

Work Suspended, London: Chapman and Hall, 1942

Brideshead Revisited: The Sacred and Profane Memories of Captain Charles Ryder, London: Chapman and Hall, 1945

When the Going was Good, London: Duckworth, 1946

Scott-King's Modern Europe, London: Chapman and Hall, 1947

Wine in Peace and War, London: Saccone and Speed, Ltd, 1947

The Loved One, London: Chapman and Hall, 1948

Helena, London: Chapman and Hall, 1950

Men at Arms, London: Chapman and Hall, 1952

The Holy Places, London: Queen Anne Press, 1952

Love Among the Ruins, London: Chapman and Hall, 1953

Officers and Gentlemen, London: Chapman and Hall, 1955

The Ordeal of Gilbert Pinfold, London: Chapman and Hall, 1957

Ronald Knox, London: Chapman and Hall, 1959

A Tourist in Africa, London: Chapman and Hall, 1960

Unconditional Surrender, London: Chapman and Hall, 1961

Basil Seal Rides Again or the Rake's Regress, London: Chapman and Hall, 1963

A Little Learning, London: Chapman and Hall, 1964

Sword of Honour (the one-volume recension of the war trilogy), London: Chapman and Hall, 1965

The Diaries of Evelyn Waugh, ed. Michael Davie, London: Weidenfeld and Nicolson, 1976

The Letters of Evelyn Waugh, ed. Mark Amory, London: Weidenfeld and Nicolson, 1980

Articles and essays by Waugh have been quoted, when possible, from:

Evelyn Waugh: A Little Order, ed. Donat Gallagher, London: Eyre Methuen, 1977

Two uncollected articles have been quoted:

'Commando Raid on Bardia', *Life*, 11, 17 November 1941

'Sloth' in 'The Seven Deadly Sins', London: *Sunday Times* magazine, 7 January 1962

OTHER REFERENCES

Acton, Harold, *Memoirs of an Aesthete*, London: 1948

— *More Memoirs of an Aesthete*, London: 1970

Allsop, Kenneth, 'Pinfold at Home', *Scan*, London: 1965

Bradbury, Malcolm, *Evelyn Waugh*, London: 1964

Cameron, J. M., 'A Post-Waugh Insight', *Commonweal*, 83, 29 October 1965

Carens, James F., *The Satiric Art of Evelyn Waugh*, Seattle and London: 1966

Donaldson, Frances, *Evelyn Waugh: Portrait of a Country Neighbour*, London: 1967

Doyle, Paul A., *Evelyn Waugh*, Grand Rapids: 1969

Dyson, A. E., 'Evelyn Waugh and the Mysteriously Disappearing Hero', *Critical Quarterly*, 2, Spring 1960

Eagleton, T., *Exiles and Émigrés*, London: 1970

Felstiner, J., *The Lies of Art: Max Beerbohm's Parody and Caricature*, New York: 1972

Fleming, Peter, *Brazilian Adventure*, London: 1933

Fussell, Paul, *Abroad*, New York and Oxford: 1980

Green, Martin, *Children of the Sun: A Narrative of 'Decadence' in England after 1918*, New York: 1976

Greenblatt, Stephen J., *Three Modern Satirists: Waugh, Orwell, and Huxley*, New Haven, Conn.: 1965

Heath, Jeffrey, *The Picturesque Prison: Evelyn Waugh and his Writing*, Kingston and Montreal: 1982

Jebb, Julian (interviewer), 'The Art of Fiction XXX: Evelyn Waugh', *Paris Review*, 8, Summer—Fall 1963

Kermode, Frank, 'Mr Waugh's Cities', in *Puzzles and Epiphanies: Essays and Reviews 1958—61*, London: 1962

Lampedusa, Giuseppe Tomasi di, *The Leopard (Il Gattopardo)*, Milan: 1958

Lapicque, F., 'La Satire dans l'oeuvre d'Evelyn Waugh', *Études Anglaises*, 10, July—September 1957

Lodge, David, *Evelyn Waugh*, New York: 1971

Macaulay, Rose, 'Evelyn Waugh', *Horizon*, 14, December 1946

Meckier, Jerome, 'Cycle, Symbol, and Parody in Evelyn Waugh's *Decline and Fall*', *Contemporary Literature*, 20, Winter 1979

Medcalf, Stephen, 'The Innocence of P. G. Wodehouse' in *The Modern English Novel*, ed. Gabriel Josipovici, London: 1976

O'Donnell, Donat (Conor Cruise O'Brien), *Maria Cross: Imaginative Patterns in a Group of Modern Catholic Writers*, London: 1954

Oldmeadow, Ernest, 'New Books and Music — to Buy or Borrow or Leave Alone', *Tablet*, 7 January 1932

— 'A Recent Novel', *Tablet*, 18 February 1933

— 'News and Notes', *Tablet*, 19 October 1935 (on Waugh's reporting of the Italian—Abyssinian war)

Phillips, Gene D., *Evelyn Waugh's Officers, Gentlemen and Rogues: The Fact behind his Fiction*, Chicago, 1975

Powell, Anthony, *Messengers of Day*, London: 1978

Priestley, J. B., 'What was Wrong with Pinfold', *New Statesman*, 54, 31 August 1957

Pryce-Jones, David (ed.), *Evelyn Waugh and his World*, London: 1973

Rolo, Charles J., 'Evelyn Waugh: The Best and the Worst', *Atlantic Monthly*, 194, October 1954

Russell, Bertrand, *Portraits from Memory and Other Essays*, London: 1956

Savage, D. S., 'The Innocence of Evelyn Waugh', in *Focus Four: The Novelist as Thinker*, ed. B. Rajan, London: 1947

Stopp, Frederick J., *Evelyn Waugh, Portrait of an Artist*, London: 1958

Sykes, Christopher, *Evelyn Waugh: A Biography*, Harmondsworth: 1977

Waugh, Alec, *My Brother Evelyn and Other Profiles*, London: 1967

Waugh, Arthur, *One Man's Road*, London: 1931

Welsford, Enid, *The Fool*, London: 1932

Index